ESSAYS ON NATIONALISM

BY CARLTON J. H. HAYES

A BRIEF HISTORY OF THE GREAT WAR

A POLITICAL AND SOCIAL HISTORY OF MODERN EUROPE
    Volume I. 1500-1815
    Volume II. 1815-1924

MODERN HISTORY
    (In collaboration with Parker T. Moon)

ESSAYS
ON
NATIONALISM

BY

CARLTON J. H. HAYES

PROFESSOR OF HISTORY IN COLUMBIA UNIVERSITY

New York
THE MACMILLAN COMPANY
1933

TO
E. C. H.

CONTENTS

ESSAYS ON NATIONALISM

I

WHAT IS NATIONALISM?

1

THE most significant emotional factor in public life to-day is nationalism. Of the current age it is the mark at once intense and universal.

Look you at the state of popular feeling in France in respect of Germany, or in Germany in respect of France; look you at the zeal of the Italians for the newer, greater Italy, at the enthusiasm of the Poles for a Poland restored and unified, at the determination of a Turkey for and by the Turks. Observe the outcome of the latest and greatest war in human annals: on one hand, the smashing of the non-national empires of the Tsars, the Habsburgs, and the Sultans, and, on the other, the building of the sovereign independence and national unity of Czechoslovakia, of Esthonia, of Finland, of Greece, of Latvia, of Lithuania, of Rumania, of Yugoslavia. Note the patriotic ardour of Englishmen in behalf of the British Empire and the no less nationalist reaction against it of Irishmen, East Indians, and Egyptians. Perceive in the United States the pursuit of a policy of national isolation, the heightening tariff, the increasing restrictions on foreign immigration, the picturesque activities of citizens in masks and nightgowns, the vogue of Americanism and Americanisation.

Study the sentimental background of diplomatic intrigues, competitive armaments, and economic rivalries, not only in general as abstract causes of hypothetical war, but specifically as concrete predisposing causes of the late

1

World War and as definite motive forces in contemporary international tensions, exemplified most pertinently perhaps in the strains and stresses of Americo-Japanese relations. The background of all these things and of much else is nationalism. Hardly a cloud appears nowadays on the horizon of domestic politics, social action, and international affairs, which is without a lining of nationalism. This fact should at once be obvious, though some painful reflection may be required to determine whether the lining be of silver or of brass.

2

Peculiar difficulties confront the student who essays to deal with the impressive and vital phenomenon of nationalism. There has been, especially of late, a good deal of "popular" writing on various aspects of it, and several scholarly treatises have recently dealt with its history among particular peoples, but no profound systematic treatment of the whole subject—the nature and history of patriotism, nationality, and nationalism—exists in any language.[1] To undertake such a treatment would be, of course, a gigantic task: one would have to know a vast amount of history, and history of ideas quite as much as of actions; further, since patriotism is a matter more of feeling than of thought, one would have to be trained in social psychology as well as in philosophy and history; and, finally, alas, before one could advance into the very heart of contemporary nationalism one would be forced to traverse the wide fields and devious paths of anthropology. Small wonder that publicists have bungled and professors have been afraid! Lacking scientific investigation and scholarly analysis, the phenomenon appears vague and intangible and mysterious. There is no agreement as to precisely what it is or as to whether it is good or bad, transitory or eternal.

Reluctance to deal adequately with nationalism is ascrib-

[1] See the Bibliographical Note, Appendix, p. 277, below.

able not only to the complexity of source-materials and the paucity of scientific treatments but also to the deep and powerful emotions with which the whole subject is charged. Nationalism touches all manner of current popular prejudices—personal, national, religious, and racial—and he who would expose the mainsprings of nationalist thought and action must guard particularly against his own emotional bias and at the same time face courageously the distrust and opposition of a large number of his fellows whose own manifold prejudices are enshrined in a collective herd-prejudice. It is almost inevitable that thoughtless persons—the bulk of mankind—should accuse the thoughtful national critic of being an "internationalist" or a "radical," an "anarchist" or a "bolshevist"; at least they will call him "unpatriotic." And what sane man likes to be called unpatriotic? The flushed faces of those who resent imputations upon contemporary forms of patriotism and the cold shivers which run up and down the spine of him who is denounced for making such imputations, are the most eloquent tributes to the strength and force of nationalist feeling. They are the most difficult hurdles in the course of the scholarly study of the phenomenon of nationalism.

A minor difficulty, but a troublesome one, must be dealt with at the outset of our study. I refer to the different and sometimes conflicting uses and connotations of the words "nation," "nationality," "nationalism," and "patriotism." Yet, if we are to comprehend and eventually to judge the phenomena which these words express, we must seek some mutual understanding of what they mean and how they are related one to another. We must endeavour to assign to them fairly precise definitions, no matter how tentative or arbitrary such definitions may be. We must speak the same language and employ the same terms in the same sense.

The word "nation" is tantalisingly ambiguous. It is an old word and has gathered much moss with the lapse of centuries. As derived from the Latin "natio" it meant birth or race and signified a tribe or social grouping based on real or fancied community of blood and possessed presumably of unity of language. Later it was used in certain mediaeval universities to designate a division of students for voting purposes according to their place of birth.[1] Edmund Spenser in the *Faery Queen* spoke of a "nation of birds"; Ben Jonson styled physicians "a subtile nation"; and Samuel Butler referred to lawyers as "too wise a nation t' expose their trade to disputation." Since the seventeenth century "nation" has been employed by jurists and publicists to describe the population of a sovereign political state, regardless of any racial or linguistic unity, and this description still enjoys general sanction. Thus, not only the relatively homogeneous peoples of Denmark and Portugal are called nations, but the polyglot peoples of the Habsburg Empire until the close of the last war were collectively called the Austrian or the Austro-Hungarian nation, and the bi-lingual Belgians and the tri-lingual Swiss are still called nations. In the United States a special usage obtains, for here the word is frequently applied to the whole body of the people coming under the jurisdiction of the federal government.

It was in part to atone for the abuse of the word "nation" that the word "nationality" was coined in the early part of the nineteenth century and speedily incorporated into most European languages. Thenceforth, while "nation" continued chiefly to denote the citizens of a sovereign political state, nationality was more exactly used in reference to a group of persons speaking the same language and observing the same customs. The jurists have done their best to corrupt the new word "nationality," just as they had corrupted the old word "nation"; they have utilised

[1] For example, the "nations" at the University of Paris were France, Normandy, Picardy, and England; at the University of St. Andrews they were Fife, Lothian, Angus, and Britain; at the University of Vienna they were Austria, Saxony, Bohemia, and Hungary. *Cf.* Hastings Rashdall, *The Universities of Europe in the Middle Ages,* 2 vols. (1895).

"nationality" to indicate citizenship. For example, they speak of a person of British nationality though thereby they may mean any subject of King George V, a subject mayhap who, in the non-legal sense, belongs to the Boer nationality of South Africa or to the French-Canadian nationality of North America.

In general, however, "nationality" is far less ambiguous than "nation" and is most commonly and can be most properly used to designate a group of people who speak either the same language or closely related dialects, who cherish common historical traditions, and who constitute or think they constitute a distinct cultural society. In this sense, a nationality may exist without political unity, that is, without an organised sovereign state of its own, and, *vice versa,* a political state may embrace several nationalities, though the tendency has been pronounced in modern times for every self-conscious nationality to aspire to political unity and independence. A nationality which is not politically independent and united is metaphorically styled an "oppressed" or "subject" or even "enslaved" nationality. A nationality, by acquiring political unity and sovereign independence, becomes a "nation," or, to avoid the use of the troublesome word "nation," establishes a "national state." A national state is always based on nationality, but a nationality may exist without a national state. A state is essentially political; a nationality is primarily cultural and only incidentally political.

The word "nationalism" appeared in European vocabularies about the same time as, or shortly after, the appearance of "nationality" and has acquired several shades of meaning. It stands in the first place for an actual historical process, that of establishing nationalities as political units, of building out of tribes and empires the modern institution of the national state. Secondly, the term indicates the theory, principle, or ideal implicit in the actual historical process. In this sense it signifies both an intensification of the consciousness of nationality and a political philosophy of the national state. Thirdly, it may mean, in such phrases as "Irish nationalism" or "Chinese nationalism," the activities of a particular political party, combining an historical process and a political theory; this meaning is clearer when the adjective "nationalist" is employed, for example, in speaking of the historical Irish Nationalist Party. A fourth and final use of "nationalism" is to denote a condition of mind among members of a nationality, perhaps already possessed of a national state, a condition of mind in which loyalty to the ideal or to the fact of one's national state is superior to all other loyalties and of which pride in one's nationality and belief in its intrinsic excellence and in its "mission" are integral parts. Though hereafter we shall give some consideration to nationalism as an historical process, we shall chiefly be concerned with nationalism as the condition of mind just indicated. For this is the nationalism which in the twentieth century is most in evidence. It is this nationalism which colours thought and conditions action in political, social, and cultural spheres, in our domestic politics and in our foreign relations.

3

Nationalism is a modern emotional fusion and exaggeration of two very old phenomena—nationality and patriotism. There always have been, so far as historians and anthropologists know, human entities that can properly be called nationalities. There has been from ancient times the love of country or native land, which is patriotism. But nationalism is a modern, almost a recent, phenomenon. This point is so impressive in itself and so fundamental to our study as to merit and require some detailed explanation.

Let us begin by considering the basis of nationality. We have already defined nationality as "a group of people who speak either the same language or closely related dialects, who cherish common historical traditions, and who constitute or think they constitute a distinct cultural society." But what is the historical and anthropological basis of such a grouping? What determines nationality in general and distinguishes one nationality from another?

Human nature, it has been suggested. In a certain sense this is perfectly true, for man is by nature gregarious and has always lived and laboured and fought in groups, and nationalities are certainly human groups. But nationalities are not the only groupings in which man has fought, laboured, and lived; outside of national limits man's gregariousness has repeatedly been exhibited in religious or economic groupings. It is no more an expression of human nature for citizens of France to display a distinguishing community of interest than for French and Polish Catholics, for Dutch and Scottish Protestants, for Rumanian and Galician Jews, for Russian and Italian Communists, or for American and German bankers.

It has been contended that geography makes nationality. The fact that Britain and Japan are islands separated from large continents and that the United States covers a large part of a continent widely distant from Eurasia has doubtless had something to do with the formation of the British, Japanese, and American nationalities. But geography alone will not explain why the British Isles are parcelled out among at least four nationalities, or why the Philippines are not Japanese, or why the Rio Grande rather than the Mississippi or the Rockies is the boundary between the American and Mexican nationalities. When we consider that some four nationalities—Portuguese, Castilian, Catalan, and Basque—coexist in the geographic unit known as the Iberian Peninsula, that the Polish and Magyar nationalities occupy parts (and only parts) of great plains, that the Greek nationality inhabits rocky coasts and islands, that Norwegian geography is similar in many significant aspects to Swedish, Yugoslav to Bulgarian, and even German to French, we must conclude that the idea of natural frontiers between nationalities is a myth.

A myth likewise is the notion, often advanced by uninformed or unreflective persons, that nationality is determined by race. While scientists are not at all agreed as to what precisely are the races of man, they are in complete agreement that every modern nationality consists of racial mixtures. Racially, modern Germans, Frenchmen, Englishmen, Irishmen, Russians, Italians—almost all Europeans, and the Jews as well—alike comprise mongrel descendants of long-heads and round-heads, blonds and brunets, tall persons and short, stout and slim. The mixture may vary in the relative strength of its component elements from one part of Europe to another, but the degree of racial variation does not change abruptly at national borders. Even the Japanese and Chinese, though marked off by certain physical characteristics from Europeans, afford clear evidence of racial admixture, and the peoples of India, who of late have been developing a consciousness of common nationality, are a veritable hodge-podge of racial strains. Purity of race, if it exists at all, exists nowadays only among uncivilised tribesmen. Nationality actually cuts through and across race, though it must be confessed, in deference to racial propaganda, that an imaginary belief in blood relationship, that is, in race, has been an effective force in building and cementing nationalities.

Then there is the "soul of a people," the theory that every nationality has a group-mind with peculiar and constant mental qualities and endowments. Group-mind, in this sense, is a metaphysical concept, and we may be pardoned for wondering at the simple faith with which many recent writers, including some who deny or doubt the existence of the individual soul, have ascribed eternal fullfledged souls to the several nationalities. It is an obvious fact that in social customs nationalities do differ from one another: the English probably drink tea more commonly and inveterately than any other Europeans; the Germans are more addicted to especially tasty brands of beer; the Italians flavour their culture more pungently with garlic;

and there are doubtless other and even greater national distinctions. Besides, it is a fact amply demonstrated by competent psychologists that human beings may behave in one way in a crowd and in another way when they are alone, in a certain manner when they are subjected to group-pressure and in a different manner when such pressure is removed, that, in other words, there is a group-mind which is a part of, but in its effects distinct from, individual minds. In this sense we may admit the existence of a "national mind," a psychological force which impels the members of a nationality-group toward some community of thought and action, but to dub this national mind a "soul" is literary license. As a matter of fact, the group-mind of a nationality is demonstrably fickle and inconstant. Most characteristics ascribed to a given nationality are found on investigation to belong to several nationalities, and what is characteristic of a particular nationality at a given time is not necessarily characteristic of it at other times. The Greeks of the age of Pericles doubtless reeked with garlic quite as much as the Italians of the nineteenth century. The Germans who fought Caesar had not yet associated great music and profound philosophy with the refinements of Pilsener or Culmbacher. The king who signed Magna Carta and the barons who drove him to it did not drink tea.

Much buncombe has been talked and written about national characters. From examples which are legion, note may profitably be taken of a quotation from an otherwise informing essay by Mr. Charles Roden Buxton: "Just as England contributes her sense for political liberty, France her intellectual honesty and lucidity, Germany her industry and discipline, Italy her aesthetic aptitude, so Finland has her advanced democracy, Poland her music and art, Bohemia religious independence, the Serbs their warm poetic temperament, the Greeks their subtlety and their passion for the past, the Bulgarians their plodding endurance and taciturn energy, the Armenians their passion for education

and progress." [1] The fallacies here are numerous and prodigious. It is implied, absurdly implied, that all Englishmen have a sense for political liberty and that only Englishmen are so endowed, that all Frenchmen are intellectually
honest and clear-headed, that all Germans are industrious,
that all Italians are artists or art-critics, that all Finns are
ultimate democrats, that all Poles are musicians, that all
Czechs are religious independents, *etc.* It is doubtful in
some instances, as in that of the Czechs, whether the characteristic mentioned may be ascribed to any considerable
section of the nationality. It is certain in every instance
that the characteristic assigned to a nationality may be attributed with equal propriety to other nationalities, ancient
as well as modern. Modern France is no more marked by
intellectual honesty and lucidity than was ancient Italy;
modern Italy possesses no greater aesthetic aptitude than
Spain, France, southern Germany, or Japan; Finland has
advanced along democratic highways no further than New
Zealand, Switzerland, or Oregon; the thermometer of poetic
feeling records no higher temperature in Serbia than in England, Ireland, Germany, and Arabia; Greek subtlety is out-
classed by Armenian, and in passion for the past Greeks
are surely equalled by Jews and Chinese; "plodding endurance and taciturn energy" have conventionally been ascribed
less to Bulgarians than to Scots; and to anyone who gives
a thought to the national traits of Americans, Japanese,
Germans, or Australians it seems utterly ridiculous to hit
upon the "passion for education and progress" as a
peculiarity of Armenians.

It is but fair to Mr. Buxton to quote later and wiser words
from his essay: "Peoples are not, in fact, to be distinguished
from one another by a single mark, detaching itself from a
background of pure similarity. It is the total combination
of qualities, of historical events, of natural surroundings,
which makes them what they are—conglomerations of vari-

---

[1] "Nationality", in *Towards a Lasting Settlement,* ed. by C. R. Buxton
(1916), p. 51.

ous and conflicting personalities and parties, touched nevertheless with some unifying character which makes even
their very divisions distinctive.' With much of this I for
one am in agreement, but I would warn against rash imaginings and easy generalisations as to what precisely may be
the "unifying character" of a nationality, and at the same
time, I would re-emphasise the point that national traits
undergo radical alterations, often in a relatively brief time.
Voltaire, writing in the first half of the eighteenth century,[1]
contrasted the English and the French: the English he
thought to be changeable and revolutionary, beheading one
king and exiling another, perpetually tinkering with government and religion, forever fermenting; the French he stig-
matised as conservative and as being too fondly attached
to the past and to the moss-covered traditions of divine-
right monarchy and orthodox Christianity, stolid and stag-
nant.   The late Mr. J. E. C. Bodley, writing at the end of
the nineteenth century,[2] again contrasted the English and
the French: the English, to him, were a conservative, anti-
revolutionary, and substantial people, among whom liberty
slowly broadened out, with the emphasis on "slowly," whilst
the French were fickle, volatile, and revolutionary, beheading one sovereign and expelling several others, fitfully ex-
perimenting with constitutions, and feverishly repudiating
religious orthodoxy.   Both Bodley and Voltaire possessed
no little critical acumen, and the explanation of their widely
divergent estimates must be sought in a change, within two
centuries, in the "group-minds" of the French and English
nationalities.

Summing up the objections against the concept of peculiar and constant "souls" in the several nationalities, Mr.

---

[1] Voltaire, *Letters Concerning the English Nation* (London, 1733),
especially letters v-ix.

[2] J. E. C. Bodley, *France,* rev. ed. (1899). A somewhat different emphasis
appears in the same author's *Romance of the Battle-Line in France* (1919).
Apparently the national "soul" of France underwent still another profound change within twenty years. *Cf.* Abbé Dimnet, *France Herself
Again* (1914).

Israel Zangwill has wittily remarked: [1] "The Bulgarians anciently had a word *pravit*, meaning 'to say'. It now means 'to do'. They had a word *dumat*, 'to think'. It now means 'to speak'. Similar changes, as of Hamlets into Othellos, occur in the souls of every people. The Mongols turned from agriculture to militarism and back again. The Magyars were Oriental shepherds before they came prancing westwards as mounted archers. The Germans were once meek and musical; a native editor of Schiller's 'Robbers' opined that 'even the Germans' could produce great passions and characters. . . . The people of Magna Carta clamours daily for more bureaucracy. The heirs of Mazzini demand court-martialling of free-spoken Deputies. The oldest monarchy in the world has just turned into a Republic, and Bushido-bound Japan has acquired a National Debt."

The conclusion is forced upon us that the basis of nationality is not to be found in inherent mental or spiritual differences among human groups, or, for that matter, in racial heredity or physical environment. Nationality is an attribute of human culture and civilisation, and the factors of zoölogy and botany are not applicable to it. The forms and behaviour of animals and plants are explicable in terms of environment and heredity, because animals and plants have no civilisation. It is not that heredity and environment do not apply at all to man, but that they apply only indirectly and remotely to his civilisation. "This fundamental fact has often been overlooked, especially in modern times, because the biological sciences having achieved successful increases of knowledge and understanding, the temptation was great to borrow their method outright and apply it without serious modification to the human material [of the social sciences]. This procedure simplified the situation, but yielded inadequate and illusory results. For a very long time the idea that man possessed and animals lacked a soul influenced people's thought to such a

[1] *The Principle of Nationalities* (1917), p. 43.

degree that they scarcely thought of human beings in terms of biological causality, of heredity and environment. Then when a reaction began to set in, less than two centuries ago, and it became more generally recognised that man was an animal, the pendulum swung to the other extreme and the tendency grew of seeing in him only the animal, the cultureless being, and of either ignoring his culture or thinking that it could be explained away by resolving it into the factors familiar from biology. The just and wise course lies between. The biological aspects of man must be interpreted in terms of biological causation, his cultural aspects in terms first of all of cultural causation." [1]

Nationality is certainly an aspect of culture, and the causation of national groupings and national traits must be sought in the factors of the social and essentially humane sciences rather than in those of botany and zoology. The distinctive marks and qualities of Russian, Greek, German, Japanese, or any other nationality are no mere appanage of race or incident of geography; they are the creation of social circumstance and cultural tradition.

4

Among the cultural characteristics of nationality, language is, and always has been, pre-eminent. Anthropologists tell us that with primitive men tribal distinctions

---

[1] A. L. Kroeber, *Anthropology* (1923), pp. 186-187. *Cf.* Clark Wissler, *Man and Culture* (1923), p. 297: "The evolution the zoologists talk about is based upon inheritance and so is a matter of germ plasm. On the other hand, culture as we have defined it is not inherited and so cannot have the same kind of an evolution"; *cf.* also A. A. Goldenweiser, *Early Civilisation* (1922), p. 399; R. H. Lowie, *Primitive Society* (1920), p. 3; and F. Boas, *Mind of Primitive Man* (1911), p. 29. John Stuart Mill asserted earlier that "of all vulgar modes of escaping from the consideration of the effect of social and moral influences on the human mind, the most vulgar is that of attributing the diversities of conduct and character to inherent natural differences" (*Principles of Political Economy*, 1849, vol. i, p. 390), and his assertion received the immediate and cordial assent of Buckle (*History of Civilisation in England,* "World Classics," vol. i, p. 31). What a pity that the wisdom of Mill and Buckle and the authority of the most distinguished contemporary anthropologists are ignored or flouted by a host of "popular" scribblers!

coincide with linguistic differences, and that the occurrence
of two tribes with precisely the same speech is so rare that
it may be regarded merely as a transient condition.[1] With
more highly civilised peoples, as historians can testify, the
tendency is the same. The ancient Hebrew nationality had
a distinctive language, and so did the Egyptian, the Punic,
the Greek, the Latin, the Armenian, the Japanese, *etc*. The
formation of most modern nationalities has been historically
dependent upon the development of particular languages.
There was no such thing as the English nationality which
we know until Anglo-Saxon had been fused with Norman
French to produce the English language. There was no such
thing as the French nationality until the Germanic Franks,
mingling with the Latinised Gauls, had modified the Latin
speech so far as to give rise to a new and different language
called French. The rise and decline of nationalities and
tribes have always been closely paralleled by the rise and
decline of their respective languages, and both processes
still go on together.

Language as a determining mark of nationality has been
criticised by some writers, who usually cite in support of
their contentions such facts as that Switzerland has three
official languages and Belgium two, that the Canadians of
Quebec speak French and the Basques and Bretons of
France do not, that English is spoken in the United States
and Welsh and Gaelic in parts of Great Britain.[2] These
citations might be multiplied but they would be of the
same kind and equally beside the point. For the difficulty
of the critics arises either from a confusion of nationalities
with political entities or from a failure to perceive the fluid
and dynamic nature of nationality.

No nationality is fixed and static. Just as in the middle
ages the long survival of Norman French at the court of
the English kings served to unite the fortunes of the English

---

[1] *Cf.* especially Clark Wissler, *op. cit.*, p. 48, and A. van Gennep, *Traité
Comparatif des Nationalités*, vol. i (1922), ch. iv.

[2] For example: J. H. Rose, *Nationality in Modern History* (1916), pp.
140-143; Israel Zangwill, *op. cit.*, pp. 40-41.

royal house with those of France and to militate against the development of a distinctively English nationality, so in modern times the use of the English language in the United States tends to link American thought and action with that of England and at the same time to obstruct the growth of an absolutely separate American nationality. Language is not the only mark of nationality, but if we will forget for the present the division of the world into sovereign political states we shall be in a better position to recognise that English-speaking peoples, wherever they may be, constitute a nationality in contradistinction to the French, the German, or the Chinese nationality. Within a given nationality differences of dialect may become in time so pronounced that, in conjunction with other separatist factors, they may exalt what have been, so-to-speak, mere "sub-nationalities" into true and distinct nationalities. Time alone will tell whether the American nationality is truly distinct from the English, and the French-Canadian from the French. The old Slav-speaking Prussian nationality long ago lost its language and was absorbed into the German nationality; as yet the languages of Welsh, Gael, Basque, and Breton survive and the nationalities which they severally represent have not been completely absorbed by the English or the French.

On the other hand, despite the artificial attempts to promote a sense of social solidarity, akin to nationality, among all the Swiss and among all the Belgians, the real fact remains that the citizens of Switzerland differ in social consciousness and in certain elements of culture according as their speech is French, Italian, or German, and that the Belgian Flemings differ similarly from the Belgian Walloons. During the World War the cleavage of Swiss sympathies along linguistic lines was patent, and of late Belgium has been torn by dissensions between Walloon and Flemish nationalities.[1] From the recent disintegration of the Austro-

---

[1] *Cf.* Louis Dumur, *Les deux Suisses* (1917), and Jules Destrée, *Wallons et Flamands, la Querelle Linguistique* (1923).

Hungarian Monarchy into its several component nationalities, it may not be utterly fantastic to draw a lesson which
may at some future time be applicable to Belgium and to
Switzerland, and even to the British Empire. Just as
Austria-Hungary was dissolved by the last World War into
its constituent national elements, so in another world war
the British Empire and other non-national states, such as
Switzerland and Belgium, may be broken into several
independent and mutually exclusive national states.

It is readily comprehensible why language should be an
important, probably the chief, factor in forming and sustaining a nationality. Uniformity of language tends to
promote like-mindedness, to provide an inclusive set of ideas
as well as of words, and like-minded persons tend to develop
group-consciousness, to experience a sense of common interest, to constitute a tribe or nationality. Members of
such a group naturally regard persons who speak a strange
and alien language as "unlike" or different from themselves
and hence as inferior and not entitled to belong to themselves. The historical antitheses between Jew and Gentile
and between Greek and Barbarian have analogies in all
languages and among all peoples.

Language, too, is the medium in which is expressed the
memory of successful achievement or distressing hardship
shared in common, and thereby it acquires cementing value
for a nationality. It is the bridge between the present and
the past. In the words of Ossian, "It is the voice of years
that are gone; they roll before me with all their deeds." [1]
And this brings us to the second distinguishing attribute of
nationality—the cherishing of common historical traditions.

History is essentially human. To men, as to no other
animals, have been vouchsafed a sense of time and an endowment of memory. Not only do human beings naturally
recall certain outstanding events in their own lives and in
those of their immediate family, but also, being gregarious,
they preserve and embroider the recollection of past crises

---

[1] "Oina-Morul," in *Tembra* (1763), p. 211.

in the life of the linguistic group to which they belong. They are especially prone to celebrate the memory of the group's heroic figures and collective fighting prowess. Indeed, man's innate tendencies to hero-worship and group-combat, tendencies which doubtless are closely connected psychologically with his gregariousness, combine with his time-sense and his memory-endowment to fashion the traditions upon which nationality most conspicuously thrives.

In the crudest forms of nationality, the tribes of primitive men, a more or less official body of elders or priests or wise men or medicine men constitute the recognised custodians of the tribal experiences and legends, and elaborate ceremonies usually attend the initiation of youths into the "mysteries" of the past. With historic peoples it is similar. The sagas of the Norsemen, the vedas of the Hindus, the pentateuch and the chronicles of the Hebrews, the Homeric poems, the Virgilian hexameters, all the famed deeds of the brave men before Agamemnon, no less and no more than the heroes and battles cherished in memory and embellished in the telling by present-day peoples, have served to inspire linguistic groups with corporate consciousness and to render them true nationalities.

With the garnering of historic traditions appears the tendency to personify the group, to view the nationality as an historical personage. Sometimes the personification is symbolised by means of a flag or other emblem signifying the life or the spirit of a nationality. More often it is a mental image derived from the hearing of legends or the reading of tales in which scientific facts have been consciously or unconsciously subordinated to the purposes of art and romance. All such personification operates emotionally upon individuals, presenting them with a glorified picture of the spirit, the principle, the ideal of their group and thereby persuading them to a deeper loyalty to their common nationality.[1] Not only this, but in the romantic history and in the idealised personification of one's national-

---

[1] *Cf.* G. E. Partridge, *Psychology of Nations* (1919), p. 85.

ity, one fancies to discover something eternal, the life of a group which existed without beginning long before any of its present members and which, by the same token, will exist without end long after its present members are gathered to their fathers' dust. Man's powerful longing for immortality receives aid and comfort from historic traditions which center in nationality.

The third distinguishing mark of nationality (after language and historic tradition) is the belief of its members that they compose a distinct, cultural society. It is but natural that a group which is cut off by difference of language from direct and general intercourse with other human beings and which has developed a peculiar attitude towards its past should feel that it is a unit distinct from others not only, but different. And as one surveys the history of nationality one is struck by the extent to which this feeling, this belief, is borne out by observable facts. Every nationality has a culture-pattern of its own, a distinctive complex of institutions, customs, and art, and the same is true even more strikingly of primitive tribes. Certain types of family relationship and social organisation, certain modes of artistic expression, certain religious tenets and observances, certain habits of work and play, certain forms of clothing and shelter, are found among primitive peoples in all the continents, but no two tribes, speaking different languages, show the same combination of such habits, observances, modes, and types. The component elements may be identical, but the *tout ensemble*, in every instance, is distinctive.

Too much emphasis as well as too little, may, of course, be put upon cultural variations among tribes and nationalities. Certainly in modern times, improved means of travel and communication have given an impetus towards uniformity of culture throughout the world, and undoubtedly in all ages what has distinguished one nationality from another has been much less vital and valuable than what several nationalities have had in common. Yet it is true that each nationality still persistently regards itself as the tabernacle of a unique civilisation. Perhaps what any group thinks itself to be is quite as significant as what it really is. It is assuredly so with a nationality.

Among elements of cultural differentiation, religion, at least in the past, has been prominent. It was in and about religion that the social customs of primitive tribesmen and of most ancient peoples were woven, so that with them religion was a peculiarly tribal or national affair. It provided a psychical content for their group-life and lent to nationality a grave dignity. In the historical case of the Hebrews it has always been very difficult to separate their religion from their nationality, and it is hardly less difficult to determine whether the Armenians, the Copts, and the Japanese owe their nationality to their religion or their religion to their nationality. Yet religion of itself cannot be deemed an invariable attribute of nationality, for the rise and propagation of "world religions," such as Graeco-Roman Paganism, Buddhism, Christianity, and Mohammedanism supplanted to a considerable degree tribal and national religions and, by creating cultural areas which overlapped—and still overlap—national borders, proved inimical rather than favourable to the principle of nationality. Besides, most modern nationalities manage to flourish without insisting upon uniformity of religious belief or practice.

Political institutions, like those of religion, may be an important factor in crystallising a nationality. Among primitive men tribe differs from tribe not only in language and religion but in form of government. With the development of civilisation loyalty to a chieftain has been merged in loyalty to his law and this in turn has been merged in loyalty to the political institutions of the state. Frequently a dynasty has become the connecting link between the tribal chieftain and the abstract idea of the political state; and the prestige and all the supernaturalism contained in the notions of divine right and divine descent have been extended to the state and its government. In this way, the idea of the political state has commanded among historic peoples a very high degree of loyalty,[1] and in many instances the expansion of a state by peaceful growth or violent conquest has served to unite various tribes in common allegiance to a common polity, to infuse all with a sentiment of solidarity, to promote the use of a uniform language, and thus to transform several small tribes into one large nationality. Such, at any rate, was the experience of the Hebrews, the Egyptians, the Latins, and many another ancient people; politics powerfully aided the transition from tribe to nationality. Such, too, was a fairly frequent occurrence in the middle ages; the growth of the French and English and Spanish nationalities was preceded by the expansion of the political sway respectively of the monarchs of France, England, and Spain.

Yet, as in the case of religion, political independence is not an indispensable condition of nationality. Many a nationality, in the long course of human history, has been engulfed by a "world-empire," such as the Egyptian, the Assyrian, Alexander the Great's, the Roman, the Turkish, the Russian, the Austrian, the British, and has thereby been deprived of its distinctive political institutions without losing its identity as a nationality. Many another nationality, such as the Phœnician, the Greek, the German, and the Polish, has continued obviously to be a nationality despite the fact that for centuries it was parcelled out among a number of states and possessed neither uniformity of political institutions nor unity of political allegiance.

5

We have now investigated at some length, though at no greater length than the subject requires, the bases and attributes of nationality; and we have satisfied ourselves that it is not dependent on an eternal "soul", that is, on con-

---

[1] G. E. Partridge, op. cit., pp. 84-85. Cf. A. E. Zimmern, Nationality and Government (1919), ch. ii, and Bertrand Russell, Why Men Fight (1917), ch. ii.

stant and inherent mental variations, or on race (though a belief in community of blood may enhance it), or on geography (save in a very general way), or on human nature (except as all forms of human gregariousness depend ultimately upon the nature of man). Rather, we have confirmed our hypothesis that nationality rests upon cultural foundations, that a nationality is any group of persons who speak a common language, who cherish common historical traditions, and who constitute, or think they constitute, a distinct cultural society in which, among other factors, religion and politics may have played important though not necessarily continuous rôles.

Thus defined, nationality has existed from the earliest times of which history and anthropology can treat. Most of the tribes described by anthropologists and most of the peoples whom we encounter in history, are nationalities. But this is not to say that a given nationality has always existed or always will. Nationalities wax and wane, rise and fall, appear and disappear. Most of the contemporary nationalities of Europe may be said, in relation to the enormous span of human life on this globe, to be of recent birth; and today, before our very eyes, numerous nationalities of American Indians are dying.

Besides, a nationality, as we have defined it, may embrace several sub-nationalities. For example, the English, the Scots, and the Welsh, in so far as they use the English language, cherish traditions of joint action against non-Britishers, and constitute, or think they constitute, a common cultural society in contradistinction to that of Frenchmen or Germans, are one nationality, but the Scots and the Welsh in so far as they possess languages or dialects of their own, in addition to the King's English, and in so far as they retain peculiar historic traditions at variance with some of their English neighbours', are nationalities distinct from the English. Wherefore it may properly be maintained that the English, Scottish, and Welsh are sub-nationalities of a British nationality. Again, the Catalans and Provençals once formed a nationality with a distinctive language and literature, with distinctive historic traditions, and with a belief that they possessed a distinctive culture, but during centuries of French rule in Provence and of Spanish sway in Catalonia they have been so permeated by the language and traditions of other and dominant nationalities that the Catalans have been reduced to the position of a sub-nationality within the Spanish nationality whilst the Provençals, though still differing from the French in minor respects, are in major matters "good Frenchmen."

On the other hand, difference of historic traditions and emphasis upon cultural contrasts, real or fancied, especially when they are reënforced by political separation, may outweigh identity of language and thereby create a sub-nationality which becomes almost, if not quite, an absolutely independent nationality. The Portuguese who first went to Brazil, the Spaniards who first settled in Mexico and Peru, the English who first colonised Virginia and Massachusetts, were certainly of the Portuguese, Spanish, or British nationalities. Their descendants have used the same national languages, but adaptation to a new and different environment, economic quarrels with the mother-countries, and forceful political isolation have tended to create and exalt among these descendants peculiar historic traditions so powerful as to give rise to Brazilian, Mexican, Peruvian, and American nationalities. In one sense, these are now independent nationalities; in another sense, they are still sub-nationalities.

Nor can it be maintained that among historical peoples the consciousness and "drive" of nationality have always been of the same intensity. The facility with which "world-religions" and "world-empires" have been superimposed upon nationalities, the rapidity with which nationalities have been broken into sub-nationalities and dissolved into an urban or a feudal society, betoken that in many ages the claims of nationality upon man's allegiance have been slight. As a matter of fact, man's gregariousness has

assumed many forms other than national, and similarly his
sense of loyalty, which springs from his gregariousness, has
not been limited to national objects; it has been displayed
in a bewildering multiplicity of ways. Sometimes it has
been loyalty to persons, as to tribal chieftains or to supposedly divine monarchs or to feudal lords or to fellow
members of a caste, a clan, a guild, a trade-union, or a club.
Sometimes it has been loyalty to places, as to grove or
stream, to thatched cottage or marble palace, to natal home
or tomb of the ancestral dead, to pastoral hillside, fertile
plain, or great busy city. Sometimes it has been loyalty to
ideas, as to a religion, a political philosophy, a scheme of
science, a programme of social reform, or an economic system. At all times man has simultaneously applied his sense
of loyalty, quite naturally and without nice discrimination,
to ideas, places, and persons. He has so applied it both
within and without his nationality. He now applies it
primarily to his nationality and his national state, but
throughout a large part of his recorded history he has
applied his sense of loyalty less to nationality than to other
objects.

Patriotism, which nowadays we connect with nationality,
has been historically more closely related to other loyalties
of man. Patriotism means literally the love of one's *terra
patria* or natal land. As such it must have been of slight
significance to the member of an early nomadic tribe or nationality, who, as Professor J. H. Robinson has said, "can
hardly have had any sweet and permanent associations with
the tree or rock under which he was born." [1] Patriotism did
become a marked feature of ancient fixed and civilised life,
but even then it was seldom a patriotism which reached
throughout the length and breadth of the country where
people of like speech had their homes; it was rarely a national patriotism. Usually the patriotism which existed
was local: it was applied, for example, by the Greeks not

[1] "What Is National Spirit?" *The Century Magazine*, vol. xciii (Nov.,
1916), p. 59.

indiscriminately to all Greek-speaking lands, but to a fragment of land such as Athens, Sparta, Corinth, or Smyrna; by the Phoenicians not generally to Phoenicia but specifically to Tyre, Sidon, or Carthage; by the Romans first and foremost not to the orbit of the Latin language but to the city of Rome.

This sort of patriotism is natural enough. Everybody who is born and reared where his ancestors have lived from time immemorial is almost certain to feel a sentimental attachment to that locality. It was easy for a mediaeval peasant to evince patriotism for the manor on which he was born and from which he derived his sustenance. It is easy for a modern French peasant to experience some patriotic emotion about the soil and scenery of his *pays*. It is less artificial for a native-born American to love a familiar little village in Massachusetts or Louisiana or California than to cherish impartially and equally all the United States.

Patriotism at an early date was extended in application from one's native locality to one's political country, from an immediate *place* to the *person* of a military or political leader, and thence to the *idea* of a state. But among ancient peoples, and mediaeval also, the sway of political and military chieftains infrequently coincided with any particular nationality, and consequently patriotism often changed from local sentiment into imperial pride without passing through an intermediate national stage. Perhaps it would be more accurate to say that on top of natural local patriotism was superimposed a more artificial imperial patriotism. At times in the history of certain ancient peoples, notably the Egyptians and the Hebrews, there was something resembling national patriotism, and doubtless, for the building and maintenance of many of the empires of the past, military conquerors and governors could rely on the special support and encouragement of the self-conscious nationality which constituted the core of an empire. But members of such a conquering self-conscious nationality could not experience quite the same emotion of patriotism about the extended empire as they felt about their own regions; and the conquered peoples, whilst they might come to regard the empire as a necessity, even as a blessing, and therefore as deserving of a kind of artificial patriotism, were certainly not inclined to bestow any particular affection upon the exclusively native land of their conquerors.

Imperial patriotism is necessarily much more artificial, more dependent on socially inherited knowledge and conscious effort, than is local patriotism. "In order to realise this, we must, again and again, remind ourselves of the quantitative limitations of all the factors in the human type. We are apt to think of human societies as we think of equilateral triangles. We can imagine an equilateral triangle with sides either an inch long or a hundred miles long, and in either case its qualities as an equilateral triangle will be the same. But if we imagine a heap of sand composed of sand-grains, each grain being about a hundredth of an inch in diameter, we must remember that a change of size in the heap may change the relation between the grains, and therefore the character of the heap. A heap of twenty grains of sand will behave differently from a heap of twenty million grains. It will, for instance, have a different 'angle of repose.' " [1]

Ancient political philosophers, notably the greatest Greek minds, recognised this principle and argued from it that the ideal state (of which true patriotism should be an attribute) could not have an extensive territory or a numerous population; Plato in *The Laws* fixed the maximum number of free citizens at 5040. Hence, to them, a huge empire was a monstrosity and even the political union of a large nationality appeared undesirable and impractical. Whatever may have been the influence of the Greek philosophers, it is a fact that in ancient and middle ages strictly national states were rare and consequently national patriotism was unusual.

It is different in modern times. Nowadays there is

[1] Graham Wallas, *Our Social Heritage* (1921), pp. 77-78

preached and practised a twofold doctrine, (1) that each nationality should constitute a united independent sovereign state, and (2) that every national state should expect and require of its citizens not only unquestioning obedience and supreme loyalty, not only an exclusive patriotism, but also unshakable faith in its surpassing excellence over all other nationalities and lofty pride in its peculiarities and its destiny. This is nationalism and it is a modern phenomenon.

6

As we have seen, it has been a mark of nurture, if not of nature, for human beings since the dawn of history to possess some consciousness of nationality, some feeling that the linguistic, historical, and cultural peculiarities of a group make its members akin among themselves and alien from all other groups. But not until very modern times have whole peoples been systematically indoctrinated with the tenets that every human being owes his first and last duty to his nationality, that nationality is the ideal unit of political organisation as well as the actual embodiment of cultural distinction, and that in the final analysis all other human loyalties must be subordinate to loyalty to the national state, that is, to national patriotism. These tenets, again, are the essence of modern nationalism.

Antiquity knew not nationalism as we know it. Ancient Egyptians were united in the bonds of a common loyalty to the sacred River Nile and to the sun-sprung Pharaoh, but the ordinary dwellers in Thebes and Memphis, though probably quite aware of common nationality, hardly felt that the claims of their nationality were superior to the claims of their Pharaoh and their priests; theirs was not exclusively a national state, and nationalism was not encouraged by the long line of Pharaohs, whose constant hieroglyph, chiselled on tomb and temple thousands of years ago, still reminds us that they aimed at a dominion on which the sun would never set. Phoenicians and Greeks alike were human in that they manifested the sense of loyalty in many ways, especially in worship of certain deities and in devotion to particular cities, but neither people was modern: they never constructed national states and their wars were chiefly interurban rather than international. The Romans had intense patriotism, but their patriotism was an expression of loyalty not to all persons who spoke the Latin language, but to the city of the seven hills with its legendary gods and heroes; and with the expansion of the city-state of Rome into an empire which encircled the Mediterranean and embraced Egyptian and Celt, Parthian and Moor, Teuton and Greek, the local patriotism of the Roman changed to pride in world-imperialism without passing through the intermediate stage of nationalism, whilst among the subject provincials the assurance of the *Pax Romana* by Roman law and Roman legions became an object of general loyalty, which, however, was always supplementary to local loyalties rather than a substitute for them.

The Jews were no exception to the rule of antiquity, despite the perfervid rhapsodies of contemporary Zionists. A re-reading of the Hebrew scriptures should show that the "chosen people" did not think of themselves as singularly blest and set apart simply because they spoke Hebrew and lived in Palestine and constituted a national state. As a matter of fact, Palestine was not their original home; they had to conquer it and at a date when Egypt was already old; and even the semblance of a united national state survived with them an exceedingly brief time. The Jews were a "chosen people" because they believed in Yahweh and the law revealed by Him, and the foreigner who would proclaim in the words of Ruth to Naomi that "Thy God shall be my God" was admitted to full membership without embarrassing questions as to racial stock or linguistic accomplishment, or as to whether the quota of immigrants from the applicant's nation was full. Historically, both in ancient times and throughout the middle ages, and even down into modern times, the Jews have been not so much

a nationality infused with nationalism as adherents to
a religion.

During the thousand years which separate Luther and
Machiavelli from Pope Gregory the Great and which we designate, for lack of a better term, the middle ages, there were
few signs of nationalism anywhere in Europe. The Europeans during this long period had many loyalties—to Catholic Church, to bishop or abbot, to parish priest, to lay lord,
to tribal chieftain, to duke or count or baron, to guild of
merchants or of craftsmen, to manor or town, to realism
or nominalism, to St. Francis or St. Dominic, to pope or
emperor, to Christendom in arms against Islam. Nationalities surely persisted throughout the period and undoubtedly
there was an acutely nascent consciousness of national differences towards the close of the middle ages, the result of
the crusades, of the rise of vernacular literatures, and of the
ambitious efforts of monarchs in western Europe, but if
there was an object of popular loyalty superior to all others
it was not the nation but Christendom. If a man whose
native tongue was French encountered a fellow Christian
whose native tongue was English, both men were fully
aware of a difference, but they were quite as aware of a
similarity; and it should be remembered that Joan of Arc,
who is now hailed as a saint of French nationalism, appeared
on battlefields of the Hundred Years' War, not in response
to the appeals of a nationalist press or the pressure of a
patriotic draft-board and not in conformity with the example of national heroes as set forth in hundred per cent.
French textbooks of history, but simply and solely in answer
to "voices" which she heard from saints of God. It should
be remembered, moreover, that Joan of Arc fought for one
claimant to the throne of France against another, who,
though simultaneously King of England and Prince of
Wales, reigned over half of France and was supported by
many French-speaking people. It should be remembered,
too, that Joan of Arc was condemned to death, not by Englishmen but by Frenchmen, not for being a foreigner, a

sort of forerunner of Edith Cavell, but for being an obstinate heretic and an advanced feminist; she dressed like a man and was, therefore, "possessed of the devil."

Nationality has always existed. Patriotism has long existed, either as applied to a locality or as extended to an empire. But the fusion of patriotism with nationality and the predominance of national patriotism over all other human loyalties—which is nationalism—is modern, very modern. How it has come about, we shall presently try to understand.

II

THE RISE OF NATIONALISM

1

In Europe, the smallest but in modern times the most influential of the continents, nationalism has had its rise; and the way for it was prepared by a quickening of national consciousness among European peoples towards the close of the middle ages. The crusades were especially significant. In general, an unprecedented number of Europeans travelled extensively and learned to surmount their earlier localism; they acquired a surer knowledge not only of large aggregates of people who spoke their own language or kindred dialects but also of other large aggregates who conversed in alien tongues; they developed a greater pride in their own nationality and a more pronounced rivalry with other nationalities.

Specifically the major crusades, in which Frenchmen were the foremost participants, stimulated French national feeling; the so-called Fourth Crusade peculiarly fostered the jealous rivalries and national enmities of Latin and Greek Christians; the Albigensian Crusade exalted the nationality of the French in measure as it abased that of the Provençals; and from the conflict between Christians and Moslems in the Iberian peninsula emerged a lively national consciousness of Castilians, Portuguese, and Catalans. It was the crusading efforts of the Teutonic Knights against pagan Slavs which, in conjunction with commercial activities of the Hanseatic League and political endeavours of the rulers of the Holy Roman Empire, stimulated the German *Drang nach Osten* and eventually aroused the national feeling of Czechs and Poles. Effects similar to those of the crusades were produced by the protracted conflicts between secular princes and the papacy and also by the Hundred Years' War between the French and the English.

The quickening of national consciousness in the middle ages did not immediately give rise to nationalism. Nationalism, as we know it, was hardly more in evidence in mediaeval Christendom than in the mediaeval Asiatic empires of China, India, and Turkey, or in the mediaeval American empires of Mexico and Peru. Too many factors still militated against the ultimate expression of national feeling. There was a universal lack of safe and easy means of travel and communication. There was an almost universal divorce between literary and vernacular languages. There was an almost universal influence of international and "world" religions. There was an almost universal nonexistence of strictly national states.

2

National consciousness, already quickened among European peoples in the middle ages, was mightily exalted at the dawn of modern times. The way which had been prepared for nationalism was now paved wide and deep. For in the fifteenth, sixteenth, and seventeenth centuries were enhanced certain crucial differentiations of nationalities. These differentiations can conveniently be grouped as (1) linguistic and literary, (2) political, (3) commercial and economic, and (4) ecclesiastical, religious, and cultural.

Greek and especially Latin had long been the predominant literary languages of European nationalities. Prevailing within the Roman Empire, they had early become the official languages respectively of the Eastern Orthodox and Western Catholic Churches, and so long as most writing was done by Christian priests and missionaries, it was done in Latin or Greek. Of course, side by side with the written international languages persisted or arose spoken national languages —the so-called vernaculars—among which were certain tongues, such as Basque, Coptic, Armenian, Gaelic, and

Breton, that antedated and survived the diffusion of Latin and Greek, and others, such as French, Italian, Castilian, Portuguese, Catalan, and Rumanian, that gradually developed from Latin dialects, and still others, such as the Teutonic, Slavic, and Finno-Magyar, that derived from tribal "barbarian" speech, and finally the curious medley of Teutonic and French languages that we call English. But literary production in these vernaculars was at first relatively slight in quantity and religious rather than national in content; even the requisite alphabets and forms of letters were borrowed and adapted from Greek or Latin.

In western and central Europe—the cultural area of Catholic Christianity—all educated persons throughout the middle ages knew Latin as well as their native tongue. They thus belonged not only to diverse nationalities but also to an international society. They possessed a common literary tradition, a single medium for oral and written communication, and a mutual understanding, which transcended national differences. Erasmus, for example, was a Dutchman by birth, but his mastery of Latin made him an international figure: he lived among educated Frenchmen, Englishmen, Italians, Germans and Belgians, with all of whom he could correspond and talk in Latin; he lectured for a time in Latin at the College of France; and he wrote Latin letters to the pope, to the kings of England, France, and Spain, to his famous publisher at Venice, and to his numerous critics in all parts of Europe.

Before the time of Erasmus, however, educated men were already beginning to write in the vulgar tongues and not by any means exclusively on religious subjects; and presently literary masterpieces appeared in the vernacular languages of the masses as well as in the ancient languages of scholars. In the fourteenth century, Dante wrote in Italian and Chaucer in English. Thenceforth one vernacular after another became the vehicle of splendid and distinctive literary expression. Two events of the fifteenth century aided the process. The one was the attempt of the Humanists to purify Latin of its mediaeval developments. which had been in the direction of greater simplicity, and to restore ancient classical Latin with its involved sentence-structure and its complicated grammar, an attempt which did much to discredit Latin as a living literary language and to restrict its use to the class-room, to ecclesiastical services, and to scientific treatises. The other was the invention of printing, which served to stereotype the common spoken languages, to fix for each a norm of literary usage, and to render possible the dissemination of national literature among the masses.

The rise of vernacular literatures in the fifteenth and sixteenth centuries tended to emphasise nationality, for not even a well educated person could be expected to know all the languages spoken in Europe, and the large majority of Europeans were familiar only with the language of their own nationality. Writers in English naturally began to stress what was peculiar to England, French writers did the same for France, and Italian writers for Italy. Gradually national characteristics were imaginatively depicted and national aspirations were poignantly voiced. In the sixteenth century, Machiavelli made eloquent national appeals to the Italians, Camoens celebrated glorious national exploits of the Portuguese, Luther addressed stirring patriotic letters to the Germans, Cervantes played fancifully with Spanish character, and Shakespeare penned the praises of England:

> "This royal throne of kings, this scepter'd isle,
> This earth of majesty, this seat of Mars,
> This other Eden, demi-paradise;
> This fortress built by Nature for herself
> Against infection and the hand of war;
> This happy breed of men, this little world,
> This precious stone set in the silver sea." [1]

From Shakespeare to the present day national literature has accentuated what is peculiar to a linguistic group rather

[1] Richard II, act ii, sc. 1.

than what is characteristic of Christendom or of the world. "This little world" has been echoed and reëchoed in drama, epic, ode, essay, and novel. National literature, in its many forms, has brilliantly illumined to human beings their nationality, but it has darkened and obscured to them their common heritage.

Literary differentiation of nationalities was accompanied, at least in western Europe, by political differentiation, that is, by the erection of sovereign national states. The creation of such a group of states was the achievement largely of a succession of able and ambitious monarchs in England, France, Spain, Portugal, and Scandinavia. The Tudor dynasty in England, the Valois and Bourbon kings in France, the Habsburgs in Spain, the Avizes in Portugal, the Vasas in Sweden were, as a rule, strong-willed and energetic. They busied themselves, towards the close of the middle ages and the opening of modern times, with efforts to increase their personal power and to establish autocratic sway. On the one hand they sought to lessen the authority of the Catholic Church, which had preserved many of the universal traditions of the ancient Roman Empire, and on the other hand they laboured to repress their feudal vassals—dukes, counts, and barons—who personified the localism of a more recent age. In their efforts they were assisted by the change in the methods of warfare which the use of firearms involved and which enabled them to put effective armies in the field against domestic and foreign foes, and likewise they were aided by the revival of the Roman civil law, by the political maxims of Machiavelli, and by the interested coöperation of many of their subjects. The upshot of the whole movement was the building and consolidation of fairly large, fairly homogeneous, and absolutely independent states in western Europe—England, France, Spain, Portugal, Sweden, and Denmark. In eastern Europe Russia emerged in like manner as a national state.

That these states were national is attributable less to design on the part of their presiding autocrats than to chance. It was a fortune of war that obliged the English monarchs in the fifteenth century to abandon their possessions in France and to devote their energies to Britain. It was a marriage alliance which united Spain under Ferdinand and Isabella. The kings of the sixteenth, seventeenth, and eighteenth centuries waged many wars for family reasons, either to place a member of a particular royal house on the throne of another country, or to obtain richer inheritances for their wives and children. These kings, moreover, were none too scrupulous about confining their ambitions to peoples of their own language and nationality. They frequently conquered territory inhabited by "foreigners," and they bartered people to and fro like so many sheep and cattle. Yet in all such royal conflicts and family transactions, the core of each monarchy continued to be a nationality of common language and common traditions, imbued with common patriotism. The autocrat could count on the patriotism of the majority of his subjects to support him, more or less unquestioningly, in the pursuit of his personal and family interests. Many a soldier of the time, inspired by loyalty to king and country, sacrificed his life on a battlefield which settled a royal succession or added a province to his autocrat's dominion.

Monarchy played a leading rôle in exalting national consciousness and national sentiment. The monarch was the symbol of national unity and independence, and in him resided national sovereignty. Indeed, "monarch" and "sovereign" were interchangeable terms. It was the monarch who coined money, levied taxes, maintained the army, declared war, and made peace. It was the nation that patriotically acquiesced in these acts of its sovereign. It was about the institution of monarchy that national traditions grew up, and it was under the patronage of individual monarchs that much national literature was produced. In the seventeenth century, it is true, England denied or narrowed the sovereign rights of her monarch, but the elaboration of constitutional government did not lessen the national

patriotism of Englishmen. It merely transformed the object
of patriotism. Autocratic monarchy had already accomplished its national function in England. Loyalty to a king
had passed into loyalty to his law and thence it was now
passing into loyalty to the national state.

It is an interesting fact that the great economic and commercial expansion of Europe at the close of the middle ages
and the beginning of modern times was closely associated
with the rise of national states. It was rulers or citizens of
Portugal, Spain, Holland, France, and England, who patronised novel voyages of exploration and discovery, who colonised distant places, and who profitted most by overseas
trade and exploitation. And the effects in the economic differentiation of nationalities and in the exaltation of national
consciousness have been striking.

Previously the economic undertakings of Europeans the-
oretically had been subject to the moral theology and canon
law of the international Catholic Church and practically
had been directed and controlled by local authorities, mu-
nicipal or guild. Not nations, but cities—Venice, Genoa,
Bruges, Antwerp, Lübeck, *etc.*—had been the units of economic life. But with this great commercial and colonial
expansion, both localism and universalism, both town and
church, were subordinated to the theory and practice of
national mercantilism. The government of every national
state sought to make it a self-sufficing economic entity, in
which the wealth and power of the nation as a whole should
be assured, and to this end many laws were enacted and
ordinances decreed. Foreign importation was prohibited
or protectively taxed. Domestic production was encouraged in various ways, notably by bounties. Colonies were
drawn into the monopolistic commercial system of the
mother-country. National navies were built and utilised
for the protection and forceful extension of national trade.
And national mercantilism, though couched in terms of national idealism, naturally led to international wars. As an
ecclesiastic of the seventeenth century quaintly confessed,

"In all the Strugglings and Disputes, that have of late years befallen this corner of the World, I found, that although the pretence was fine and Spiritual, yet the ultimate end and true scope, was Gold, and Greatness, and Secular Glory." [1]

The quest of gold in the European expansion of that time, and the national mercantilism which attended it, certainly contributed to the greatness and glory of nationality. As prosaic dynastic wars in Europe were merged with more colourful fighting on the high seas and in fantastic lands beyond the seas, national patriotism responded to a new and potent stimulus. Those persons who enriched themselves from the operation of national mercantilism were properly disposed to lead the chorus of national praise and thanksgiving, but they had a truly national following. To the masses in every national state a vast galaxy of new national heroes appeared—hardy mariners and daring discoverers, conquistadores and padres, smugglers and pirates and bold buccaneers. Even the enormous financial profits which accrued to individuals were represented as assets to the whole nation, and it seemed but meet and right that any distant economic undertaking of an individual European should be applauded by his compatriots and protected by his national government.

Ecclesiastical differentiation of many European nationalities synchronised with economic, political, and literary differentiation. Already, organised Christendom had been cleft asunder along the lines of linguistic differences between West and East. In the East, from an early date, the Christian churches had fallen under the direction and domination of temporal rulers and had become state or national churches, with variations in belief and ceremony and with differences of liturgical language. Thus had arisen the Armenian, Coptic, Greek, and Russian churches, each

---

[1] William Sancroft, archbishop of Canterbury, writing under the pseudonym of W. Blois, in *Modern Policies taken from Machiavel, Borgia, and other Choice Authors* (1690), p. 1.

employing its own national language and either contributing to the unity and distinctiveness of a national state in victory and success, as was the case with Russia, or, as exemplified by the Armenian and Coptic churches, cementing and preserving a nationality in defeat and subjection. In western and central Europe, on the other hand, the Catholic Church for centuries had been international rather than national; its liturgy and official literature were uniformly in Latin, its teachings were everywhere the same, and its organisation centred in a supreme spiritual institution, the papacy, which kept itself distinct from, and in a sense superior to, temporal states and national ambitions. Popes and Catholic bishops had always recognised the principle of nationality and had made minor concessions to it, but in general they had rigorously withstood anything which might savour of nationalism. They and their Church had builded an international, if not a cosmopolitan, culture and civilisation.

The international character of this civilisation was threatened in the later middle ages by several heretical movements, which, under the influence of quickening national consciousness, took on a national complexion, such as the Albigensian heresy among the Provençals, the Lollard in England, and the Hussite in Bohemia, and it was all but destroyed by the religious and ecclesiastical upheavals of the sixteenth century. The exaltation of nationality was in part the cause of the Protestant Revolution, and in turn the Protestant Revolution and the Catholic Reformation too were landmarks in the development of national patriotism. One cannot adequately understand why religious reformers secured the numerous and widespread popular following which they did secure unless one reads the national appeals which Luther addressed to Germans, Calvin to Frenchmen, and Knox to Scotsmen. Nor can one fully appreciate how the pope managed to retain a hold upon large numbers of Christians, except as one studies the increased favours which he accorded to national sovereigns, notably to those of Spain, Portugal, and France, and the national appeals which were made in his name.

The national results were impressive. The Protestant Revolution, by disrupting the Catholic Church and subjecting the Christian community to national variations of form and substance, dissolved much of the intellectual and moral cement which had long held European peoples together and at the same time gave religious sanction to the notion, already latent in each people, that it and it alone possessed a pure faith and a divine mission. The so-called religious wars of the sixteenth and seventeenth centuries, though by no means exclusively religious in origin or outcome—they were, in fact, primarily economic or dynastic,—were popular because they were fought in the name of religion and for a supposedly national religious ideal; and they certainly engendered a livelier sense of patriotism. Adherence to the Reformed Faith united the northern Netherlands in rebellion against the Catholic King of Spain; and the long conflict which they waged against him not only made them independent but stimulated among their inhabitants a sturdy Dutch patriotism. Simultaneously fidelity to Catholicism led the southern Netherlands to separate from their northern neighbours, to halt their own rebellion against the Spanish monarch, and to develop a distinctive Belgian patriotism. Furthermore, the general acceptance of Lutheranism by Scandinavians exalted the national monarchies of Denmark and Sweden and rendered the Swedes the special crusaders of Protestantism on the Continent. Allegiance to Presbyterianism aroused the national enthusiasm of the Scottish people. In England Protestantism assumed from the outset a national form: national monarchs established the Anglican Church, and national patriotism maintained it. When, for a variety of reasons, political, economic, and religious, Philip II of Spain sent his Grand Armada against England in 1588, the English people rallied wholeheartedly to the support of Good Queen Bess; and the destruction of the Armada was hailed as a glorious victory equally for English Protestantism and for the English nation, and as such it has ever since been extolled in patriotic poetry and religious legend.

In Protestant countries Catholics were long suspected of being unpatriotic because they did not prize the religious customs and traditions of the majority of their fellow countrymen. This was one of the reasons undoubtedly why Catholics suffered persecution at the hands of Protestants, and a similar reason may be assigned for the persecution of Protestants by Catholics. Catholicism was as much a symbol of national patriotism in Spain and France as was Protestantism in England and Scotland. The retention of the Catholic faith by the Irish at the very time when the English became Protestant, served to continue and to emphasise between these nationalities differences which the diffusion of the English language and the decline of Gaelic had promised to bridge. The more rigorously the English monarchs attempted to Anglicise the Irish by forcing Protestantism upon them, the more stubbornly the Irish clung to Catholicism as a sign of their continuing existence as a distinct nationality.

3

From the middle ages dated among European peoples a quickened and quickening national consciousness. In the sixteenth and seventeenth centuries, in many parts of Europe, religion, economics, politics, and literature were nationalised. By the seventeenth century, in western Europe, the states of Sweden, Denmark, Holland, France, Spain, Portugal, and England, were really national. Each of these states comprised a definite geographical area inhabited by populations that were marked off from their neighbours by a difference of speech; each possessed an independent political organisation and pursued an independent economic policy; and the citizens of each cherished peculiar customs and traditions. The process of nationalism—the process of transforming local, feudal, and imperial states into national states—had already begun.

But it was still dubious whether the process of nationalism would advance or recede. Localism rather than nationalism was still embodied in the political institutions of Germany and Italy, and international imperialism was actually supplanting nationalism in Austria, Russia, and Turkey. The Catholic Church had not fully approved of the new order in western Europe, and the Jesuits were manfully combatting its introduction into central Europe. Even in the West, the absence of national education, of universal military training, and of cheap and influential journals, and the presence of class-distinctions and class-privileges, prevented an exalted national consciousness from coming to full fruition, and national patriotism continued to be associated chiefly with loyalty to a monarchial sovereign.

Certain intellectual developments of the seventeenth and eighteenth centuries tended, however, to confirm and strengthen the nationalist process in western Europe, particularly in France and England. One was the philosophising about the popular overthrow of autocratic government in England and about the means of providing a more popular basis for government in France. Another was the rationalist spirit of the age, which sought in natural science and natural religion, in natural law and natural right, substitutes for supernatural religion and which, indirectly and temporarily at any rate, weakened international Christianity; but not even eighteenth-century rationalists could altogether abolish human sentiment and human emotion, and, beginning with attacks upon Christian superstitions, some of them ended with almost superstitious respect for the institution of the state and reverence for the emotion of patriotism.

A third development was the vogue of classicism, the fashionable reading (often in translation) of ancient Greek and Latin writers, from whom was derived, among other things,

the notion that patriotism is a noble virtue, that its proper
object is the impersonal country instead of the personal sovereign, and that its inevitable fruits are love of liberty and
hatred of tyranny. Plutarch's "Lives," which ran through
many editions in the original Greek and more in vernacular
translation, supplied much patriotic feeling, and patriotic
feeling was stiffened by the application of Stoic philosophy.
That devotion to the commonweal is commanded and
blessed by God was conned from the civics of Cicero in the
"Dream of Scipio," and that fidelity to the state and to
freedom is its own reward and can dispense with temporal
success or public recognition was learned from Lucan
and Tacitus.[1]

To be sure, the patriotism about which the Romans and
Greeks wrote, as has been pointed out, was not national patriotism, but the classicists of the seventeenth and eighteenth centuries did not hesitate to adapt it to the fancied requirements of their own, much larger and more artificial
states. Perrot d'Ablancourt, in a curious collection of
apothegms "taken from Plutarch, etc.," and published in
1664, described the patriotic chant of the Spartans in a
manner which suggests the *Marseillaise* of a later day, at
least in the disposition of its verses. D'Aguesseau's celebrated panegyric before the Parlement of Paris on the death
of Louis XIV (1715) was rich in classical allusion and redolent of antique patriotism. Alfieri, the foremost Italian
litterateur of the eighteenth century, bowed down in worship before the Greek and Roman picture of popular liberty
in arms against the tyrant. The great Frederick of Prussia
condescended, albeit in French, to indite "Letters on Patriotism" in style and spirit which he thought Athenian or,
more probably, Spartan. The fathers of American independence rolled classic patriotic phrases on their tongues,
and the histrionic "Give me liberty or give me death" of
a Patrick Henry was reminiscent of a Brutus's "Sic semper

[1] Stewart and Desjardins, *French Patriotism in the Nineteenth Century*
(1923), p. xix.

tyrannis." On the classical background of the leaders of
the French Revolution it is unnecessary to dwell; an heroic,
Cato-like patriotism was unmistakably manifest in the utterances and actions of a Vergniaud, a Madame Roland, and
a Camille Desmoulins.

For a time and to a degree the vogue of patriotic classicism ran counter to contemporary rationalism. Many intellectuals of the eighteenth century imagined that their rationalism was leading not toward nationalism but toward
cosmopolitanism; they took their cue, so far as antique
ideals were concerned, less from Cato than from Marcus
Aurelius; and they looked forward to a very near future
(they were incorrigible optimists) when the shadows of
national difference should vanish in the clear light of reason
and national citizenship give way to world-citizenship. "No
more," Rousseau pontifically proclaimed, "are there Frenchmen, Spaniards, Germans, or even Englishmen; there are
only Europeans. All have the same tastes, the same passions, the same customs." "The whole world being only one
city," confessed Goldsmith, "I do not much care in which
of its streets I happen to reside." "Love of country," Les-
sing declared, "is at best but an heroic vice, which I am
quite content to be without." "The world is my country,"
added Thomas Paine, with becoming pride; "mankind are
my brothers."

But these were spectacular flashes of cosmopolitan light-
ning which did no damage and served merely to herald a
drenching downpour of nationalism. For theories of cosmopolitanism and super-national humanitarianism were
speedily dampened and extinguished by the storms in politics and society, in industry and commerce, which swept
western and central Europe at the close of the eighteenth
and the opening of the nineteenth century. In the French
Revolution, in the Industrial Revolution, and likewise in
the romanticism which succeeded rationalism, are dis-
coverable the factors that finally resolved all doubts about
the future of national states and the currents that ulti-

mately galvanised national consciousness everywhere into
the nationalism which we know. To appreciate these currents and these factors, then, we must note certain features
of literary and philosophical romanticism and certain facts
in the story of the Industrial Revolution and in that of the
French Revolution.

4

The French Revolution promulgated to Europe and then
to the world the dogma of national democracy. It asserted
the right of individuals not only to determine their form of
government but also to choose the state to which they would
belong. In other words, it enunciated both the doctrine of
popular sovereignty and the doctrine of national self-determination. The theoretical basis of popular sovereignty
had already been prepared by Locke, Rousseau, and Jefferson, and by even earlier political philosophers. Something
which resembled the right of national self-determination,
moreover, had already been invoked by groups of Frenchmen and Poles as early as the fourteenth and fifteenth centuries, by the Dutch in the sixteenth century, by the Czechs
in the seventeenth century, and by Americans in 1776. But
it was the French Revolution which first put these doctrines into successful operation on a large scale. Political
democracy was substituted in France for monarchial autocracy, class-privileges were broken down, local and provincial
distinctions were swept away, and all French-speaking people in Europe were incorporated into the national state and
infused with the national spirit. All Frenchmen became
brothers, and together they embodied the national sovereignty of "la belle France."

The French Revolution also proclaimed the altruistic and
messianic character of the new nationalism. Of many per-
tinent citations which might be made, the following from
an official report of Lazare Carnot, the revolutionary and
patriotic "organiser of victory," is particularly informing: [1]

---

[1] "Rapport au Comité diplomatique du 13 février 1793," *Correspondence
générale de Carnot,* ed. Étienne Charavay (1892), vol. i, p. 363.

"Let us follow the law which is written on the heart of all men, and let us try not to abuse it; let only national honour and French generosity be for all peoples of the world the certain guarantee of the justice which you owe them and which you should render them; in breaking the chains of oppressed nations, let such sublime sentiments surpass their hopes and their desires. . . . The ancient and natural boundaries of France are the Rhine, the Alps, and the Pyrenees; the parties who have dismembered them have done so only by usurpation; hence, following ordinary rules, there would be no injustice in regaining them, no ambition in recovering those brothers who were ours formerly or in reëstablishing the bonds which were broken only through ambition.

"But these diplomatic claims, based on ancient possession, are null in our eyes as in those of reason. Every nation has the right to live by itself if it pleases or to unite with others, if they wish, for the common good. We Frenchmen recognise no sovereigns but the peoples themselves; our system is not at all one of domination, but one of fraternity."

So convinced were the French of the blessings of the new nationalism for themselves that they could not conceive how it could fail to bless all other peoples. It was a peculiarly French mission, they believed, to spread the new gospel—by the sword if necessary. They would undertake a modern crusade, a crusade in behalf of democratic nationalism. In December, 1792, the National Convention decreed: "The French nation . . . will treat as enemies every people who, refusing liberty and equality or renouncing them, may wish to maintain, recall, or treat with a prince and the privileged classes; on the other hand, it engages not to subscribe to any treaty and not to lay down its arms until after the establishment of the sovereignty and independence of the people whose territory the troops of the [French] Republic shall have entered and until the people shall have adopted the principles of equality and founded a free and democratic government." [1] Other peoples did not immediately heed the call of the new messias. Large numbers of them—Germans, Englishmen, Dutchmen, Spaniards, and Italians—actually supported their respective monarchs in armed attempts to suppress what they were pleased to term the "excesses" of the French Revolution. Probably, as so often happens to missionary enterprise, what seemed altruistic and messianic to the crusaders appeared to their beneficiaries (or victims) selfish and downright satanic. At any rate, the French Revolution precipitated a series of great international wars, in the protracted course of which the French themselves subordinated political democracy and individual liberty to military dictatorship (in the person of Napoleon Bonaparte), won glory for themselves more than freedom for others, and allowed the new nationalism to become identified with selfishness and militarism quite as much as with peace and altruism. The wars, both in their earlier Revolutionary aspects and in their later Napoleonic phases, stimulated enormously the national patriotism and national pride of the French people; eventually also they evoked among other European peoples the spirit of nationalism, but this was accomplished not directly through the French as gospellers of the right of national self-determination so much as indirectly against the French as foes of national independence and national sovereignty. In the long run the French Revolution shewed that nationalism might be associated with monarchial institutions almost as closely as with those of political democracy.

The French Revolution made many definite and signal contributions to the subsequent, almost universal, practice of nationalism. It strengthened the lay state at the expense of the church and, while allowing to individuals a considerable latitude of ecclesiastical affiliation, it inculcated the doctrine that all citizens owed their first and paramount loyalty to the national state and it prescribed quasi-religious rites before altars of *la patrie* and over the remains

[1] J. B. Duvergier (ed.), *Collection complète des Lois, etc.*, vol. v, p. 84.

of the dead fallen "pour la patrie." It inaugurated such
nationalist forms as the national flag, the national anthem,
and national holidays. It insisted upon linguistic uniformity.

About the last point a few reflections may be illuminating. Until the French Revolution no attempt had been
made by any government to force its citizens or subjects
to use a particular national language. Never had French
or English kings or Holy Roman Emperors thought it needful or desirable to insist upon linguistic uniformity. French
was spoken at the court of Queen Elizabeth, Italian at the
courts of Francis I and Henry IV, and even Slovene was
one of the languages recognised and spoken at the Viennese
court. Latin long remained an official language in Hungary; and when the princes of Lithuania became masters
of White Russia they adopted the latter's speech to the
detriment of their own. True, there were decrees of Spanish monarchs against the use of Hebrew and Arabic, but
these decrees had religious rather than national significance.
French Revolutionaries, however, recognising the linguistic
basis of nationality and determined to exalt national loyalty above all other loyalties, and mindful too, in a specific
way, of the rebellious behaviour of many Bretons, deemed
it necessary to impose on all French citizens the "central
or national language." To Barrère and the Abbé Gregoire
belong the distinction of having been the first political
theorists to adumbrate a policy of linguistic oppression and
persecution for the benefit of a sovereign national state.[1]

It was the French Revolution, moreover, that elaborated
the first general scheme of national elementary education,
which should be state-supported and state-directed, compulsory and universal, and in which national patriotism
and national duty should be taught equally with the three
R's. It was the French Revolution, too, that adopted and
gave effect to the principle of the "nation in arms," the

---

[1] Cf. A. Van Gennep, "La Disparition et la Persistance des Patois,"
Religions, Moeurs et Légendes, vol. iv (1911), pp. 241-268.

principle that all able-bodied male citizens should be trained for war and liable to conscription for military or naval service. And, finally, it was the French Revolution that gave impetus and character to nationalist journalism, to the publication of newspapers, pamphlets, and magazines so cheap and so demagogic that they would appeal to the masses of the whole nation, to the half educated even more than to the well educated.

From the days of the French Revolution to the present, the democratic dogma has proved a most helpful bolster for nationalism.[1] Individuals cannot feel quite the same loyalty to a nationality in which they are subjects as to a nationality in which they are citizens, for, as Rousseau pointed out a century and a half ago, we love what is ours more than what is another's. Of course, Rousseau nowhere said that the doctrine of popular sovereignty is applicable only to a nationality; he talked about "the people" in the vaguest way; but events soon demonstrated that political democracy could be far more effective in a country which was a linguistic unit, or at least in which the large majority of people used the same language, than in a polyglot empire. If people were to govern themselves, they must understand one another and be able to speak and read a common language. Nationality has thus provided a practical basis for democratic government, and democratic government, or the striving for it, has fostered nationalism.

The democratic dogma has everywhere carried with it more or less obvious corollaries. One has been the requirement that a people who would govern themselves must be

---

[1] Professor William T. Laprade has argued against the contention that "democracy brought nationalism in its wake" (*Annual Report of the American Historical Association*, 1915, pp. 226-227), and if we were to accept his definition of nationalism as "modern national feeling" we could hardly dissent from his conclusion. But nationalism as defined above (p. 26) certainly appeared first in the wake of doctrines of popular sovereignty; generally and powerfully it has been abetted by political democracy; and most countries which have become nationalist have at least aspired to political democracy. Nationalism in some cases has preceded democracy, but that there is a close relationship between these phenomena admits, I think, of little doubt.

literate and hence should be compelled to learn in democratic schools how to read and write the national language. Another has been the conviction that a people who would shape their own policies and destiny must be constantly informed of the domestic and foreign problems affecting their country and familiarised with the plans of their representatives for solving such problems, and hence should be supplied frequently and readily with national news. A third has been the obligation that a people who would enjoy the rights and privileges of self-government must likewise assume its duties and burdens and hence should be prepared and willing to fight for their country and to pay the supreme sacrifice. In practice political democracy has invariably created a demand for state-directed systems of popular elementary education, for state-controlled systems of universal military training, and for the multiplication of public journals and newspapers. But these agencies are the very agencies which have done most in the nineteenth and twentieth centuries to propagate nationalism.

It is difficult to imagine the operation of democratic government in a country devoid of national schools, national journalism, and national armaments, but it is easy to think of countries in which national armaments, national journalism, and national schools have existed without political democracy. It would seem that the democratic dogma as accepted by the French Revolution was immediately reenforced by instruments which proved to be instruments of nationalism, and that these instruments were then appropriated by other peoples with or without the original political dogma. In the nineteenth century democracy spread fast, but nationalism spread faster.

5

Synchronising with the political revolution in France was the beginning in England of that application of power-driven machinery to manufacturing and to commerce, which, continuing throughout the nineteenth century and down to our own day and permeating all civilised countries, has wrought a veritable revolution in industry and in society, in customs of living, working, and travelling. This Industrial Revolution is, quite as much as democracy, a mark of the present age.

On first thought it may seem that the Industrial Revolution has had little or no connection with nationality or nationalism, that, on the contrary, it has been laying economic foundations for internationalism and cosmopolitanism. Obviously it has shrunken the earth and tied as by ropes of steel all sorts of men together. By means of steamship and locomotive, telegraph and telephone, motor car and airplane, cinema and radio, it has brought most nationalities of the whole world in closer contact with one another than were the thirteen English-speaking American colonies a century and a half ago. It has plainly established an international market of supply and demand for capital, raw materials, finished products, labor, and ideas. Has it not broken down the last barriers of local isolation and self-sufficiency?

Yes, so far as local isolation is concerned. But it has not overcome national isolation. Closer observation of the Industrial Revolution should disclose the fact that its effects, important though they may have been on the world at large, have been much more important within the territorial confines of national states. It was a national state in which the Industrial Revolution had its beginnings, and it was chiefly to national states that the Revolution spread in the nineteenth century, and in almost every instance these states were already imbued with traditions of mercantilism. By means of the new machinery production of goods was vastly augmented, but the organisation of production remained on a national basis. The principal instruments of improved communication, both national and international, were sometimes owned and always controlled by national governments. Foreign consumption of goods increased, but domestic consumption increased more rapidly.

International trade grew, but trade within an industrialised nation grew faster. Money and credit and banking, the life-blood of industrial capitalism, had international aspects, but they too rested on national foundations and were utilised primarily within a nation. Labour, also, though held by Marxian Socialists and other internationalists to be nonnational, tended to crystallise along national lines and to evince, at least in times of stress, a national patriotism as vigorous and vehement as that of bankers and manufacturers.

Traditions of mercantilism were not the only reason for the appropriation of the Industrial Revolution to national purposes. It was easier and more natural for one to do business with persons who spoke and read one's own language than with others. Even the enormous transit of ideas and news which the Industrial Revolution made possible, assumed, for linguistic reasons, a complexion predominantly national. News-gathering agencies were organised on national bases, and the publication of news was necessarily in a language comprehended by the readers. Any idea, no matter how cosmopolitan, was likely to be variously coloured by the several linguistic media through which it must be expressed, and thus to be received by the members of each nationality as an idea peculiar to themselves.

Then, too, the Industrial Revolution rendered possible and practical the permanent establishment and rapid extension of that national democracy which the French Revolution indicated as ideally desirable. Forms of political democracy had obtained long before the eighteenth century, as, for example, in ancient Athens, or among primitive Teutonic tribesmen, but never had they been connected with our present-day institutions of the ballot and of responsible, representative government or deemed applicable to a large national state. Only a radical improvement in the means of transportation and communication and a revolutionary change in the social life of the masses could introduce the type of political democracy which would foster nationalism.   Nationalism as a world-phenomenon could come, as it were, only by machinery, and actually by the machinery of the Industrial Revolution it has come.

In a special sense the Industrial Revolution has contributed incalculably to the elaboration of the most effective instruments of nationalist propaganda, whether in democracies or in monarchies.   Population has prodigiously increased with the advent of power-driven machinery, and the very vastness of our modern cities, a natural accompaniment of factory-production and wholesale trading, has provided favourable and fertile fields for popular mass-education.   Time and space have been so lessened by railway and motor car and so nearly annihilated by telegraph, telephone, and radio, as to bring rural communities within the educational orbit of capital cities.   Journalism and warfare, like education, have been revolutionised both by mechanical developments and by increased numbers of human beings. It has become possible since the Industrial Revolution to print newspapers rapidly and cheaply and to sell them widely.   It has become practical since the Industrial Revolution to arm an entire nationality against another and to kill on a large scale scientifically.   The armaments, the journalism, and the national education which flourished so conspicuously in all national states before and during the recent Great War would have been unthinkable without the Industrial Revolution.

6

Nationalism as a more or less unconscious process was certainly quickened by the Industrial Revolution and by the French Revolution, but nationalism as a purposeful doctrine received its chief impetus from the philosophical and literary "Zeitgeist" of the first decades of the nineteenth century—the Age of Romanticism. Romanticism, as exemplified by its great apostles, Herder and Schlegel in Germany, Chateaubriand in France, and Sir Walter Scott in Britain, represented an intellectual and aesthetic reaction against the "Enlightenment" of the seventeenth and eighteenth centuries, both against its pseudo-cosmopolitanism and against its classicism. Romanticism was a protest against the dictum that man lives by reason alone, and it was also an imaginative escape from the frightful realities of the Revolutionary and Napoleonic wars. It prized emotion, extolled common things and common men, and found in the idealised past, more in the history of the middle ages than in that of ancient times, the most ennobling ideals for a glorious future of liberty and peace.

Romanticism had a pronounced nationalist bent. Its interest in common men and common things stimulated the study and revival of folk-ways, folk-legends, and folk-music. Its appeal to history meant an appeal to folk-history, to adorned tales of the "good old days" of fanciful national independence and national integrity. Being a literary movement, romanticism exalted folk-language and folk-literature and folk-culture; being philosophic, it attributed to every folk a soul and inherent mental qualities and distinguishing manners and customs; being emotional, it tended to consecrate the peculiarities of national life and to inspire a popular worship of nationality.

In criticism of Joseph II, that outstanding imperial cosmopolite of the late eighteenth century, the romantic Herder wrote: "Has a people anything dearer than the speech of its fathers? In its speech resides its whole thought-domain, its tradition, history, religion, and basis of life, all its heart and soul. To deprive a people of its speech, is to deprive it of its one eternal good. . . . As God tolerates all the different languages in the world, so also should a ruler not only tolerate but honour the various languages of his peoples. . . . The best culture of a people cannot be expressed through a foreign language; it thrives on the soil of a nation most beautifully, and, I may say, it thrives only, by means of the nation's inherited and inheritable dialect. With language is created the heart of a people; and is it not a high concern, amongst so many peoples—Hungarians, Slavs, Rumanians, *etc.*,—to plant seeds of well-being for the far future and in the way that is dearest and most appropriate to them?" [1]   Friedrich Schlegel, lecturing in 1812, declared: "Every important and independent nation has the right, if I may say so, of possessing a literature peculiar to itself; and the meanest barbarism is that which would oppress the speech of a people and a country, or exclude it from all higher education; it is mere prejudice which leads us to consider languages that have been neglected, or that are unknown to ourselves, as incapable of being brought to a higher perfection." [2]   Said Jan Kollár, the Slovak patriot-poet, in 1824: "It is a mistake to call the country in which we dwell by the holy name of fatherland; the true undying homeland, against which might and deceit cannot prevail, is custom, speech, and concord." [3]

By the romantic movement scholarship itself was impelled into new channels.   The interest which romanticists aroused in folk-language led to a marked development of national philology.   Their appeal to folk-history called forth the type of national history which predominated throughout the nineteenth century.   Their emphasis on folk-customs gave a powerful impetus to anthropology, comparative jurisprudence, and comparative religion.   The great majority of social scientists proceeded to devote themselves to the exposition, in one form or another, of national distinctions.   By accentuating nationality and providing it with a "scientific" basis and a "scholarly" justification, they were repaying their debt to romanticism and at the same time they were assembling the stone and mortar for the impressive modern temple of nationalism.

---

[1] *Briefe zu Beförderung der Humanität*, Br. 10, vol. i (Riga, 1793), pp. 146-148.

[2] *Geschichte der alten und neuen Literatur, Vorlesungen gehalten zu Wien im Jahre 1817*, in *Sämmtliche Werke*, vol. ii. (1846), p. 24. Of these lectures, i and x are particularly illuminating.

[3] On Kollár, see Alfred Fischel, *Der Panslawismus bis zum Weltkrieg* (1919).

The influence of romanticism was not confined to literary declamation or scholarly exegesis. The romantic songs of an Arndt and a Körner among the Germans and of a Kollár among the Slavs and the no less romantic prose-poems of a Mazzini among the Italians were effectual incitements to popular action in behalf of national unity and national independence. The active participation in the War of Greek Independence of a Lord Byron, a Francis Lieber, and many another Philhellene, was a sacred symbol of the universal troth which romanticism had plighted to the new nationalism.

7

We have now observed how the consciousness of nationality was greatly exalted in Europe, at least in western Europe, by literary, political, economic, and religious differentiations in the sixteenth and seventeenth centuries, and how it began to be transformed into nationalism at the close of the eighteenth and opening of the nineteenth century by the French Revolution, the Industrial Revolution, and the vogue of romanticism. Throughout the nineteenth century and to date in the twentieth, the process of nationalism has assumed a threefold aspect. First, thanks to the Industrial Revolution, it has ceased to be restricted to western Europe; it has affected in time every nationality in Europe and most nationalities in all the other continents. Secondly, it has advanced apace in states, such as England and France, which had already more or less fortuitously become national states. Thirdly, and perhaps most strikingly, it has invaded non-national states, such as the Habsburg, Muscovite, and Ottoman Empires, and broken them into national fragments.

The French became nationalist during their great political and social revolution at the end of the eighteenth century; and the advantages which they derived shortly afterwards from the Industrial Revolution enabled them to perfect their political democracy and with it those instruments of democracy which, as we have seen, were likewise instruments of nationalism—national education, national journalism, and national armaments. Thereby the French not only retained but intensified their nationalism. To Carnot, Danton, and Bonaparte succeeded Thiers, Napoleon III, Gambetta, Poincaré, and Foch.

The English had, if anything, a livelier national consciousness in the eighteenth century than the French, but the strong national prejudices of Englishmen for a time prevented them from appropriating the political democracy which was the ally and abettor of modern nationalism in France. The English, however, welded their national feeling and sentiment in the crucible of the Revolutionary and Napoleonic War, and eventually a particularly abundant harvest from the Industrial Revolution assured to them what they had refused to garner directly from the French Revolution. Gradually the nationalising influences of armaments, newspapers, and public schools, and of national democracy too, were manifest in Great Britain. After Burke, Pitt, Nelson, and Wellington, followed Canning, Palmerston, Disraeli, Salisbury, Chamberlain, and Kitchener.

English-speaking people in America established a strong national government for themselves in the very year in which the French Revolution began. Some of them were devoted to earlier English traditions of liberty; others were impressed by the contemporary democratic and egalitarian principles of the French; all were united by the memory of recent common suffering and success in a war against the "tyranny" of a British king. This community of interest was strengthened not only immediately by the creation of a common government but subsequently by the building of railways and the stretching of telegraph wires, by the universal use of print-paper and the ubiquitous erection of "little red school-houses." Came naturally therefrom a thoroughgoing political democracy, and, though a horrible civil war supervened, came quite as naturally a real nationalism. The United States might not comprise a single nationality wholly distinct from every other nationality, but in the zeal of its citizens for nationalism, no matter how artificial such nationalism might be, it was not to be outdone by any European country.

For a century and more the principles of political democracy and national self-determination were jointly invoked by romantically inclined leaders of peoples throughout Europe and America. Old nationalities which had long been subject to the rule of alien nationalities were induced to struggle both for political liberty and for national independence. Nationalities which had long been broken into political fragments were moved to seek national unity and national democracy. Nationalities which had been burdened by monarchial despotism were prevailed upon to revolt and to set up a democratic government which would be more intensely national. In the 1820's appeared in Europe the embryonic national states of Greece and Serbia (Yugoslavia) and in America a group of Spanish-speaking republics. In the 1830's the Belgians successfully freed themselves from Dutch sovereignty, whilst the Poles unsuccessfully rebelled against Russia, and the Italians against Austria. In the 1840's the Germans attempted to erect a democratic national state. In the 1850's and 1860's the Italians and the Rumanians alike established their national independence. In all these instances, the resurgence of a nationality was in part a romantic invocation of the past; it was, historically, a movement backwards. But the actual driving force was the revolutionary sentiment of liberty, equality, and fraternity, and the popular conviction that every people had the right to dispose of itself as it pleased.[1] And the effect in every instance was the fostering of nationalism.

The rise of nationalism was normally attended by a striving for national democracy; democrats and liberals

[1] *Cf.* Bertrand Auerbach, *Les Races et les Nationalités en Autriche-Hongrie,* 2nd ed. (1917), p. xvi.

were ordinarily the vanguard of nationalist movements.
But not always. In some cases, notably in that of Germany, national unification was eventually achieved, not
by a democratically minded assembly but by a militarist
king and an aristocratic statesman. But even in Germany,
Bismarck and William I could hardly have succeeded where
the Frankfort Assembly had failed, had it not been that
ready to their hands were compulsory education, patriotic
journalism, and what amounted to a national army. These
very agencies of German, and European, nationalism were
borrowed, moreover, almost simultaneously by Japanese
aristocratic statesmen, who utilised them in conjunction
with the national Japanese religion and in lieu of political
democracy for the furtherance of Japanese nationalism.
In autocratic Russia, too, nationalism emerged; here there
was no assistance from national democracy and little from
national education, but the Orthodox Russian Church
proved itself a peculiarly efficacious instrument of
nationalism.

For many years within the nationalist empires of Russia
and Germany agitation of "oppressed" nationalities proceeded. The more the Germans endeavoured to Germanise
their empire, the more the subject minorities of Poles, Danes,
and Alsatians sought to preserve their national individual-
ity. The more the Russians tried to Russify their domain,
the more the subject peoples—the Poles, the Finns, the
Esths, the Letts, the Lithuanians, etc.—worked for national
emancipation. In the Austrian Empire the dominant Germans and Magyars were actually outnumbered by the subject peoples—Czechoslovaks, Poles, Yugoslavs, Rumanians,
etc.—and as these became nationalist, they made of the
Empire an absurdly anachronistic and ramshackle structure which the Great War of 1914 at last brought down in
a miserable heap of ruins. Before the Great War, the
Turkish Empire, as everybody knew, was the "sick man of
Europe," and his sickness was primarily the prevalent epi-
demic of nationalism: not only his Christian subjects—

Greeks, Serbs, Bulgars, and Armenians—but a Mohammedan "oppressed" nationality, such as the Arab, were
delirious with nationalist fever, whilst he himself, once
fairly sane and tolerant, was insanely bent on reducing a
most polyglot dominion to Turkish unity.

To the ardent nationalist of the nineteenth and twentieth centuries it was not necessary that his nationality be
numerous. Indeed, to him littleness had a sentimental and
romantic value which mere bigness lacked. Nor was it but
a temporary inconvenience that his little nationality should
have become adepts in the use of a "foreign" tongue and
ceased long since to speak or read the distinctive language
of their forebears. They should and could have their own
language artificially revived, and forthwith it was done.
The bulk of the Irish knew only English in the eighteenth
century, but in the twentieth, under the influence of nationalism, they have been learning, almost as though it were
a foreign tongue, their aboriginal native Gaelic. Artificial
Irish nationalism must be rendered natural by artificial
respiration. Latterly, also, Norwegian nationalists have
emphasised their dialectic differences from other Scandinavian speech, have effected a political separation from
Sweden, and changed the Latinised name of their capital
Christiania to the old Norse form of Oslo. Icelanders are
behaving in similar fashion. And so the story goes with
the budding little nationalisms of Catalans, Provençals,
Basques, Wends, Flemings, White Russians, Manxmen, and
Maltese!

During the nineteenth century the tide of nationalism
rose steadily. Perhaps flood tide has been reached in the
Great War of the twentieth century. But who knows?
The mighty surge of nationalist propaganda still booms
loud.

Romanticism, the French Revolution, and the Industrial
Revolution together made possible and perhaps inevitable
the general nationalist process, of which some outstanding
landmarks have just been indicated. But the historical

process could not have taken the precise shape it did take, and the present nationalist state of mind, so universal throughout the world, could not be exactly what it is, without the aid of special engines of propaganda forged chiefly by doctrinaires and used with telling effect upon the masses of mankind. To these engines of propaganda, to their structure and their function, it is important to direct attention.

III

THE PROPAGATION OF NATIONALISM

1

THE sentiment of nationality is not new. The sentiment of patriotism is not new. But nationalism is new. Only since the eighteenth century has there been a conscious and purposeful attempt to redraw the political map of the whole world on national lines and to instill in the hearts and minds of all human beings a supreme loyalty to their respective nationalities and to their several national states.

That this attempt should have been crowned with brilliant successes in so brief a time is attributable not merely to certain highly favourable circumstances in recent times—the Industrial Revolution and the vogue of romanticism and the democratic dogma—but quite specifically to the zeal with which nationalism has been propagated first among intellectuals and then among the masses. Events of the eighteenth century predisposed some countries to nationalism. Propaganda during the nineteenth century rendered nationalism a universal phenomenon.

Propaganda, despite the opprobrium which in some quarters has been heaped upon it by reason of its association with questionable devices latterly employed by war-time governments in order to raise the patriotic temperature of their peoples to the boiling point, should still be deemed at least a neutral, if not a wholly respectable, word. There may be propaganda of truth as well as of falsehood, that which is evangelic as well as that which is diabolic. Certainly, so far as the propaganda of nationalism is concerned, it was inaugurated and carried forward by scholars and idealists who were moved by the noblest and most altruistic feelings and who would have been inexpressibly pained to learn of some of the uses to which their preachments were subsequently put. Propaganda may be good or bad, moral or immoral, but it always involves a more or less conscious effort to influence the thought and action of one's fellows. This is the true meaning of the word, obviously appropriate to nationalism. For nationalism, as we have defined it, is not a natural, instinctive thing; it is artificial, and its growth and spread are traceable to artificial stimulation, in a word to propaganda.

In the propagation of nationalism three factors or sets of factors must be considered. First and fundamental is the elaboration of a doctrine of nationalism by an eminent company of "intellectuals"—philologists, historians, anthropologists, economists, philosophers, and litterateurs. Second and very influential is the championing of the doctrine by groups of citizens who discover in it a satisfaction and refreshment for their souls and sometimes an advantage to their pockets. Thirdly, the doctrine finds lodgement in the popular mind by means of new and curious, but singularly universal, forms of mass-education.

2

The work of the intellectuals has been basic and various. It has comprised scholarly treatises on philology, scientific national histories, annotated speculations on politics and economics, artistic representations of national idiosyncrasies and national distinctions, and likewise innumerable popularisations of all these learned and elegant tomes in the form of compendia, text-books, pamphlets, magazine articles, and newspaper items. Many of the real savants have not been avowedly nationalist, but their work, naturally reflecting in subject-matter the interests and aspirations of the age in which they lived, has been of a sort that their cousinly intellectuals, the vulgarisers, could seize upon and utilise in the service of nationalism.

The scientific and comparative study of language hardly antedates the French Revolution. In was in 1786 that Sir William Jones in his *Asiatick Researches* called the attention of scholars to similarities between Sanskrit, on the one hand, and Greek and Latin and German, on the other. Thenceforth philology advanced rapidly. German savants, such as J. C. Adelung, A. L. von Schlözer, the Grimms, and Max Müller developed the theory of an original Aryan language, from which not only Sanskrit, Latin, Greek, and German had been derived but also Persian, Armenian, and the Celtic and Slavonic tongues. It was assumed that these Aryan languages were better than any other, and, inasmuch as Max Müller and certain of his colleagues took the trouble to identify language with race, it was soon assumed that the Aryan peoples were superior to all others.

But which of the modern Aryan peoples was closest in speech and therefore in virtue and valour to the original pure Aryans? Here was a golden opportunity for the esoteric closet science of philology to play a rôle in the propagation of nationalism, and if some of its anointed devotees were too self-effacing or too self-respecting to participate in the sport, pseudo-philologists there were in plenty who undertook with courage and conviction to prove that the Germans were the purest and most valiant people on earth or that the Greeks were the purest and most valiant, or mayhap the Rumanians or the Lithuanians! And in the meantime scholarly philologists and philologists who were not so scholarly were alike busied with research into the origin and development of their respective national languages. The ponderous German dictionaries of Adelung and Jakob Grimm were paralleled in national consequences if not in bulk by the Polish dictionary of Linde, the Czech dictionary of Jungmann, the Russian grammar of Lomonossov, the Greek studies of Korais, and so on *ad infinitum*.

To the aid of the philologists rallied the students of comparative law and jurisprudence, both those who investi-

gated legal and customary likenesses between Hindus and
Europeans and those who exhaustively traced the rise of
national institutions. On the one hand, the study of similarities in custom and law gave seeming support to the
contention that the Aryan peoples were related to one
another and superior to all other peoples. On the other
hand, the study of peculiarities in institutional life provided
many a powerful prop for the contention that every nationality had had a long, useful, and distinguished existence,
that its "soul" was to be found in its institutions as much
as in its language.

Until the latter part of the eighteenth century no one
seems to have doubted that man, so far as he could be
regarded as animal at all, formed a single indivisible species. But with the rise of anthropology a new opinion was
advanced. At the very beginning of the nineteenth century the prominent French naturalist Virey urged [1] that
the races of mankind are so different from one another
that they must have had separate origins. Virey's polygenist theory was duly endorsed by reputable members of
his guild, notably by Lawrence in England and by Nott
and Gliddon in America,[2] and was curiously applied by the
German romanticist Schlegel to the blossoming science of
philology. *Quot linguae, tot gentes,* was Schlegel's dictum,
and though later anthropologists pointed out the gross fal-
lacy of the equivalence of speech and breed, it long dominated European thought on the subject and reënforced the
sentiment of nationality. A distinct racial body had been
discovered, or invented, for every national "soul." And
inasmuch as it followed from the polygenist theory that
races are unequal, it was likewise argued that national
souls are unequal, that some have a better, purer, and

---

[1] Jules Joseph Virey, *Histoire naturelle du genre humaine,* 2 vols.
(1801) ; 2nd ed., 3 vols. (1824).

[2] Sir William Lawrence *Lectures on the Physiology, Zoölogy, and
Natural History of Man* (1817) ; J. C. Nott and G. R. Gliddon, *Types of
Mankind* (1854) ; *cf.* J. L. Myres, *Influence of Anthropology on the Course
of Political Science* (1916), pp. 68-73.

healthier racial embodiment than others. This was the argument, for example, of the Comte de Gobineau, that opinionated pseudo-anthropologist and pseudo-litterateur of the mid-nineteenth century; it was essentially the argument of that strangely fanatical *fin de siècle* Germanophile Stewart Houston Chamberlain; it is still, with variations and improvisations, the argument of those diverting American publicists, Messrs. Madison Grant and Lothrop Stoddard.

The general run of present-day anthropologists do not trouble themselves with polygenism; they have become extraordinarily critical of generalisations about "race"; and they give slight succour to the cause of nationalism. But we may hazard the guess that it will be a long time before their doubts and indifferentism will receive the same public recognition as the fallacious certitudes of their predecessors. At any rate, all anthropologists, those of today as well as those of yesterday, may be assured of grateful remembrance on the part of nationalist posterity for having centred much scholarly attention upon folk-ways and folk-customs, the very heart-beats of nationality.

Both comparative law and comparative philology—to say nothing of romanticism and the stirring events at the close of the eighteenth century—gave a new turn to the writing of history. The pursuit of Clio is a very old vocation or avocation of man, but, prior to the nineteenth century, very little history of a strictly national character had been produced. It had been local history or "world" history or religious history, chronicles of kings, biographies of warriors or saints, philosophical disquisitions upon the course of God's dealings with man, but almost never national history as such. During the nineteenth century, however, very little history was written which was not national in scope or import. Some of it was "scientific," but most of it dealt with material which was grist to the mill of nationalism. It treated of the past of one's nationality, of national politics, national life, national heroes, national wars, national diplomacy. In Germany, the quickening of national consciousness at the beginning of the century was attended by the projection of the *Monumenta Germaniae Historica,* that vast collection of all the sources for German history; and presently appeared the giant figures of the Prussian school of patriot-historians—Giesebrecht, Häusser, Droysen, Sybel, and Treitschke.

Germany has had no monopoly of nationalist history. In almost every country collections of source-material for the writing of national history have been made, national historical associations have been formed, and great national epics have been produced. If we were to list the historians of the nineteenth century who have been most widely read and popularly esteemed, we would record everywhere the names of national historians—Martin, Thierry, Michelet, Guizot, Thiers, Hanotaux, and Fustel de Coulanges in France; Macaulay, Green, Stubbs, Freeman, Froude, and Seeley in England; George Bancroft, Motley, Prescott, Parkman, Fiske, and Roosevelt in the United States; Botta in Italy; Palacky in Bohemia; Lafuente in Spain; Carvalho in Portugal; Xenopol in Rumania; Blok in Holland; Pirenne in Belgium.[1] And these would be but a slight indication of the overwhelmingly nationalist trend of recent historiography.

Even more directly nationalist than the political historians have been the historians of national literatures. Taine, whose brilliant work on English literature is the type and example of a multitude of nineteenth-century books of this kind, perceived something almost mystical in the continuous distinctiveness of English prose and poetry and advanced the hypothesis that this something was the product of, and inherent in, the admixture of Celt and Anglo-Saxon. Such an hypothesis is quite unten-

[1] *Cf.* H. Morse Stephens, "Nationality and History," *American Historical Review,* vol. xxi, pp. 225-236 (January, 1916). Says the late Professor Stephens, "The historian is influenced by the prevailing spirit of his age, and he feeds the spirit of national intolerance to-day as his predecessors fed the flames of religious intolerance in days gone by" (p. 236).

able in the light of later anthropological study, for Taine, like Max Müller, was confusing a linguistic group with a biological race. But literary historians, and litterateurs in general, have gone on, in blissful ignorance of scientific anthropology, blandly advertising Celtic mysticism, Slavic melancholy, Mongolian cunning, Teutonic fierceness, and Anglo-Saxon common-sense, as if such qualities were hereditary within the limits of fixed races. And they have had their reward in popular approval, because for every person who peruses a learned treatise on race there are at least ten thousand who read a novel or see a play in which national character is depicted as indelible and unchangeable.

Among litterateurs of the nineteenth century, poets, dramatists, and novelists have been conspicuously successful propagandists of nationalism. At their hands national traits and national characters have been as rigidly conventionalised as was the chorus on the ancient Greek stage. The average man's notion of a Frenchman or of a German or of an Irishman or of a Jew is gotten not from extensive personal observation but from antitypes supplied by versifiers, story-tellers, and playwrights. There is something infectious about all this. It stimulates a people to live up to the character ascribed to them, and in turn as they shew forth the traits expected of them their literary critics and interpreters become more enamoured of the original conventions and more eloquent in expressing them. No doubt nationalities do differ from one another at any particular time, but the point which we are here trying to make is that litterateurs have tended to overemphasise these differences, to simplify and stereotype them, and thereby to provide a literary basis for the current popular belief that every nationality has a "soul" and a "mission."

The popular belief that every nationality has a right to sovereignty and statehood sprang naturally, as we have seen, out of the precepts and practices of the French Revolution and the Napoleonic era; and throughout the nine-

teenth century a galaxy of philosophers and jurists were
weaving out of the truths, half-truths, and guesses of philology, anthropology, and history the doctrinal garment of
political nationalism. Fichte eloquently proclaimed the
linguistic basis of nationality and the national foundation
of the true state. Schleiermacher zealously maintained that
a clearly defined geographic unit is naturally the abode of
a state. Hegel mystically conceived of the state as an end
in itself, as a divine person, as an organism comprehend-
ing a folk. Savigny painstakingly studied "folk" (he might
have called it "nationality") and defined it as an aggregation of individuals living a definitely indicated kind of life
and permeated by a common spirit whose most obvious
manifestations are language and law; a folk, he added,
tends always and irresistibly to reveal its inner and in-
visible spirit in outward and visible form, and this form
is the national state, by means of which a folk attains to
true personality and the power to act. Bluntschli prettily
summed up the earlier German speculation on the subject
by declaring that a national state is an aggregation of men
united, as government and subjects, on a definite territory,
into a social-ethical, organic, masculine personality, whilst
a nationality is a union of masses of men of different occupations and social strata in an hereditary society of common spirit, feeling, and race, bound together especially
by language and customs in a common civilisation which
gives them a sense of unity and distinction from all foreigners, quite apart from the bond of the state.

Here, then, was the essential doctrine—the sacred exclusive nationality, marked by peculiar language, race, customs, and civilisation, and destined to enshrine a sovereign
deified national state. To this doctrine some glosses were
added. On the one side, Friedrich List, following in the
footsteps of Alexander Hamilton, pointed to economic advantages of national unity and shewed how a national state
might strengthen itself by pursuing a policy of economic
isolation and self-sufficiency; to him as to many politicians

tariff protectionism was a bit of nationalist *realpolitik*. On the other side Mazzini glowingly idealised nationality and talked incessantly about its divine mission and human duties, about its service to humanity; and the optimistic view of the Italian was shared to greater or less degree by all the prophets and seers who rose in numbers legion among oppressed and subject nationalities. It was also shared by numerous liberals among other and presumably happier peoples, by Ernest Renan in France, by Émile Laveleye in Belgium, by John Stuart Mill in England, by Francis Lieber in America.

Subsequently, a few advanced liberals grew suspicious of the practical operation of the new gospel and diverted their energies and enthusiasms, just as Marxian Socialists were doing, to the evangel of internationalism. But this only served to bring out in bolder relief the extreme nationalist doctrines which flourished at the close of the nineteenth century and in the first decades of the twentieth and which found expression not only in the writings of Maurras and Barrès, Treitschke and Bernhardi, Homer Lea, J. A. Cramb, and Theodore Roosevelt, but also in the activities of ultra-patriotic societies the world over. Doctrines whose origin lay in speculation in the varied fields of philology, comparative law, anthropology, national history, literature, and social psychology, had been crystallised into a fairly coherent political philosophy, which, Janus-like, might present a peaceful and idyllic appearance to sentimentalists and at the same time a ferocious frenzied mien to realists.

3

The doctrine of nationalism was primarily the work of intellectuals—of scholars and litterateurs. But it was more than a closet philosophy for intellectuals. It was for the classes and for the masses.

The classes took to it first. Especially from the upper middle class came its stanchest disciples and apostles, and naturally so. The upper bourgeoisie—bankers, merchants, and professional men—were as a rule men of money and brains. In Europe throughout the nineteenth century and in America latterly they were usually trained in colleges and universities where nationalist professors through lectures and personal contacts exercised an enormous influence. From their training and their class-traditions, moreover, they were likely to possess an inquiring turn of mind and to pride themselves upon "keeping up with the times." If new times brought new doctrines, then the bourgeois élite must know a bit about the novelties and pay at least lip-service to them. Members of the upper middle class could afford to buy new books, even expensive books, books of erudition as well as of belles-lettres; and an interest which one first felt within the sombre walls of a university lecture-hall could subsequently be sustained in the graceful comfort of one's private library.

It was the upper middle class which had been most affected by the eighteenth-century philosophy of natural law, natural rights, and natural perfectability of mankind and which had gone farthest in doubting supernatural religion and repudiating organised Christianity. What more natural than that the same class should descry in the doctrine of nationalism at once an emotional substitute for Christianity and a reasoned extension of the principles of nature? They were fond of science, perhaps fonder of the word than of the reality, and the doctrine of nationalism came to them from "scientists" in the name of "science." If they had any sentimental weakness, it was a weakness for what they were pleased to think of as "humanity," and nationalism, particularly its Mazzinian version, consolingly suggested that nationalities were the stepping-stones to humanity. The upper bourgeoisie, as a class, were liberals —some of them were democrats—and the doctrine of nationalism, it may here be reiterated, was historically related to the dogmas of liberty and popular sovereignty.

If we were to review the actual course of nationalism in any European country in the nineteenth century, we would be struck by the early prominence of professors, lawyers, physicians, merchants, and bankers. The most conspicuous nationalists in France during the Restoration and the Second Empire were of those callings, and so were the bulk of the deputies in the German National Assembly at Frankfort in 1848 and in the Slav National Assembly at Prague in the same year. Alike in national states which were developing nationalism and in nationalisms which eventually produced national states, members of the upper middle class were active. In France, Spain, and England, and also among Germans, Italians, Greeks, Poles, Czechoslovaks, and Yugoslavs, it was the same story.

Almost invariably it was from the ranks of the bourgeoisie that the professional nationalists were drawn, persons who were so imbued with the doctrine of nationalism that they devoted considerable time and resource to its propagation. They patronised societies for the preservation or revival of the national language. They founded museums for the collection of national relics. They supported national athletic associations, Turnvereins and Sokols. They subsidised nationalist newspapers. They gave prizes for the best rendition of national songs and national dances. They encouraged the donning of national costumes. They applauded every effort to improve or inaugurate native industry. "Ourselves alone!" was the motto of these professional nationalists, or, as recently phrased in the revivified Gaelic of Irish nationalism, "Sinn Fein!"

Was there an economic element in the spiritual devotion of the bourgeoisie to the new doctrine of nationalism? Perhaps, though in many individual instances it is difficult to detect. To be sure, the large majority of the middle class, being men of money and brains, were notoriously impatient, for perfectly valid financial reasons, with many features of autocratic government and were naturally impelled by economic self-interest to demand a share in the conduct of public affairs. They were anxious not to bear the whole burden of taxation and eager to have some say in the spending of the taxes which they paid. In the France of the old régime they came to resent the wastage of their sustenance in the riotous living of a group of noble and indolent courtiers and to believe that if their own wishes were consulted and their own advice followed, the state might be saved from sinking into bankruptcy and ruin. They ended by espousing the revolutionary doctrine of popular sovereignty, the dogma that government rests upon the consent of the governed. In the English Revolution of the seventeenth century and yet more strikingly in the American and French Revolutions of the eighteenth century the bourgeoisie ground their economic axes upon the whetstone of popular sovereignty. But popular sovereignty had nationalist implications.

The "people," whoever they might be in theory, turned out in practice to be a nationality. Political democracy, as applied to a nationality, involved representative government. And the chosen representatives or deputies or commoners (call them as you will) of every country whose government was based upon popular sovereignty, whether the franchise was restricted or not, were chiefly middle-class patriots, notably lawyers and business-men.

The middle class, so soon as they were entrenched in public office and charged with the guidance of public business, proceeded to think of the state, of the national state, as peculiarly their own and to love the nation as it had never been loved before. To quote Rousseau again, "one loves what is one's own more than what is another's." Nor was it long before the liberal and democratic middle class discovered that the rewards of love were not merely love. They found that they could use their preëminent position to obtain state-action favourable to their economic desires and at the same time could so apply their love as to guarantee their preëminent position. By preaching nationalism to the masses they acquired in marked degree that respect and veneration which worthy disciples are wont to pay to spiritual leaders. By securing the trust and confidence of the masses they were the better enabled to identify national aspirations with their own interests.

In such states as were already national, the nationalist proclivities of the bourgeoisie found expression in the glorification of the state and eventually, as the Industrial Revolution progressed, in the development of a kind of neomercantilism—a governmental favouring of national industry, national trade, and national banking. This kind of mercantilism swept Germany, France, Italy, the United States, and many another national state in the last quarter of the nineteenth century; and potent in it and profitting by it were bourgeois patriots. If England did not go to the lengths of other national states in according bounties and tariff-protection to her citizens, it was not because middle-class nationalists were less influential in England than elsewhere; it was rather because England still had an industrial lead over other countries and the English middle classes thought they could best serve their economic interests by retaining freedom of trade.

Among so-called subject or oppressed nationalities the bourgeoisie tended to inveigh against the economic policy of their imperial state, on the ground that it cramped them and prevented the rise of a salutary national system of banking, trade, and industry. In the struggle of Italians for national unity and national independence, in the corresponding struggle of the Germans, in those of the Magyars, the Czechoslovaks, the Yugoslavs, the Poles, the Finns, the Norwegians, the Irish, etc., it was always the same. Middle-class agitators against an imperial Austria or an imperial Russia or an imperial Sweden or an imperial Britain were in every instance propagandists of nationalism, and whether they said so or not, the nationalism which they propagated had for themselves economic significance.

Some of the bourgeoisie, particularly bourgeois politicians, made a very interesting discovery about the phenomenon of nationalism. They found that the masses when brought under its spell not only were less inclined to criticise their leaders but also were more disposed to accept the *status quo* in economic matters. On the multitudes nationalism could be made to act as a sort of laughing gas. If a labourer could be induced to take a long deep breath of it, he would feel quite exhilarated and for a time at any rate he would forget about overwork and underpay in factory, field, or mine, and lose the reality of his own squalid habitation in the dream of national greatness. A sustained inhalation of nationalism, as in time of national election or international war, might even deaden the noise of socialists, anarchists, and other apostles of social revolution or economic unrest.

It should not be concluded that bourgeois patriots have always been conscious of economic advantages to themselves in the propagation of nationalism. It is too crass, too strabismic, a view to perceive in financial profit a direct and all-compelling motive for every piece of human conduct; and in this respect the middle classes are not different from other classes. Most of the bourgeoisie who espoused nationalism did so for a great variety of reasons, chief among which were reasons of sentiment and altruism. Some of the bourgeoisie might discover that the doctrine could serve an economic end, but such a discovery would usually be a later reasoned justification, rather than a conscious original purpose, of their championship of nationalism.

4

The middle class was not the only class which produced effective propagandists of the new nationalism. In Great Britain the landed aristocracy—the peers of the realm and the country squires—were glowingly patriotic. They felt that they were the group who had made England what she was, and it is a fact that the English aristocracy possessed fine traditions of continued public service in church, in army, and in state. Throughout the nineteenth and twentieth centuries they furnished many a nationalist hero and exemplar. In Germany, too, the Prussian Junker had served his king so long and so faithfully in army, civil service, and church that with the rise of nationalism he found it fairly easy to extend his unquestioning and unswerving loyalty to the consolidated realm whose national emperor was his king. For like reasons many nobles in Russia, and in Spain too, were nationalists. So were Polish noblemen and Magyar noblemen. In France the nobles had been despoiled of property and privilege by revolution, but nothing could seemingly rob them of national patriotism. In fact, as the nineteenth century progressed, it appeared as if scions of the old French nobility were seeking in nationalist propaganda a rehabilitation of their former prestige. Both the "nationalist" movement which developed around the banner of General Boulanger in the 1880's and the ultra-nationalist "Action Francaise" which flourished in the twentieth century charged the government of the Third French Republic with national inefficiency and patriotic cowardice; both were patronised by noblemen.

Among many subject nationalities the landed aristocracy were less patriotic, less nationalist. But wherever such a situation existed, it could usually be explained by reference to the fact that there the nobility belonged in social affiliation if not in blood to the nationality of the conquerors rather than to that of the conquered. Numerous nobles in Bohemia were German, not Czech, in sympathy. The nobility among the Rumanians in Transylvania or among the Yugoslavs in Dalmatia were German or Magyar in feeling and social ties. The Lithuanian nobility were largely Polish, and the nobility in Ireland had more in common with Englishmen than with Irishmen. Among these subject peoples "alien" nobles were usually upholders of imperialism, friends of a "foreign" nationality, and inveterate foes of the nationalism of the people among whom their estates were located. Nationalist agitation in such localities was directed almost as much against the "alien" aristocracy at home as against the "alien" imperial government afar.

Clergymen participated in nationalist propaganda in widely varying degree. The clergy of churches which already had been nationalised were likely to be zealous advocates of the new doctrine. The clergy of the Russian Church, of the Anglican Church, of the Greek Church, of the Reformed Churches of Holland and Scotland, and of the Evangelical Churches of Prussia and Scandinavia were, as a class, prominent in the new apostolate. The Catholic clergy, as a class, were not so prominent; many of them entertained grave doubts about the tenets of the new faith; and Pius IX and his papal successors had enough personal experience of the practical operations of Italian nationalism to suggest to them that extreme nationalism might prove even more troublesome and dangerous to the Church in the twentieth century than the quickening of national consciousness had proved to be back in the sixteenth century. And yet, nationalism among "oppressed" peoples, among Croats, Slovenes, Slovaks, Poles, and Irish, was certainly abetted in the nineteenth and twentieth centuries by Catholic priests and even by Catholic bishops. In traditional Catholic countries which had long possessed national states, such as France, Spain, and Portugal, the clergy found it difficult to breast the mounting waves of nationalism and frequently deemed it prudent to swim with the tide. In the United States and certain other countries where Catholics constituted a minority, and a minority mainly composed of relatively recent immigrants, the Church was so often rabidly assailed as foreign and unpatriotic that many of its clergy adopted, probably unconsciously, a sort of defense-mechanism and proceeded to preach a very intense nationalism.

Of clergymen everywhere, whether Catholic or Protestant or Orthodox, it may be remarked that some emotionalism is apt to be associated with their calling and their office, and that the altruism with which the doctrine of nationalism was originally clothed called forth from many of them an emotional response. Certainly such clergymen as accepted nationalism were highly emotional propagandists of it, and therefore highly effective with the masses.

With the lapse of time, special propagandists emerged from what may be termed, we trust without offense, the vested interests of nationalism. There were persons who wished to follow a political career in a national state, to sell munitions and uniforms and supplies for the national army, to superintend national schools, to dispose of flags and bunting and firecrackers, the paraphernalia and insignia of a new fad—all these persons took to nationalism as naturally as the proverbial duck takes to water.

In the propagation of nationalism as in the propagation of any doctrine, there is always an opportunity for the person who likes to stand in the limelight and to feel that he is a man (or she is a woman) of no small importance. Especially has this been true in the propagation of a continuously and rapidly effective doctrine like nationalism in the nineteenth and twentieth centuries. To preside over a patriotic society, to deliver an address at the unveiling of a monument to a national hero, to march be-ribboned and be-medalled at the head of a patriotic procession, is calculated to feed one's self-esteem and at the same time to increase one's respect for that which has enabled one to be so conspicuous and so important. Vanity may be a fault, but if so it is a broadly human fault. It crops out in clergyman, in nobleman, in business-man, in professor. It has given us of late from every class many spectacular propagandists of nationalism.

5

Nationalism as a doctrine has been evolved and proclaimed in many lands by groups of "intellectuals." Nationalism as a faith and as a guide has been accepted and advertised by numerous individuals especially in the upper and middle classes. But nationalism could hardly be the driving force in the lives of the masses of mankind which it is today had not instrumentalities of mass-education been perfected and utilised for popular propaganda. Nationalism, being a cultural phenomenon, is not "in the blood"; it cannot be transmitted biologically from one person to another; it is an "acquired character," and the method of its acquisition, as of any cultural product, is education.

Education by itself is too often thought of exclusively as formal schooling. As a matter of fact, all methods and means by which one generation consciously influences the next are educational. The family is a primary agency of education, and its educational influence is apt to be especially strong. Strong, too, may be the influence of personal associates outside of the domestic circle, both individuals and social groups—a "hero," a street-gang, a club, a moral teacher. Nor is there anything peculiarly recent or modern about this type of education. The human being of 1926 A.D., no more and no less than the human being of 6291 B.C., begins his career as a motor-sensory animal, without conceptions concerning democracy, socialism, or romanticism in art, and whatever convictions may be his when he reaches his twenty-second year will have been implanted in him by propaganda; he will have undergone a process of education, whether or not he has ever seen the interior of a schoolhouse.

For centuries popular education was obtained from personal conversation, from orations of statesmen, oral instructions of priests, and recitations of artists, from forum, arena, theatre, and church, and, for persons who could read, from manuscripts and books. By these and similar means ideas were disseminated and culture was passed from generation to generation. In places and at times all such instruments were marshalled, moreover, in support of a particular organisation or a particular philosophy. This was the case in the middle ages, when the majority of

Europeans for generations were instructed in Catholic Christianity. It was also the case in the nineteenth century when "intellectuals" and the "classes" brought to bear upon the masses in support of nationalism all the old familiar agencies of popular propaganda.

To long established and traditional agencies of propaganda and education, the era inaugurated by the French and Industrial Revolutions added novel means and emphasis. It was not until the Revolutionary and Napoleonic Wars that fighting ceased to be the distinguishing function of relatively small professional armies and became the province and duty of whole peoples; since then, in most countries compulsory military or naval training has been an ideal and usually an achievement. And among the masses universal military training has been an impressive agency of propaganda and education.

It was not until the Industrial Revolution that newspapers could be rapidly and cheaply printed and widely distributed; ever since the London *Times* in 1814 first installed power-driven printing presses, journalism has advanced in scope and influence as by geometrical progression, until the contemporary use of newsprint paper for scare-headlines, human-interest tales, cartoons, "graphics," and commercial advertisements, may lead future geologists, as Proudhon suggested, to date from our era the "papyracious" age of the earth's formation. The new journalism is obviously the greatest engine yet constructed for propaganda and education.

Both the new journalism and the new militarism were evolved in the century during which the doctrine of nationalism was formulated by intellectuals and accepted by the "classes." It is not surprising, therefore, that nationalists have seized upon these powerful agencies of propaganda, and that in turn the new militarism and especially the new journalism have performed signal services in the nationalist education of the masses.

From the new militarism have sprung, *inter alia,* a rich crop of patriotic societies [1] whose members have increasingly reminded the common people of the pride they should feel in the glorious past and manifest destiny of their particular nationality. Especially active have been these societies in the profuse peppering of the landscape with markers, memorials, shafts, and busts, commemorative chiefly of national fighting. Only spasmodically, however, are common people reminded of the existence of patriotic societies which have sprung from national militarism, and the few commoners who retain some fastidiousness about *objets d'art* may still walk in the more quiet side-streets of civilised towns without encountering an equestrian statue or votive tablet to the memory of a national warrior. But where nowadays is the commoner who can escape the newspaper with its incessant and insistent nationalism? In the grave, or in the cradle, or, if I am reliably informed, in certain newer hospitals whose humane wardens seek to provide a restful atmosphere! Elsewhere the newspaper is omnipresent, omnipotent, and usually, according to its own admission, omniscient. It may be conservative or liberal, republican or democratic, metropolitan or provincial, urban or rural, farmer-labour or capitalist, but it has everywhere become in the nineteenth and twentieth centuries, with comparatively few exceptions, nationalist. [2]

6

Journalism and militarism are novel and impressive agencies of popular propaganda, but an agency quite as novel and even more impressive is the new formal education, that is, the rising system of state-directed and state-controlled compulsory national schooling. It is difficult for us to appreciate how very new this system is. For many, many

---

[1] Other and vastly more important nationalist aspects of militarism are set forth in Essay VI, below (pp. 156-195).

[2] *Cf.* Walter Lippmann, *Public Opinion* (1922), and Lucy M. Salmon, *The Newspaper and Authority* (1923) and *The Newspaper and the Historian* (1923).

centuries and as late as the eighteenth, it was universally believed that schooling is and should be a privilege for the few, rather than a right of the many; its conduct was not within the jurisdiction of the state but was left to ecclesiastical or other voluntary guidance; its declared aim was primarily that "religion and learning might go hand in hand and character grow with knowledge"; and if it trained for citizenship it was ostensibly for citizenship in the next world as much as in this; above all, it was not compulsory and it was not national.

With the eighteenth century, however, schools assumed a new importance and a changed character. To many thoughtful persons it seemed desirable that the masses should be literate and loyal, and that to this end the state should establish and maintain schools for all its citizens. Thus, the Constitution of Massachusetts, as ratified in 1780, contained the following provision: "Wisdom, and knowledge, as well as virtue, diffused generally among the body of the people, being necessary for the preservation of their rights and liberties; and as these depend on spreading the oppertunities and advantages of education in the various parts of the country, and among the different orders of the people, it shall be the duty of Legislatures and Magistrates, in all future periods of this Commonwealth, to cherish the interests of literature and the sciences, and all seminaries of them; especially the university at Cambridge, public schools and grammar schools in the towns. . . ." [1] In France, the Constitution of 1791 contained the following provision: "There shall be created and organised a system of public instruction common to all citizens and gratuitous in respect of those subjects of instruction that are indispensable to all men. Schools of various grades shall be supplied according to need over the entire kingdom. National holidays shall be designated for the purpose of preserving the memory of the French Revolution, of developing the spirit of fraternity among all citizens, and of attaching them to the

[1] Constitution of 1780, ch. v, sect. ii.

constitution, the country, and the laws." [1]   In Prussia, King
Frederick William II promulgated in 1794 the edict:
"Schools and universities are state institutions, charged with
the instruction of youth in useful information and scientific
knowledge; such institutions may be founded only with the
knowledge and consent of the state; . . . all public schools
and educational institutions are under the supervision of
the state, and are at all times subject to its examination
and inspection." [2]

Thenceforth, and down to the present day, in all countries
influenced by democracy or nationalism, the new schooling
has taken root and put forth abundant branches. In Prussia,
a state department of public instruction was erected in
1807; elementary and secondary education was centralised
under a governmental bureaucracy and compulsory attendance prescribed [3] in 1825; the abolition of tuition fees, begun in 1833, was completed in 1888; and a uniform, nationalist curriculum was elaborated in 1872.   The other German
states imitated Prussia's example.   In France, the real foundations of a national system of primary schools were laid
by Napoleon Bonaparte; the principle of compulsion was
applied in 1833; and by the Ferry laws of 1881-1886 the
whole superstructure of free, compulsory, secular instruction was reared.   In Great Britain, the state assumed responsibility for elementary instruction in 1870, made such
instruction obligatory in 1880 and free in 1891, and erected
a national Board of Education in 1899.   Holland began the
construction of a national system of formal schooling in
1806, Greece in 1823, Belgium in 1842, Portugal in 1844,
Argentina in 1853, Brazil in 1854, Spain in 1857, Italy and
Rumania in 1859, Finland in 1866, Hungary in 1868, Japan
in 1872, Peru in 1876, Bulgaria in 1881, Siam in 1891.   The

---

[1] Constitution of 1791, tit. i.

[2] *Allgemeines Landrecht für die preussischen Staaten,* part ii, title xii,
sects. 1, 2, 9; (ed. Schering) vol. iv (1876), pp. 140-1.

[3] Compulsory attendance had been decreed by Frederick the Great
in 1763, but until 1825 it was honoured more in the breach than in the
observance.

Canadian provinces of Ontario and Quebec contracted the contagion in the decade of the 1840's, and, at the antipodes, the Australasian colonies caught it in the 1870's. If I have omitted from this painfully long list any national state, I would apologise to its patriots, for it can safely be assumed that every country which pretends to any considerable degree of political democracy or conscious nationality possesses in the present year of grace some system of state-supported and state-directed national schools.

The United States is no exception to the general rule. In fact, so implanted in the American mind is devotion to free public schools supported by public taxation, dominated by public officials, and innocent of religious teachings, that the average American citizen imagines the whole system to have been always distinctively American and harbours a little doubt only regarding its origin, whether it sprang from Plymouth Rock at the magical touch of the Pilgrims, or leaped from the Nordic brain of Leif Ericson in the mysterious pre-prohibition region of Vineland. The truth of the matter is that the venerated fathers of American liberty were not trained in secular public schools and that the elaboration of national schooling in the United States has occurred not faster and not slower than the elaboration of systems of national education in numerous foreign countries. It is difficult to assign precise dates to the process in America by reason of the constitutional circumstance that the development has been registered not by specific action of one Federal Government, but by desultory activity of forty-eight Commonwealths. In establishing state-supervision of all elementary schools, New York led the way in 1812 and Illinois followed in 1825. The practice of levying general taxes for the support of public schools, begun relatively early in New England, did not spread widely until after 1824. Tuition fees were gradually abolished between 1834 and 1870. The secularisation of the public schools, that is, their separation from ecclesiastical connections and the establishment of the principle that no public funds should be expended on private and denominational schools, was wrought in many commonwealths, amid great strife, between 1825 and 1855. High schools were not associated with the elementary schools, under state control, until after 1840. Not until the period of the Civil War did there come unmistakably into view, and then only in the North, the complete outline of that system which is styled today the American public-school system. Its filling-in has been the work of the last sixty years. Though operated technically by forty-eight constituent parts of the American federation, the school system in the United States is now almost, if not quite, as national in scope and effect as the centralised systems of France and England.

Wherever the gospel of political democracy has been preached, in the United States, France, Great Britain, or elsewhere, there has the new education been promoted. The relationship between education and democracy is obvious and natural. The coming generation must be taught not only to respect and cherish the principles of democracy, but also to participate in its practice, and this requires as a minimum the literacy of the whole citizenry. But the new education has flourished in the nineteenth century quite as notably in an autocracy like Prussia as in democracies like France and the United States, and it is reasonable to suspect, therefore, that democracy is not the sole or even the chief *raison d'être* of state-supported, state-directed compulsory schooling. In truth, the more one reflects on the subject, the clearer to one is the perception that the ubiquitous rise of the new education has paralleled less closely the spread of democracy than the propagation of nationalism.

Prussia took the most significant steps toward the inauguration of state-controlled compulsory education in the midst of the national awakening and reaction against Napoleon Bonaparte, in the period aptly termed in German history "the era of national regeneration," and the uniform nationalist curriculum of the German schools was the product of the wars of national unity from 1866 to 1871. In

France it was the democratic and nationalist Revolutionaries who outlined the programme of national schools, but it was the stridently nationalist Napoleon who began to realise it and the even more vociferously nationalist victims of the Franco-German War of 1870-1871 who carried it to fruition. Count Cavour was the champion of Italian nationalism more than of Italian democracy; Count Cavour was the sponsor of national education in Italy. Despite the gradual growth of a democratic spirit in Great Britain it was not until the last third of the nineteenth century was reached, not until the era of the new nationalist imperialism was in sight, the era of Disraeli, Salisbury, Rosebery, Joseph Chamberlain, Cecil Rhodes, and Rudyard Kipling, that the British schools were taken over by the state and nationalised.

It is an arresting fact, too, that among all so-called subject or oppressed nationalities of the nineteenth and twentieth centuries, leading nationalist agitators have invariably directed attention to the schools. The loudest demands made on the Austrian government by the earliest exponents of Czech nationalism were in behalf of national schools in Bohemia and Moravia, in which the Czech language and Czech history should be taught, and over which Czech nationalists should preside. Slovaks, Serbs, and Croats vied with one another in beseeching the Hungarian government to accord them the right of separate national schools. The German Poles begged for a distinct administration of the compulsory state-schools in their localities by means of a separate Polish bureau in the Ministry of Education at Berlin. The founders of the Sinn Fein movement in Ireland originally put greater emphasis on the need of a national system of schools than on political separation from England, and the founding of the National University of Ireland nicely antedated the Dublin insurrection of 1916 and the recognition of the Irish Free State.

In the United States, the vaunted system of free public schools did not proceed immediately from Mr. Jefferson's

Declaration of Independence [1] or from the gentlemen of the
Constitutional Convention or from General Washington's
Farewell Address or from Mr. Monroe's Doctrine. Its evolution curiously paralleled the subsequent westward expansion of the American people and the rising wave of foreign
immigration which began to beat with might on their eastern shores in the 1840's and 1850's. To assure national
unity between West and East and to guard national customs and ideals against foreign contamination, these, rather
than mere *à priori* reasoning about political democracy, were
the effective, if somewhat unconscious, motives for the building of the American system of national education. The
system was definitely fashioned by the generation which
participated in the nationalist War for the Union, and its
later minor amendment has been conditioned less by the
New Freedom than by the New Nationalism.

7

Nationalists everywhere have demanded and secured the
establishment and extension of state-schools. In return, the
state-schools have been the basic and most reliable agencies of nationalist propaganda among the masses. Such
schools may fall short now and again of achieving what
professional educators tell us on pompous occasions is their
goal of "drawing out" the pupils, but they have proved
marvellously successful at "pumping in" a most exaggerated
worship of the pupils' nationality and national state. It is
much the same wherever these schools exist, and where now
do they not exist? In France, they inculcate French nationalism. In Germany, they inculcate German nationalism.
In Japan, they inculcate Japanese nationalism. In Massachusetts, New York, Virginia, Illinois, and California, they
inculcate American nationalism. The general process, like-

---

[1] Mr. Jefferson personally, it may be recalled, was an early proponent
of state-directed universal education; as early as 1779—only three years
after the Declaration of Independence—he presented to the Virginian
Legislature a scheme of universal education. Mr. Jefferson lived long
but not long enough to see the adoption of his scheme.

wise, is much the same, in America and Japan, in Germany and France, though there are numerous variations of detail.

Everywhere nationalists have influenced the content of the new education, the curriculum of the state-schools. So fundamental a subject as reading has, of course, been given premier place, often in the name of democracy, social as well as political, and always it has been made to serve admirably the purposes of nationalist propaganda. Nationalities vie with one another nowadays in boasting, not only of material wealth and physical power, of virtue and valour, but also of extensive literacy, and some people cite comparative statistics of the literacy of, say, Spain and Prussia as proof that the culture of the Prussians is much greater than that of the Spaniards. Mere literacy, however, does not make humans humane or critical or even intelligent; and in literate nationalities, the majority of boys and girls, who do not pass beyond the earlier grades of elementary schooling, acquire only sufficient mastery of the art of reading to render them the gullible victims of penny dreadfuls, graphics, newspaper headlines, advertising posters, movie captions, and in general the cheaper sort of journalism which is apt to reek with nationalism. The minority of boys and girls, who graduate from secondary schools, should be qualified to read more and better things, but inasmuch as they have been exposed for a longer time to the nationalist influence of the schools, their minds are likely to be set and grooved more conveniently for a life-long antipathy to any development which might weaken nationalism.

It has recently been pointed out by Professor J. M. Mecklin, of Dartmouth, that Oregon has less than two per cent. of illiteracy and a relatively high percentage of high-school graduates and yet has been a stronghold of an organisation notorious for ignorant fanaticism in the name of religion and patriotism. "There must be," he thinks, "a singular lack of independent critical public sentiment in a community that is such an easy victim of the Klan. One feels that the educational system of Oregon, in spite of [1] one and one-half per cent. illiteracy, must be after all a very mechanical affair. Her sons and daughters, as in her sister states, pass with measured tread through public school, high school, and university, assimilating the external mechanical symbols of culture, and yet these symbols remain mere symbols,—traditional, educational, and cultural stereotypes. These prospective citizens have not been schooled to the critical analysis of their intellectual heritage. So long as one is clever enough to clothe his propaganda in the familiar dress of these stereotypes he finds ready and uncritical acceptance." No wonder that nationalists applaud and abet an institution which provides a great wholesale market for the propagation of nationalism. No wonder that publishers of national journalism and leaders of national militarism and officials of patriotic societies are sincere advocates of national literacy.

Universal literacy is a primary purpose of the new education, and indirectly, as things now are, it promotes nationalism. But, under nationalist influence, an equally primary purpose, frankly avowed, is the direct inculcation of nationalism. Elementary readers are packed with nationalist poems, with ultra-patriotic legends, and with tales of the mythical and always exemplary deeds of ancestral national demigods. Geography is usually centred in the providential economic and territorial primacy of one's own country, and from its study the pupils gather that their nation is, or should be, the most favoured of all God's creation, and that it has, or should have, "natural boundaries," great "natural resources," and vast wealth. From their study of civics, the same pupils are led to believe that their country is the freest, the most liberty-loving, the most progressive, the best governed, and the happiest on earth. From their study of history (what amazing history it usually is) they derive an exaggerated notion of the bravery and worth of

---

[1] I wish Professor Mecklin had written "because of only" instead of "in spite of." I suspect it would have been more accurate.

their own countrymen and an equally exaggerated notion of the viciousness and cowardice of foreigners. It is from the school, and especially from nationalist history as taught in the schools, that the rising generation bring the catchwords and shibboleths of nationalism, such as "national honour," "national rights," "national interests," the "genius of the nation," the "mission of the nation."

Penetrating and inspiring the whole curriculum of the state-schools—history, civics, geography, reading, and writing—is the day-by-day training in nationalist observance: the singing of nationalist hymns, the round of ceremonies associated with the national flag or with national heroes and holidays, the solemnities connected with a "preparedness" week or with a "patriotism" week, the special eulogies pronounced from time to time by visiting patriots on national customs, national institutions, and national heroes.

Back of the nationalist curriculum of contemporary state-schools are all those forces in present-day social life which consciously or unconsciously abet nationalism. Politicians who conceal a paucity of convictions and ideals under the broad folds of the national flag, actors who redeem poor performances by displaying at the critical moment the national colours, employers who sense that patriotic fervour is less disturbing to the stock-and-bond market than economic criticism, individuals who make a living by whipping up popular emotion and popular prejudice, all these can be relied upon to sustain and strengthen the propaganda of nationalism in the schools.

But the chief goad to such propaganda is the new journalism. The cheaper newspapers of the present age cater to a vast number of persons who have received a nationalist education in state-schools, and the editors know that they will earn public praise (and private profit) if they focus popular attention upon the imperative need for, and any fancied lack of, nationalism in the schools. News-items, headlines, editorials, letters from "a citizen," cartoons, all are paraded with cumulative effect. From examples which

are legion in every national state, notice may here be taken
of but one, a cartoon selected at random from hundreds of
the same kind which have appeared in the *Chicago Daily
Tribune*.[1] It discloses a stern, knowing, majestical Uncle
Sam, legs planted wide and firm, one arm extended at full
length toward a huge American flag in the background, the
other arm in the foreground securely grasping and relent-
lessly shaking a poor, mean, bespectacled, little man who
is labelled "Pacifist Educator," and from whose paralysed
hands have fallen a litter of papers variously inscribed
"School Pacifism," "Anti-Nationalism," "Altruism," and
"Idealism."

If at any time there is a lull in journalist goading of the
state-schools to more intense nationalism, professional nationalist societies may be trusted to poke up both the schools
and the newspapers. For in all national states flourish numerous societies of professional patriots—army leagues,
navy leagues, associations for nationalising somebody, veterans or descendants of veterans of some war or other—and
these special and self-constituted guardians of modern
nationalism work ceaselessly, even whilst others sleep.

Under the circumstances it is not strange that national
schools have become ever more nationalist. The commis-
sioners, superintendents, principals, *etc.*—the bureaucrats of
the new education—discover that they must, from the very
nature of things, lead a kind of double life: they must be
super-teachers, raising the standards of their schools, arousing the ambition of pupils, and setting an example of the
highest idealism for their teachers; they must be, also, more
or less servile representatives of the state, holding their
teachers in check, guarding their pupils against radicalism
and novelty, and generally maintaining such standards in
the schools as reflect most faithfully the collective spirit
of the taxpayers. Some of these administrators are more
Dr. Jekyll than Mr. Hyde, and some are more Mr. Hyde

---

[1] Issue of March 25, 1924. The *Chicago Daily Tribune* modestly con-
fesses in every issue that it is "the world's greatest newspaper."

than Dr. Jekyll, but every Dr. Jekyll, if he aspires to a long tenure of office at a constantly augmenting salary, must be Hydian enough to ensure that the nationalism which is proclaimed by the public press and the professional patriots shall be taught in the schools and that the teacher or textbook that is charged by any considerable number of taxpayers with a wee lack of nationalism, despite unquestioned excellence in other respects, shall be banned and expelled. In elementary state-schools it hardly seems probable, under existing circumstances, that the instruction will rise in character or quality much above the average level of the prejudices of the whole state's citizenry. And among these prejudices nationalism is nowadays everywhere preëminent.

It should not be gathered from the foregoing pages that I am labouring under any misapprehension that public state-schools are the only schools now in existence or that they are the only schools which inculcate nationalism. The new education has not entirely obliterated the old, and in most countries throughout the world there are still numerous private schools, many of them under ecclesiastical control. In some cases, for example in England, these schools are semi-public, in the sense that they are subsidised from the public treasury. In other cases, notably in France and the United States, they are obliged to depend upon tuition-fees and voluntary contributions. Mainly they exist on sufferance, and frequently they are handicapped by one form or another of protective tariff in aid of the public state-schools. In any event they are inclined nowadays to take their tone, methods, and curriculum from the state-schools. In all important national states, the public schools are much more largely attended than the private schools, and the predominance of the former in resources as well as in numbers has helped to induce in the popular mind the conviction that the public schools are part and parcel of true, hundred-per-cent. nationalism. But, after all, the private schools are subject to much the same popular influences as the public schools, and there is little or no evidence that national patriotism is not sedulously taught alike in Protestant, Catholic, and undenominational schools. On the contrary, there are many indications that private ecclesiastical schools are acutely aware of the prejudices against them and are thereby moved to redouble their efforts to prove how patriotic they are, and there can be no doubt that private schools in the nature of military academies are even more given to specialisation in nationalism than are the public state-schools.

Compulsory national schooling—the new education—is the basic means of propagating the doctrine of nationalism among the masses. It is strikingly effective. It fertilises the mind of the rising generation for the seeds implanted by "intellectuals" in the first half of the nineteenth century and henceforth watered and tended with consummate care by a large number of middle-class and upper-class nationist gardeners, and brought to blossom and fruit by the winds of modern journalism, the rains of modern militarism, and the sap of professional nationalists. The propagation of nationalism, in truth, has been a great achievement of our age. First it inflamed visionaries; then it grew strong with the classes; and latterly it has possessed the masses. From an unconscious process, nationalism "became idea; from idea, abstract principle; then fervid prepossession; ending where it is today, in dogma, whether accepted or evaded." [1] As dogma, and as cult too, we must deal a bit more in detail with contemporary nationalism.

[1] Viscount Morley, *Politics and History*, in *Works*, vol. iv (1921), p. 47.

IV

NATIONALISM AS A RELIGION

1

THE PRESENT generation has a curious hobby of at least pretending to like a thing not because it has intrinsic excellence but solely because it is new. In some quarters this hobby is interpreted as "progress." Indeed the proverbial Man from Mars, initiated into the temper of our age and informed of the current vogue of nationalism on Earth, might reasonably conjecture that nationalism is extolled by us because it is modern. He would be right, as I have sought to shew, in guessing that it is modern; he might truthfully say that it is very modern; but he would be wrong in concluding that its modernity is the sole or chief cause of its popularity.

Contemporary nationalism has been attributed to historical events of the eighteenth, nineteenth, and twentieth centuries. It has been explained that the contact of political democracy, the Industrial Revolution, and philosophical romanticism with a long germinating popular consciousness of nationality produced a nationalist process and a nationalist doctrine—the body and the soul, as it were, of nationalism. It has also been explained that the doctrine was preached and the process made palatable to the masses of mankind by means of educational and propagandist agencies which the French Revolution deemed desirable and the Industrial Revolution rendered practical—national schooling, national militarism, and national journalism. These explanations, however, are not entirely satisfactory. They may be valid so far as they go, but they do not make perfectly clear why apostles of nationalism are characterised by a missionary zeal that is fiery and why its multitudinous disciples are possessed of a love that is consuming. Why are millions ready and willing to lay down their lives for nationalism?

There have been many historical processes and philosophical preachments which called forth no such popular response in the past as in the present age nationalism evokes. Ancient stoicism, mediaeval nominalism or realism, modern hedonism, alike have led to interesting speculation by "intellectuals," have been accepted by influential members of the upper classes, and have had at least some indirect effect upon the masses, but great aggregates of men have never fought and died for any of those philosophies. There must be something more than a philosophy, something more than a doctrine and an historical process, about modern nationalism.

This something is obviously an emotion, an emotional loyalty to the idea or the fact of the national state, a loyalty so intensely emotional that it motivates all sorts of people and causes them to subordinate all other human loyalties to national loyalty. In modern national states, of course, individual citizens still retain many if not most of the emotional loyalties to particular persons, specific places, and peculiar ideas that have marked the human race since the dawn of its history. The loyalty of the American to a political leader, a secret lodge, a church, a trade-union, a college, a New England town, a Southern plantation, or a Western ranch, is different in degree but not in kind from loyalties of ancient Roman, Jew, and Egyptian. Now as ever, too, it may transpire that an individual must choose between two loyalties: he may throw over a political leader to do the bidding of a secret lodge; he may leave the lodge at the behest of his priests; he may turn against the priests in order to follow the fortunes of a political leader. But nowadays, and herein lies the fundamental difference between us and our ancient and mediaeval and early modern forebears, the individual is commonly disposed, in case of conflict, to sacrifice one loyalty after another, loyalty to persons, places and ideas, loyalty even to family, to the paramount call of nationality and the national state. This is nationalism, and surely it must have a richly emotional content to predominate over all other emotional loyalties of the present generation.

Now, as one looks back over the multifarious pages of man's history, one is struck by the frequency and force of human movements which have had their mainspring in religious emotion. Herein is a valuable clue for us. May it not be that we shall here find the most convincing explanation of the strength of modern nationalism, the zeal of its apostles, and the devotion of its disciples? Is it not a demonstrable fact that nationalism has become to a vast number of persons a veritable religion, capable of arousing that deep and compelling emotion which is essentially religious? To this aspect of the subject let us address ourselves.

2

From the dawn of his history man has been distinguished by what may be called a "religious sense," that is, a mysterious faith in some power outside of himself, a faith always accompanied by feelings of reverence and usually attended by external acts and ceremonial. Everywhere, under the most diverse forms, you find its expression, in the caves of primitive men, in the pyramids of Egypt, in the laws of Moses and the rites of Aaron, in the words of the Delphic oracle, in the tended fire of the Vestal virgins, in the temples of Inca and Aztec, in the tabus of Eskimo and Hottentot. You find it enshrined in great religious systems, such as Hinduism, Buddhism, Christianity, and Mohammedanism, which through the centuries have counted their devotees by billions. As always, so today, man feels its spell.

Apparently the "religious sense" is so ingrained in man that normally he must give expression to it in one way or another. He may lose faith in a particular religion, but if so he usually dedicates himself consciously or unconsciously to another object of worship. It may be worship of Christ or Buddha; it may be worship of totem or fetish; it may likewise be worship of science or humanity—provided these concepts are written in his mind with capital letters. In any case it involves an experience, a reverential emotion, which is primordially religious.

Even in ages when doubt and scepticism about a popular religion have been most rampant, the very sceptics and doubters have been disposed to seek some object outside of themselves to which they might pay reverence. For example, in the early centuries of the Christian era, when Graeco-Roman Paganism was losing its hold upon the intellectual classes of the Roman Empire, there was a notable tendency to find an outlet for the religious sense, on the one hand, in Stoicism and other philosophies that proclaimed a truer and higher divinity in Duty or in Reasoned Pleasure, and, on the other hand, in mystical communion with strange and somewhat bizarre gods, with Isis and Osiris, with Mithra, or with the "spirits" of Neo-Platonism. The resultant unsettling and diversification of religion was in that instance only transitional and not at all irreligious; it inspired quaint attempts to mingle and reconcile heterogeneous objects of worship; it presently produced a kind of religious syncretism; and thereby it prepared the way for the eventual widespread diffusion and acceptance of Christianity. Christianity was, in fundamental respects, novel and revolutionary, but it did not represent a clean break with the past; it preserved much of the antique doctrine and practice of Judaism, and simultaneously it borrowed for its cult and theology many elements from pagan and Gentile religions. Christianity was a syncretic religion, as had been Graeco-Roman Paganism before it. Both Paganism and Christianity, and also the transitional steps from the one to the other, appealed to man's religious sense.

Again, in the later middle ages, doubts arose and multiplied in western and central Europe about the teaching of the Catholic Church concerning the nature and proper wor-

ship of the Christian God. Followed the rise of Protestantism. But as one studies historic Protestantism one is impressed less by the novelties which the Reformers introduced into the content of Christianity than by the conservatism with which they clung to certain central dogmas and
rites of the older Christian Church.[1] They borrowed plentifully from Catholicism, whilst at the same time they appropriated much from the intellectual movements of their
day and put themselves especially under new obligations to
ancient Judaism. Conversion from Catholicism to Protestantism in the sixteenth century doubtless betokened a
lessening faith in a particular religion, but the historical
student knows that the sixteenth century was not irreligious.
In Protestantism, as in Catholicism, or in Judaism, and likewise in the transition from one to another, man gave expression to his religious sense.

In like manner it may be argued that the subsequent
rapid disintegration of Protestantism into innumerable denominations and sects has been simply a modern parallel
to the ancient deliquescence of Graeco-Roman Paganism
and further that the syncretism latterly proceeding in the
Protestant world may correspondingly usher in a new form
of religion, which, however Christian and Protestant in
name, will depart very considerably from historic Protestantism and historic Christianity. Yet such a neo-Protestantism, if and when it appears, will be, quite as much as
historic Protestantism, and as historic Catholicism before
that, an embodiment of man's religious sense.[2]

[1] The reader will recall that long ago this opinion was voiced by Gibbon
with devastating rhetoric and mordant wit. *Cf. The Decline and Fall of
the Roman Empire,* vol. vi (ed. J. B. Bury), pp. 125-126.

[2] I do not wish to be understood as implying that there are no essential
differences between Paganism and Christianity or between Catholicism and
Protestantism or "neo-Protestantism." I explicitly disclaim any connection with that large and lazy sect of recent times who profess that "one
religion is as good or as true (or false) as another." Here, however, I am
not attempting to establish or even to assert the superiority of any particular religion; my present purpose is much more modest, merely to point
out that all these religions appeal, like "natural religion," to man's inherent
"religious sense."

Of all periods of religious scepticism and theological doubt, the most crucial in human history, at any rate for our present purpose, is the eighteenth century. It was the eighteenth century which witnessed in western Europe, especially in France, the mocking attacks of Voltaire and other "enlightened" litterateurs upon "supernatural" religion and ecclesiastical institutions. Christian tradition and the Christian Bible were alike impugned. Ecclesiastical authority was assailed. Miracles were ridiculed, and mysteries such as the Trinity, the Incarnation, and the Redemption, were rejected. Christianity was denounced as superstition and its clergy as humbugs. Nor were these opinions and judgements confined to a few philosophers. They were shared by wide circles, so that the eighteenth century clearly witnessed a pronounced loosening of the hold of traditional Christianity, whether Catholic or Protestant, upon the intellectual classes of Europe. For the first time since the Arian controversy, a large number of influential adherents to Christianity had come openly to doubt the truth and worth of its most fundamental tenets; for the first time, Christian intellectuals would abandon Christianity or subvert it wholly. Many of the eighteenth-century intellectuals perceived in the Trinity, in the God-made-Man, and in the Christian sacraments, only the vain imaginings of dupes or hypocrites. They perceived nothing in the Christian Revelation or, for that matter, in any "supernaturalism," to which man could justifiably attach any devotion or reverence. They were logical—in their fashion. They might not and they would not express their religious sense in Christian worship. They would not be Christians.

But those same intellectuals of the eighteenth century did possess a religious sense. And they shewed it in many curious ways. Most of them got excited about a God of Nature who started things which he could not stop and who was so intent upon watching numberless worlds go round in their appointed orbits and so transfixed by the operation of all the eternal immutable Laws which he had invented that he had no time or ear for the little entreaties of puny men upon a pygmy Earth. This God of Nature was obviously not much of a person and not much of a power; he was only a fraction of the God of the Christians. But he was outside of man, and eighteenth-century intellectuals managed somehow to develop quite a mysterious feeling about him. They praised him with a voice so loud that he would have heard them if he could have heard anyone, and with a voice so awed that it betrayed the religious fervour which moved them.

The God of Nature was not, of course, the only object of religious devotion on the part of eighteenth-century intellectuals. Some discovered and paid obeisance to a mysterious force outside of themselves which they termed Science—though this Science, when duly capitalised, proved to be but a theological handmaid to the God of Nature. Others found a hydra-headed monstrosity which they proceeded to worship under the title of Humanity, and these were especially devout, perhaps because the deification of all Humanity is fraught with infinitely greater mystery than the conception of a single God-Man or even a Triune God. And between the sect of the Naturalists and that of the Humanitarians many another speedily arose. These were the Rationalists, who isolated a little bit of man's being and ascribed to it a most mysterious infallibility; the Progressives, who venerated Progress as if it were a sailing vessel and who, by aid of the theological virtues of faith, hope, and charity, were eager to go wherever the wind might blow them; and the Perfectabilists, who with eyes of faith and the gift of tongues saw and proclaimed the millennium—Eden and Paradise—on this earth just around the corner.

As might be expected of any era of doubt and scepticism about popular religion, there was a good deal of syncretism among the cults of the eighteenth century. Some Humanitarians were devoted to Nature; some Naturalists adored Reason; some Rationalists worshipped at a side-altar to

Perfectability or Progress or Humanity; even some Christians who exchanged their traditional God for Nature went on styling themselves Christian and participating in Christian worship. In any event, the eighteenth century, which beheld a waning faith in Christianity, beheld a waxing faith in Deism, Nature, Law, Science, Reason, Progress, Perfectability, and Humanity. It beheld also the rise of various organisations, such as Freemasonry and Illuminism, which enshrined one or all of the cults of the day and began to spread internationally. In the whole of the new syncretism, as well as in its component elements, the intellectual of the eighteenth century was giving expression to his inherent sense of religion.

3

All the doubting and sceptical periods of which mention has here been made have been characterised by another sort of worship—the worship of the Political State. It is an interesting fact that during the second and third centuries, when pagan scepticism was prevalent among Greek and Roman intellectuals and when philosophers and mystics were toying with new cults, the deification of the Roman Emperor was completed and his worship was widely and popularly indulged. It is another interesting fact that in the sixteenth century, when doubt about Catholicism was rife, not only Protestantism appeared on the scene, but also that popular exaltation of the lay State which a host of the intellectuals of the time—Machiavelli and Erastus (to name but two)—proclaimed and idealised. It is, moreover, an arresting fact that the eighteenth century, which witnessed among the classes the growth of scepticism about Christianity and simultaneously the rise of a novel faith in Deism, witnessed also, for the masses, the enthronement of the national state—*la Patrie*—as the central object of worship. Perhaps these instances are mere coincidence; more likely they may represent causal connections.

Doubt about a particular popular religion begins with intellectuals, and intellectuals as a class are notoriously timid. They have frequently been fearful of the unsettling effects of their own doubts upon the masses, and even willing on occasion that the masses, for the sake of social peace and general security, should go on indulging in belief and worship which to these intellectuals must seem superstitious. At the same time their very scepticism denies them any leadership in the preservation of the older popular religion, and their substituted faiths are usually so diverse and so abstract as to militate against the immediate and vulgar acceptance of any of them as a new popular religion. What is more natural, under these trying circumstances, than that the masses should be encouraged to transfer a large part of their inherent awe and reverence from a "supernatural" religion which the classes deem superstitious if not degrading, to a political religion which has the two-fold advantage of being obviously real and of having physical power sufficient to club the multitudes into some semblance of social harmony? Let the masses and the classes unite to rear and dedicate a high altar to the state; the masses may then be suffered to bring a few flowers to the little side-shrines of their ancestral gods, whilst the classes in assured peace can utilise the crypt for their novel rites and gradually impregnate the whole temple with the strange sweet odors of their esoteric incense.

The French Revolution—that landmark in the history of nationalism—was a landmark in the development of nationalism as a religion. At first many a French intellectual entertained the idea of syncretising eighteenth-century philosophy with Catholic Christianity in a State Church which should be organised democratically and conducted in the national interests. "The state, it seems to me," said the Abbé Raynal, "is not made for religion, but religion is made for the state. . . . The state has supremacy in everything . . . When the state has pronounced, the church has nothing

more to say." [1]   The Civil Constitution of the Clergy, voted
by the National Assembly in July, 1790, was the formal legal
attempt to realise the Abbé's programme; it aimed to create a national clergy, under the control of the civil power,
with the same standing as other state-officials.   But the
pope and the large majority of the French clergy were not
ready for any such religious syncretism; the Civil Constitution was condemned at Rome in April, 1791; and
thenceforth issue was squarely joined in France between the
religions of Catholicism and Nationalism.   Christianity was
not formally proscribed, but only the clergy who swore allegiance to the Civil Constitution were allowed to perform
Christian services, and the Catholic churches in most parts
of France were transformed into civic temples.   Against
the refractory clergy, measures of increasing severity were
taken; but severity did not suffice, and by the summer of
1793 a real persecution of Catholicism had begun.   For in
the minds of the Revolutionaries the Catholic clergy as
a whole had committed the greatest infamy of all—they had
defied the national state.

For nationalism truly became a religion with the French
Revolutionaries.   In the "new order" they perceived a mir-
aculous regeneration for France not only, but for the entire
human race.   The Declaration of the Rights of Man and of
the Citizen was hailed as "the national catechism," [2] and
solemn profession of belief in it was prescribed by the Constitution of 1791.   Those who refused to swear to it were
cut off from the community by civil excommunication, and
foreigners who proclaimed their loyalty to it were admitted
to the ranks of the faithful and enrolled as in a communion
of saints.   The written Constitution, embodying the Declaration, became holy writ.   At the first session of the Legislative Assembly, in the autumn of 1791, "twelve old men
went in procession to seek the Book of the Constitution.

---

[1] A. Bayet et F. Albert, *Les Écrivains politiques du xviiième siècle*
(1904), pp. 388-390.

[2] The words are Barnave's. *Cf.* A. Mathiez, *Les Origines des Cultes
Révolutionnaires* (1904), p. 22.

They came back, having at their head the archivist Camus, who, holding up the Book with his two hands and resting it on his breast, carried with slow and measured tread the new Blessed Sacrament of the French. All the deputies stood up and bared their heads. Camus, with meditative mien, kept his eyes lowered." [1]

The tricolour *cocarde,* the "trees of liberty," the Phrygian cap, the tablets of the Declaration of Rights and of the Constitution, the altars to *la Patrie*—all these were symbols of the new faith. The Legislative Assembly decreed in June, 1792, that "in all the communes an altar to the Fatherland shall be raised, on which shall be engraved the Declaration of Rights with the inscription, 'the citizen is born, lives, and dies for *la Patrie.*' " [2] Two years earlier at Strasbourg was introduced the rite of "civic baptism." "Civic marriages" and "civic funerals" came later. And the new religion soon had its hymns and its prayers, its fasts and its festivals.

Whilst the masses were drawn increasingly to the faith and worship of the national state, the revolutionary intellectuals redoubled their attacks upon historic Catholicism and attempted to substitute for it various specialised cults of nationalism. In the National Convention, on November 5, 1793, Marie-Joseph Chenier proposed the formal establishment of an exclusively lay religion, that of *la Patrie.* "Wrest," said he, on that occasion, "the sons of the Republic from the yoke of theocracy which still weighs upon them. . . . Devoid of prejudices and worthy to represent the French nation, you will know how to found, on the débris of the dethroned superstitions, the single universal religion, which has neither sects nor mysteries, of which the only dogma is equality, of which our law-makers are the preachers, of which the magistrates are the pontiffs, and in which the human family burns its incense only at the altar of *la Patrie,* common mother and divinity." [3] Two days later

---

[1] A. Mathiez, *op. cit.,* p. 27.   [2] *Ibid.,* p. 31.

[3] A. Aulard, *Le Culte de la Raison et le Culte de l'Être Suprême* (1892), p. 35.

the Constitutional bishop of Paris announced to the Convention his abdication, and declared that "there should no longer be any public worship other than that of liberty and holy equality." [1] Three days more, and the worship of Reason was solemnly inaugurated in the cathedral of Notre Dame.

Reason, however, did not obtain universal or permanent adoration. It was speedily succeeded, under the influence of Robespierre, by the worship of the Supreme Being (Deism), and this in turn, after the downfall of Robespierre, by the civic cult of the Decadi and the ethical cult of Theophilanthropy. But what vitality there was in any or all of these varieties and vagaries of religious experience is attributable to their intermixture with the religion of nationalism. This religion had already lodged deep in popular consciousness, and eventually it was to emerge, in more or less curious syncretisms with older philosophies and world-religions, as the dominant religion of the nineteenth and twentieth centuries. Under the mask of *laicisation* the new religion of nationalism soon claimed the allegiance of a multitude of determined zealots throughout the world.

4

Nationalism, viewed as a religion, has much in common with other great religious systems of the past. It has, for example, a god, who is either the patron or the personification of one's *patrie,* one's fatherland, one's national state. This god resembles the Jewish Yahweh, in that he is the god of a chosen people, a jealous god, and preëminently a god of battles, but he must not be identified with Yahweh, for French and German and British and all non-Jewish nationalists have a contempt for Yahweh as deep-seated and expressive as the priests of Yahweh entertained in biblical times for Baal and his priests. Devotees of a particular national god are prone to mock and sneer at any failure of another national god to bring down fire from heaven.

On his own national god the modern religious nationalist

[1] *Ibid.,* p. 45.

is conscious of dependence. Of His powerful help he feels the need. In Him he recognises the source of his own perfection and happiness. To Him, in a strictly religious sense, he subjects himself. Moreover, the religious nationalist not only is disposed subjectively to acknowledge his dependence on the national god, but also he is ready to acknowledge such dependence objectively through acts of homage and adoration. Nationalism, like any religion, calls into play not simply the will, but the intellect, the imagination, and the emotions. The intellect constructs a speculative theology or mythology of nationalism. The imagination builds an unseen world around the eternal past and the everlasting future of one's nationality. The emotions feed the theological virtues of faith, hope, and filial love; they arouse a joy and ecstasy in the contemplation of the national god, who is all-good and all-protecting, a longing for His favours, a thankfulness for His benefits, a fear of offending Him, and feelings of awe and reverence at the immensity of His power and wisdom; they express themselves naturally in worship, both internal and external, both private and public. For nationalism, again like any other religion, is to a large extent a social function, and its chief rites are public rites, performed in the name and for the salvation of the whole community.

Nationalism as a religion first appeared among peoples that were traditionally Christian, and it is not extraordinary, therefore, that it should have borrowed and adapted to its own purposes many customs and usages of historic Christianity. In fact the current notion of the national state is so similar to the mediaeval notion of the Christian Church that the close study of the doctrine and practices of contemporary nationalism is recommended to the modern man who would comprehend the seemingly incomprehensible middle ages.

To the modern national state, as to the mediaeval church, is attributable an *ideal*, a *mission*. It is the mission of salvation and the ideal of immortality. The nation is conceived of as eternal, and the deaths of her loyal sons do but add to her undying fame and glory. She protects her children and saves them from foreign devils; she assures them life, liberty, and the pursuit of happiness; she fosters for them the arts and the sciences; and she gives them nourishment. Nor may the rôle of the modern national state, any more than that of the mediaeval church, be thought of as economic or mercenary; it is primarily spiritual, even otherworldly, and its driving force is its collective *faith,* a faith in its mission and destiny, a faith in things unseen, a faith that would move mountains. Nationalism is sentimental, emotional, and inspirational.

There are very definite and illuminating parallels between contemporary nationalism and mediaeval Christianity. Nowadays the individual is born into the national state as formerly he was born into the church, and the secular registration of birth is the national rite of baptism. Thenceforth, with tender solicitude, the state follows the individual through life, teaching him in patriotic schools the national catechism, shewing him by pious precept and solemn sacrament the beauties of national holiness, fitting him for a life of service (no matter how glorious or how menial) to the state, the Alpha and Omega of his being, the author and finisher of his blessings, and commemorating his vital crises by formal registration (with a fee) not only of his birth but likewise of his marriage, of the birth of his children, and of his death. If he is a crusader in behalf of nationalism, his place of entombment is marked forever with the ensign of his service. And the funerals of national potentates and heroes are celebrated with patriotic pomp and circumstance that make the obsequies of mediaeval bishops seem drab.

Membership in some modern national state is compulsory. The individual may withdraw from the earthly State Militant only by death or emigration, and in the latter case he finds it well nigh impossible to discover any land which does not possess some established form of the religion of nationalism. He may change his sect, so to speak, but not his religion. The fabled "man without a country" has become an up-to-date version of the "flying Dutchman." And the individual, however sceptical he may be about his national faith, knows that compulsory membership in any national state involves compulsory financial support of its maintenance and missionary enterprise, for such a state is as insistent upon the collection of taxes as ever was the mediaeval church upon the levying of tithes.

Interior devotion to nationalism is expected of all persons, though here a little allowance can appropriately be made for human frailty. So long as public rites and ceremonies are decently observed, the hearts of the individual worshippers need not be too closely searched. Human beings doubtless differ from one another in the intensity of their religious feelings, and some, perhaps, are so abnormal as not to experience any religious emotion whatever. Besides, it has long been recognised that he who prays the loudest and beats his breast with greatest ostentation may be most lacking in true interior devotion. The ways of sceptics and doubters have been notoriously subtle, and it may be questioned whether Pharisees and whited sepulchres do not exist among the hordes of sincerely devout nationalists.

There can be no question, however, of the popular and compelling character of external nationalist worship. Blasphemy and sacrilege have always been treated by man as heinous crimes, and the modern man who allows a flitting mental doubt to find expression in jest or sneer at the expense of the national cult is eligible for mad-house or penitentiary.

The ritual of modern nationalism is simpler than that of certain other great historic religions, probably because sufficient time has not yet elapsed for its elaboration, but, considering its youthfulness, it is already fairly well developed. Nationalism's chief symbol of faith and central object of worship is the flag, and curious liturgical forms have been devised for "saluting" the flag, for "dipping" the flag, for "lowering" the flag, and for "hoisting" the flag. Men bare their heads when the flag passes by; and in praise of the flag poets write odes and children sing hymns. In America young people are ranged in serried rows and required to recite daily, with hierophantic voice and ritualistic gesture, the mystical formula: "I pledge allegiance to our flag and to the country for which it stands, one nation, indivisible, with liberty and justice for all." Everywhere, in all solemn feasts and fasts of nationalism the flag is in evidence, and with it that other sacred thing, the national anthem. An acute literary critic in his purely secular capacity might be tempted to find fault with certain phrases in "Rule Britannia," in "Deutschland über Alles," or even in the "Marseillaise"; he might conceivably object, on literary grounds, to such a lame beginning as "Oh say, can you see?" But a national anthem is not a profane object and does not admit of textual criticism. It is holy. It is the *Te Deum* of the new dispensation; the worshippers stand when it is intoned, the military at "attention" and the male civilians with uncovered heads, all with external signs of veneration and respect.

Nationalism has its parades, processions, and pilgrimages. It has, moreover, its distinctive holy days, and just as the Christian Church took over some festivals from Paganism, so the national state has borrowed freely from Christianity. In the United States, for example, the Fourth of July is a nationalist Christmas, Flag Day is substituted for Corpus Christi, and Decoration Day for the commemoration of All Souls of the faithful departed, whilst in place of the saints' days of the Christian calendar appear the birthdays of national saints and heroes, such as Washington and Lincoln. Nationalism also has its temples, and he who would find the places and the buildings that are held most dear and most sacred by the vast majority of Americans, should seek not Christian cathedrals but Independence Hall in Philadelphia, Faneuil Hall in Boston, the shrine to General Lee in Lexington, and that to General Grant in New York, and the city of Washington with its stately Capitol, its White House, its great monuments to Lincoln and Washington, and its adjacent Arlington and Mount Vernon.

Moderns, especially Americans, are inclined to regard the mediaeval veneration of images, icons, and relics as savouring of "superstition," but let them replace a statue of St. George by a graven image of General George Washington, an icon of the Blessed Virgin Mary by a lithograph of the brave Molly Pitcher, and a relic of the Holy Cross by a tattered battle-flag, and they display a reverence which they deem beautiful and ennobling. If one calls to mind the images of national heroes with which every town is plentifully supplied and the icons of national fathers which adorn both the sumptuous clubs of the rich and the simple cottages of the poor, one can appreciate the basic religious appeal of modern nationalism. In 1915, when the old cracked Liberty Bell was transported from Philadelphia to the San Francisco Exposition, throngs of refined and lovely ladies met it at many a station on the long way and piously bestowed upon it their sweet kisses. By veneration of a national relic these ladies were expressing their religious sense and practicing the nationalist cult.

5

Every national state has a "theology," a more or less systematised body of official doctrines which have been deduced from the precepts of the "Fathers" and from the admonitions of the national scriptures and which reflect the "genius of the people" and constitute a guide to national behaviour. In America, the canon of national holy scripture certainly includes the Declaration of Independence, the Constitution, Washington's Farewell Address, the Monroe Doctrine, and Lincoln's addresses, but here, as elsewhere, the canon is not yet definitive. There is even now an intense rivalry between two theological schools, that which supports the authenticity of the gospel according to Theodore Roosevelt and that which attributes inspiration to the epistles of Woodrow Wilson. Such rivalries, of course, can be but transient; and it is as probable as it is desirable that in the long run our doctors of sacred theology will arrive at a compromise and will then exercise their infallible authority by incorporating into the American canon both the Woodrownine epistles and the gospel of Theodore. Nationalism can easily survive, as other religions have survived, and even profit from, some little discrepancies and minor contradictions in holy writ. An opportunity for interpretation and higher criticism is a wonderfully golden opportunity for professed theologians.

From the theologians of nationalism proceed more or less learned works, say about the Constitution or the Monroe Doctrine or the Wisdom of Abraham Lincoln, which are commented upon and simplified by publicists and textbook compilers, and the writings of these gentlemen (and ladies) in turn are piously vulgarised by sentimental journalists and emotional orators. The upshot of the whole process is that a nationalist theology of the intellectuals becomes a nationalist mythology for the masses.

Nationalist mythology is not in every detail strictly accurate and literally true—no mythology ever is—but after all its main purpose is didactic, "for example of life and instruction of manners," [1] and didacticism need not depend slavishly upon historical or scientific fact. It claims and deserves the wider range of imagination and emotion. Take for instance almost any Fourth-of-July oration delivered in any year or in any part of the United States, or almost any patriotic speech read into the Congressional Record and distributed gratis among the Representative's constituents, and you will find that objective truth and scientific detachment have been sacrificed to a more emotional appeal and a higher truth. It is not that patriotic orators and national Congressmen set out to prevaricate or lie; as a rule they are upright and honourable men. What actually happens is that they are so convinced of the sacred

---

[1] Article VI of the "Thirty-nine Articles," *Book of Common Prayer*.

truth of the nationalist teachings and myths which have
been handed down to them and so inflamed with the desire
to confirm the faith of the multitude that they unquestioningly repeat any statement favourable to the cause and may
go so far as to invent and spread a quite erroneous picture
of the nation's past. In this way they contribute to the
elaboration of a popular mythology and to its confusion
with official nationalist theology.

I have before me now a speech which my own Congressman delivered in the House of Representatives on August
15, 1916, and which with kindly thoughtfulness he had the
Government, at its expense, send to me, along with numerous packages of agricultural seeds, for my national nourishment and edification. The speech closes with an uplifting
nationalist paean:

The military annals of mankind reveal no finer discipline,
no more splendid heroism, than were displayed on every
battlefield of the Revolution and the War between the
States. The soldiers of Washington were no craven spirits,
no mercenary hirelings, imported from the shambles of
Europe to do battle for filthy lucre at the bidding of tyrant
kings. They were freemen, champions of human liberty,
as brave and gallant warriors as ever breasted the flood of
death. No ignorant, vulgar rebels they! The Revolutionary ranks were filled with accomplished scholars, with men
who read the tragedies of Aeschylus in Greek as easily as
the tragedies of Shakespeare in English. Government, philosophy, and religion were themes of daily and familiar
converse around colonial camp fires. The soldiers of the
Revolution knew the richness of their blood. They traced
their lineage along a noble line to Crécy, Poitiers, Malpla-
quet, and Ramillies. They read the military achievements
of their race in the recovery of the holy sepulchre, in the
battle at Hohenlinden, in the capture of Quebec. They
felt no inability to multiply these brilliant deeds; and
when the battle call was sounded by the bugle's stirring
blast and the thrilling tones of the trumpet and the drum,
it was then that the heroes of Saratoga and Yorktown, of
Brandywine and Valley Forge, moved to the impetuous
charge with the victors' exultant shout. It was then they

stepped "like bridegrooms to a marriage feast," into the jaws of death, and their soldier spirits joined in eternity that band of warrior souls that, in every age from the mountain pass of Thermopylae to the battle plains of Cuba and Mukden, have died for the liberties of their fellow men. Such was the character and such the conduct of the soldiers of Washington.

More than fifty years ago civil war broke upon the country. The most momentous struggle in history called to the field of battle the finest armies of the world. Men from the North and men from the South rushed to the dividing line in serried ranks, with martial step, and with hearts that beat like kettledrums; and whether dressed in blue or clad in gray, at Gettysburg and Antietam, at Cold Harbour and the Wilderness, they sent to generations yet unborn a message of perfect discipline and deathless valour. . . .

Mr. Speaker, I have an abiding and an unbounded faith in the great destiny and in the undying glory of my country. I believe that the time is not far distant when we shall have complete military and naval, economic and industrial, intellectual and spiritual preparedness; when American genius and American influence will dominate the nations and overshadow the earth; when our Constitution and our Declaration of Independence will be the mould and model of free institutions among all the tribes of men; when the torch of freedom which was lit at the flame of the American Revolution will be a beacon light to the oppressed of all mankind; when our soldiers and our sailors will be feared and respected on every land and on every sea; when the drum beat of our country will be heard around the world; when freedom's flag will illumine all the skies; and, whether proceeding from the mouth of an ambassador or from the hot throats of Federal guns, the mandate of the great Republic will be heard and obeyed throughout the earth. [Applause.]

Such a peroration is nobly dithyrambic, but it does propagate some myths. The trained historian knows that there were battles in the Revolutionary War and in the War between the States (for instance, the First Battle of Bull Run) in which no sort of discipline or heroism was displayed. He also knows that the Revolutionary ranks were not exactly filled with men who read the tragedies of

Shakespeare (or anything else) in English, to say nothing of men who read Aeschylus in the original Greek. Nor is it easy for a severe logician to perceive just how freedom's flag will illumine all the skies at the very time when American soldiers and sailors are feared on every land and on every sea. But these and many other criticisms which the scientist or the literalist might level at the quotation are beside the point.

What gives rise to popular myths about modern nationalism, as, for example, the myths associated with the American Revolution, the myths fashioned and disseminated by our Congressman, is the same as what gave rise in the middle ages to the "Donation of Constantine" and the "pseudo-Isidorian decretals." These mediaeval documents, supercilious and unsympathetic moderns have branded by the ugly name of "forgeries," but they are forgeries only in the sense that many nationalist writings and speeches of recent times are forgeries. Both have sprung from a lively faith and a glowing imagination, and both have been justified on the common ground that they meet a contemporary need so perfectly that they must be true. They are products of piety, and how can piety be immoral? How can edification be untruthful? What really matters is that they are received by the masses on faith and are reverently embodied in the popular mythology.

The school-system of the national state is held to strict accountability for any lapse from the official theology or for any slur upon the popular mythology. Here and there a bold teacher or a tactless textbook writer may suggest an explanation of some episode in early national history not in full harmony with the nationalist faith; such a person, as is well established in these latter days, is liable to denunciation by some zealous patriotic society and to trial and degradation by an Inquisitorial Board of Education—functioning as a kind of modern Dominican Order—and the offensive texts are put on a nationalist Index Librorum Prohibitorum and thenceforth the civil arm may ban them from public libraries and burn them in public squares amid the plaudits of the faithful.

For there is a chronic fear among nationalists, as among most religious enthusiasts, that the masses are on the point of losing their faith, and a firm determination, therefore, that only such information should be imparted to them as will strengthen that faith and promote popular devotion to it. As the "Committee on Studies and Textbooks" of the public schools of New York City (consisting of principals and teachers) declared in their report of March 27, 1922: "The textbook must contain no statement in derogation or in disparagement of the achievements of American heroes. It must not question the sincerity of the aims and purposes of the founders of the Republic or of those who have guided its destinies. . . . [In discussing the American Revolution], everything essential is accomplished when it is made plain to the pupils: that the Colonists had just grievances; that they rebelled because they could obtain no redress; that they were inspired by a fierce love of liberty; that they counted neither the cost nor the odds against them; that the dominating spirit of the Revolution is found in the words of Nathan Hale: 'I regret that I have but one life to lose for my country.' " [1] Thus is it sought to keep the minds of the young pure and uncontaminated from knowledge of the full truth which, it is assumed, might weaken, if not destroy, the nationalist faith. For the preservation of the faith, the common people should be kept in ignorance. The argument has been imputed to mediaeval Christians less justifiably than to modern nationalists.

6

Human beings do not normally and willingly give their lives for economic gain. The supreme sacrifice is oftenest paid in behalf of an ideal and in response to the "religious sense." And perhaps the surest proof of the religious character of modern nationalism is the zeal with which all

[1] *The Historical Outlook*, vol. xiii, pp. 250-255 (October, 1922).

manner of its devotees have laid down their lives on battlefields of the last hundred years. At this very moment there
are hundreds of thousands of little whitewashed crosses all
over northern France, each bearing the simple black inscription "Mort pour la Patrie."   Vastly more men per-
ished in the recent four-years War of the Nations than in
the four centuries of mediaeval Christian Crusades.

A faith that inspires the noblest sacrifices is apt to be
intolerant in some of its manifestations, and the similarity
in this respect between modern nationalism and mediaeval
Christianity is striking. The mediaeval Christian was not
the supremely intolerant person that prejudiced moderns
imagine; he distinguished between various kinds of unbe-
lievers, and treated them accordingly; he was harsher to
heretics than to infidels, pagans, and Jews; he dealt more
severely with the ignorant than with the learned and more
excitedly with the popular propagandist than with the
closet philosopher. And it is even so with the modern
nationalist.

Towards pagans and infidels in their own distant homes,
that is, towards inhabitants of foreign countries, our attitude varies all the way from amused interest or contempt
to dislike and fear and hatred; if we think our vital
interests or our "national honour" to be threatened we
preach a crusade against them, but otherwise we tolerantly
let them survive as curious aberrations of Providence.
Towards pagans and infidels in our midst, that is, towards
unnaturalised immigrants, our attitude differs according as
they are few or numerous. If they are few, we pity or
despise them, but we do not directly persecute them; rather,
we hope and work for their conversion to our faith, for
their naturalisation in our national state. On the other
hand, if they are numerous, and especially if they are re-
calcitrant about conversion, we grow fearful, lament the
failure of the "melting-pot," and erect social, sometimes
legislative, barriers against them.

Heretics are fellow countrymen who have lapsed from

the pure faith and gospel, depraved beings who, having had the advantage of belonging to us and of experiencing our nationalism, have failed to appreciate it and have fallen into error or doubt. There are several gradations of national heresy. The outright traitor—the apostate who fights against us in our crusades—is the worst; he excites in us hatred and horror. If we catch him we put him to ignominious death, and if we don't catch him we use his name forever after as a by-word. In popular American thought Benedict Arnold has long since ceased to be human and become a satanic spirit. The heretic who is a plain and simple pervert, that is, who lives abroad and takes out naturalisation papers in a foreign country, is exceptional and can be merely despised and reproached; we assuage our wounded vanity by imagining that he did the wicked thing under compulsion or for financial profit.

But the most perplexing and troublesome kinds of heretic are the crypto-heretics, the persons who are so indecorous in their external acts of devotion, so critical of the "Fathers" and "scriptures," or so indifferent to their patriotic obligations, that they are suspected of harbouring interior devotion to some other nationality, or, what is worse, to no nationality at all. These unfortunates in times of great excitement, as in our modern national crusades, we ferret out by methods which would astound a Torquemada or a Cotton Mather, and either banish or jail, often on the flimsiest evidence. In ordinary times, however, we allow crypto-heretics some freedom of physical movement and even a little liberty of speech and publication, provided, of course, that they are university professors or other "cranks," far removed from public life and without direct influence on the formation of public opinion. But even in ordinary times, we must take cognisance of crypto-heretics who teach children or write for the masses; these are very dangerous, for they imperil the nationalist souls of the little ones; they may lawfully be penalised by the officials of the land, or they may be left to be handled beyond the law by ultra-patriotic private organisations, such as Black Hundreds or Fascisti or Ku Klux Klans.

"My country, right or wrong, my country!" Thus responds the faithful nationalist to the magisterial call of his religion, and thereby he intends nothing dubious or immoral. He is merely making a subtle distinction between governmental officials who may go wrong and a nation which, from the inherent nature of things, must ever be right. It would sound pedantic for him to say, "my nation, indicatively right or subjunctively wrong (contrary to fact), my nation!" Indeed, to the national state are now popularly ascribed infallibility and impeccability. We moderns are prepared to grant that all our fellow countrymen may individually err in conduct and judgement, but we are loath to admit that our nation as a whole can make mistakes. We are willing to assail the policies and even the characters of some of our politicians, but we are stopped by the faith that is in us from doubting the Providential guidance of our national state. This is the final mark of the religious nature of modern nationalism.

The most impressive fact about the present age is the universality of the religious aspects of nationalism. Not only in the United States does the religious sense of the whole people find expression in nationalism, but also, in slightly different form but perhaps to an even greater degree, in France, England, Italy, Germany, Belgium, Holland, Russia, the Scandinavian and Baltic countries, Poland, Hungary, Czechoslovakia, Spain, Portugal, Ireland, the Balkans, Greece, and the Latin-American republics. Nor does the religion of nationalism thrive only on traditionally Christian soil; it now flourishes in Japan, Turkey, Egypt, India, Korea, and is rearing its altars in China. Nationalism has a large number of particularly quarrelsome sects, but as a whole it is the latest and nearest approach to a world-religion.

7

Nationalism is a religion now common to the great majority of mankind. But this is not to say that older religions have been obliterated by nationalism. Buddhism and Hinduism still exist. So does Mohammedanism. So does Christianity—Catholic, Orthodox, and Protestant. What is actually occurring is a new religious syncretism, by virtue of which very many persons continue nominally to adhere to the faith of their ancestors and even to practice its cult, whilst they adapt it to the exigencies of nationalist worship and discipline. Some extreme (and, let us grant, logical) nationalists abandon and assail other religions. Some devotees of other religions criticise and condemn nationalism. But the bulk of nationalists, and a growing number of Christians, Mohammedans, and Buddhists, proceed more or less unreflectively to effect a compromise between the old faith and the new. And the compromise is increasingly favourable to the religion of nationalism.

Judaism is still a potent force in the lives of many Jews, but there can be little doubt that in recent times, with the development of scepticism about the divine inspiration of the Hebrew Scriptures and the rise of "reform movements" and the consequently less strict observance of the Mosaic law and of the ceremonial of the orthodox synagogue, an ever augmenting number of Jews are expressing their religious sense in nationalism, either in devotion to the nationalism of the people among whom they live or in service and sacrifice in behalf of their own peculiar Zionism. Ancient Judaism was a religion which centred the hopes and aspirations of a "chosen people" upon a supernatural God, the God Yahweh, and anyone who believed in Yahweh and abided by His commandments was "chosen." Modern Zionism is a religion which transfers the object of worship from Yahweh to the chosen people, and none is chosen who is wilfully ignorant of the Hebrew language.

Buddhism is still a powerful factor in the lives of myriad

Orientals, and in the quaint forms of Theosophy it is exerting a little direct influence upon the Occident, but in Japan, at any rate, it has latterly been subordinated to nationalist Shinto, and in China certain intellectuals are attempting an amalgam of it with Confucianism and Christianity in order to produce a Chinese national religion. Mohammedanism is still a great and aggressive religion, with far-flung missionary enterprise in the East Indies and in central Africa, but the followers of Mustapha Kemal Pasha have proved themselves Turkish nationalists first and Moslems afterwards, and Mohammedan Arabs are fraternising with Christian Arabs in a common supreme devotion to Arab nationalism against the threats of established Zionism. In India both Mohammedanism and Hinduism are ebbing before a rising Indian nationalism.

Christianity has more nominal followers today than ever before in its history, and possibly there are more sincere and devout Christians—Catholic, Orthodox, and Protestant—in the twentieth century than in any earlier century. But it is manifest to us who live in the West that Christianity for enormous numbers of people has become an adjunct to nationalism. The Orthodox Churches of the East, the Armenian Church, the Coptic Church, the remnant of the Nestorian Church, are auxiliaries to nationalist fervour and nationalist endeavour. Westminster Abbey is a holy fane of the Church of England and, much more so, of British nationalism; and the Protestant cathedrals of England and Scotland and Ireland, and of Prussia too, are adorned not so plentifully or so conspicuously with statues of Christian saints as with images of national heroes, military or naval, and with national battle-flags. In France, the sacred remains of Napoleon Bonaparte lie close to a Catholic altar, and the magnificent Christian church of Sainte Geneviève has been transformed into the National Panthéon.

Christianity in the United States is becoming more and more nationalist,—and naturally so. The Protestant majority, in holding their own and seeking the conversion of divers immigrants, constantly affirm that America is Protestant, and that Protestanism is American. The Catholic minority, not to be outdone by such an attractive plea, are bent on "Americanising" themselves and their immigrants. All this promotes the religion of Americanism, not quite as a substitute for Christianity, but rather as a most impressive supplement to it. The process is fostered, moreover, by the very fact that American Protestantism is divided into numerous sects and denominations. No Protestant sect is strong enough—and certainly the Catholic Church is not strong enough (even if it were so minded)—to establish itself as the official church of the United States. Hence there can be in a common Christianity no oneness of faith and worship for the whole American people. Consequently the spiritual unity, which almost everyone deems desirable, must be sought in nationalism. American Protestants may differ about the literal interpretation of the first chapter of the Book of Genesis, or about the manner of administering baptism, or about the orders of the ministry and the number of sacraments, but they do not differ essentially in their homage to the national state. In most Protestant churches in the United States a big American flag hangs resplendent over the pulpit or communion-table, and in most localities Protestant clergy and their faithful hold "union services" at least on Thanksgiving Day, on Decoration Day, on Washington's Birthday, and on the Fourth of July. Is there not some justification for the prophecy of Mr. Israel Zangwill that "America will doubtless be the first to fuse its 186 denominations and its countless crank creeds into a single American religion"? [1]

A good deal has been said and written of late by agnostically inclined gentlemen about the decay of Protestantism in America, and it has been pointed out that only about thirty per cent. of the American people attend church. This, in my opinion, is a most superficial estimate of the situation.

[1] *The Principle of Nationalities* (1917), p. 87.

Protestantism of the sixteenth-century Lutheran or Calvinistic type may be decaying—I don't know, and I am reluctant to guess—but Protestantism as a vehement protest against historic Catholic Christianity and as an important element in the contemporary syncretic religion of nationalism is certainly alive and thriving. In this sense far more than thirty per cent. of the American people are Protestants—and nationalists. And it is undoubtedly true that many Catholic Americans would resent any imputation that they are less devout in the worship of nationalism than are their Protestant fellow countrymen.

Syncretism of nationalism and Christianity go on apace in the United States. At one extreme, a group of Catholics of French-Canadian extraction in the diocese of Providence (Rhode Island) are so intent upon exalting nationalism as an indispensable prop for their traditional Christianity that, upon being refused the use of a Catholic church and hall for a nationalist demonstration, they denounce their bishop, call him unseemly names, defy his authority, and obtain from a priest in Quebec words of encouragement for their cause and conduct. At the other extreme the modernist pastor of a Unitarian church in New York, a clergyman of English descent, declares that it is an absurd anachronism for American children to be studying the folk-tales of the alien Hebrew people, and announces that the Sunday-school attached to his church will henceforth teach the "American Holy Bible"—the Constitution, the Declaration of Independence, and the biographies of our national heroes.[1] "Fundamentalists" appear to apprehend a prop to their literal Biblical faith in the parallel between the early chosen Hebrews and the later chosen Americans. "Modernists" seem to thicken Americanism in measure as they dilute Christianity.

From the newspaper we learn that at the Protestant Episcopal Church of St. Mark's-in-the-Bouwerie, in February, 1924, a sermon by Dr. Stuart L. Tyson, vice-president of the Modern Churchman's Union, in which he denied the

[1] Rev. C. F. Potter, *New York Times*, February 28, 1924.

divinity of Christ, and a ritual service devoted to the American flag, "engaged the attention of large congregations morning and afternoon." [1]

The ritual expressing the religion of Old Glory was taken from a book of that title published by the rector of St. Mark's, Dr. William Norman Guthrie, who says that it was authorised for use in St. Mark's on the Sunday after Thanksgiving Day, 1918, by Bishop David H. Greer, then head of the Protestant Episcopal Diocese of New York.

The worship of the flag was performed on a platform in front of the chancel, by professional actors designated as Chief Officiant, the Son; First Assistant, the Mother; and Second Assistant, the Father. The rector named the seven impersonators of the red stripes in the flag as Washington, Jefferson, Jackson, Lincoln, Cleveland, Roosevelt, and Wilson.

The white flagstaff was placed in front of the sanctuary, topped with a golden sphere over which hovered the golden eagle. The congregation was addressed as follows: "At the top of the flagstaff hovers the emblem of our sovereignty, the white-hooded eagle. He expresses our aspiration and our inspiration, our living communion with the God of our fathers." This was followed by the psalm of the eagle. After the psalm the Chief Officiant cried aloud: "Hear ye the cry of the eagle." The congregation responded, "Let us rally to obey." The flag was raised to the singing of the first stanza of the "Star-Spangled Banner", while the Chief Officiant said: "Let us raise a standard, to which the wise and the honest can repair."

In the second part of the ritual the congregation were bidden to lift up their eyes to the seven red stripes, "as they are well worthy of worship." This chorus followed:

> "Let us sing together our song
> To the red of the flag,
> The red of the flag,
> The red of the flag,
> To the red of the flag forever."

[1] *New York Times,* February 25, 1924.

In like manner was performed the ritual worship of the six white stripes, the square of the midnight blue, the five-pointed white stars. The final ceremony was the worship of the white-hooded eagle. At the conclusion the flag was allowed to drop on the flagstaff as a salute to the sanctuary, and the "Battle Hymn of the Republic" was sung.

Though it is likely to be a long time before the new religion completely ousts the old, the syncretism now proceeding is far more favourable, in our opinion, to nationalism than to Christianity, Mohammedanism, or any other supernatural world-religion. The weaker grows the element of Christianity, for example, the stronger becomes the element of *la Patrie*, "supplying as it does channels for both devotion and sacrifice, and even an after-life in the life of the nation. Thus already we see Professor Loisy, in his new book 'Mors et Vita,' reacting from his thwarted hope of a reformed Christendom, to a religion of France, and this though he himself exposes the nationalist spuriousness of French neo-Catholicism." [1]

8

I would not have anyone gather from what I have said that I condemn nationalism because it is an expression of man's "religious sense." I am too convinced a believer in the inherently religious character of man to make light of religion; and to condemn nationalism because it depends on religious emotion would seem to me as futile as to condemn vegetation because it thrives on sunlight. I would suggest, however, that there are many, many ways in which man may express his religious sense, and that religious emotion, like any other instinctive emotion, is always susceptible and often needful of conscious direction and control. Some forms of religion are superior to others, and when we recognise the religious nature of modern nationalism we have

[1] Israel Zangwill, *The Principle of Nationalities* (1917), pp. 85-86. *Cf.* also Bertrand Russell, *Why Men Fight* (1917), pp. 56-58.

still to ask ourselves whether it is the form of religion most conducive to human betterment.

Most great religious systems of the past have been unifying, rather than disintegrating, forces in the history of the human race. Buddhism gave rise to a common type of constructive civilisation among the teeming millions of Burma, Siam, China, and Japan. Mohammedanism drew together in a common bond and inspired with a common zeal the most diverse tribesmen of Arabia, India, Persia, Turkey, the Malay archipelago, and Africa. Christianity bound together in a cultural community all kinds of European peoples, regardless of their habitat, breed, and native language. And especially in the case of Christianity, the forms and ceremonies which attended the expression of man's religious sense were constant symbols of a universal striving for a kingdom that was not of this world, for the sacrifice of self, and the assurance of peace on earth to men of good will.

Modern nationalism, while evolving customs and ceremonies which externally are very reminiscent of rites and practices of Christianity, has developed quite a different spirit, and set itself quite a different goal. Despite the universality of the general concept of nationalism, its cult is based on a tribal idea and is, therefore, in its practical manifestations, peculiar to circumscribed areas and to persons of the same language. The good at which it aims is a good for one's own nation only, not for all mankind. The desires which it inspires in an Englishman or a German or a Japanese are not the same as the desires which it inspires in a Frenchman, a Pole, or an American.

Nationalism as a religion represents a reaction against historic Christianity, against the universal mission of Christ; it re-enshrines the earlier tribal mission of a chosen people. The ancient reflective Roman imagined that one chosen people—the Hebrew nation—was one too many for general comfort and safety; the thoughtful modern Christian may be pardoned for being a bit pessimistic about a world devoid of a Roman Empire and replete with dozens upon dozens of chosen peoples.

Nationalism as a religion inculcates neither charity nor justice; it is proud, not humble; and it signally fails to universalise human aims. It repudiates the revolutionary message of St. Paul and proclaims anew the primitive doctrine that there shall be Jew and Greek, only that now there shall be Jew and Greek more quintessentially than ever. Nationalism's kingdom is frankly of this world, and its attainment involves tribal selfishness and vainglory, a particularly ignorant and tyrannical intolerance,—and war. That nationalism brings not peace but the sword, we propose next to shew.

V

NATIONALISM AND INTERNATIONAL WAR

1

WAR HAS been throughout the ages the fairly constant avocation of man. If in modern times war has been interrupted by comparatively long periods of peace, it is less a sign that man has found, what William James hoped he would find, a moral substitute for war, than an indication that when man has latterly plied his avocation of war he has plied it so wholeheartedly and so furiously as to exhaust him for relatively long periods. Our wars of the nineteenth and twentieth centuries may be briefer than those of earlier times, but they are vaster and more deadly. The recent Great War, though it lasted but four years, took a larger toll of human lives and property, and wrought more destruction, than did the twenty years' conflict of the Napoleonic era, or the Thirty Years' War of the seventeenth century, or the Hundred Years' War between the monarchs of England and France, or the three centuries of Crusading in the middle ages, or the protracted series of Persian and Peloponnesian Wars of the ancient Greeks, or any number of tribal conflicts among primitive men.

Nor has the recent Great War proved itself a final and cataclysmic ending of war. There are more men under arms in 1926 than there were in 1901; there is no doubt that every large army possesses a competent general staff; it is obvious that prodigious progress (eminent authorities call it "progress") is being made in the perfecting of airplanes, submarines, and poisonous gases. As the last war was chiefly a test of artillery, so the next is likely to be principally a demonstration of chemistry. And just as every general struggle in Europe during the last hundred and fifty years has sooner or later involved the United States, so this country, despite Washington's Farewell Address, despite the Monroe Doctrine, despite the heroic rhetoric of a noble band of Senatorial isolationists, is bound to be entangled sooner or later in the tentacles of the next Great War. Then, if any bits remain of what we term modern civilisation and modern science, they will be reassembled and utilised in preparedness for yet another world war. None knows how long this process can and will continue. If it continues unchecked, it must ultimately destroy all science and all civilisation.

Why do we have war? Why, especially in the present age, when we prate so much about "progress" and "science" and "humanity"? Why have we recently had a Great War, and why now do we behold on all sides preparations for another Great War? Present-day psychologists refer us, for an answer, to man's animal mind, to man's ill-concealed cave propensities, to man's combative instinct. Present-day economists refer us, for the answer, to trade-rivalries, to the competitive search for coal and iron and oil, to the greedy and quarrelsome exploitation of backward regions; in a word, to economic imperialism.

Economists and psychologists are doubtless right—so far as they go. Economic imperialism in one form or another has certainly paved the way to most wars, and without a combative instinct in the participants no war would be possible. But real civilisation—true culture—has always implied the suppression, or rather the sublimation, of primitive instincts, and it is a significant fact that that country is accounted most cultured and most civilised whose citizens, controlling their combative instinct, live most peacefully and most amicably one with another. Within our country we punish anyone who allows his combative instinct to express itself in robbery or murder. Apparently we reserve full expression of the combative instinct for dealings with foreigners. Yet if we can control our primitive nature in domestic matters, why may we not control it in international relations?

Nor is it tenable that economic imperialism is alone the cause of war. Undoubtedly there are now, as always, greedy and grasping men who contend with one another in cornering the world's supply of this or that necessity, of this or that luxury, and greedy and grasping men are likely to be so blind to the welfare of the world at large as to get their fellows to fight in behalf of their selfish interest. But our economic imperialists, stupid and near-sighted and even perverse, as some of them are, know better than to make economic gain the avowed *casus belli*. The ordinary normal man will not lay down his life for his own economic gain, and surely not for the financial profit of some anonymous fellow citizen who has foreign investments; the supreme sacrifice is paid only for an ideal. American investments in Cuba, actual or contemplated, had something to do with the Spanish-American War, but the masses of the American people gave support to that war not because of the investments, but because of their own idealism. A considerable number of Americans had, or thought they had, financial stakes in the recent Great War, but the American people as a whole went into the war because they were incorrigible idealists. And it is so with every people and in every war. Economic imperialism may create a situation favourable to war. The unrestrained combative instinct may make war possible. But war is not fought without idealism in the hearts of the masses and shibboleths on their lips.

2

It is a curious fact that the best part of man—his idealism, and particularly his religious idealism—has continually been played upon by the mercenary ambition of a minority of his kind and has frequently unloosed the worst that is in him, his fighting passion, his lust for gore and glory. Tribal gods and tribal religions have inspired their devotees with warlike zeal and fighting prowess. "Let us sing to the

Lord, for he is gloriously magnified, the horse and his rider he hath thrown into the sea." [1] "Though he slay me, yet will I trust in him." [2] Great world religions, too, have supplied excuses, and aroused enthusiasms, for human slaughter. The "Allah wills it" of the Moslem and the "Deus vult" of the Christian Crusader were expressions of a widespread popular conviction, which was none the less sincere because it precipitated a protracted contest that enabled a Saladin to rebuild a puissant Mohammedan empire and permitted in Christendom certain feudal landlords and enterprising merchants to enrich themselves with this world's goods. The sixteenth-century wars between Spaniards and Dutchmen and between Spaniards and Englishmen were of financial consequence to a few important personages, but for the masses they possessed no economic implications at all: on the one side, they constituted a noble, gallant struggle against overwhelming odds in order to preserve national liberties and the pure Protestant faith, and to break the power of bigoted, brutal Spain; on the other side, they represented a struggle quite as noble and gallant and against odds quite as overwhelming, in order to safeguard Christian civilisation and the Catholic faith from the onslaughts of fanatical rebels and unprincipled heretics.

In the nineteenth and twentieth centuries historic religions have played no such war-inspiring rôle as they played in earlier times. Neither ancient tribal gods like Baal or Yahweh, nor great world religions such as Mohammedanism or Christianity, have furnished, at least directly, the shibboleths for recent warfare. In the latest Great War, for instance, millions of human beings fought and died not because Allah willed it and not because Christian orthodoxy must be defended against heresy. Yet, despite the lessening influence of those types of idealism which moved most earlier generations to mortal combat, it is a self-evident

[1] The song of the Hebrew women, sung "with timbrels and with dances." *Exodus*, xv, 21.
[2] *Job*, xiii, 15.

truth that the wars of the last century have been more popular, that is, a larger percentage of the world's population have participated in them, and more destructive both of life and property, than the wars of any previous century.

It is our contention that in recent times nationalism has been substituted for other religion as the impelling source and object of that idealism which renders war popular. And such a substitution must be taken into account in any attempt to explain the modern intensification of war. Of course, it may be maintained that recent wars have been bloodier and costlier than ancient or mediaeval wars simply because of the marked advance of the industrial arts, that, for example, the Crusades of the twelfth century would have been as destructive as the nationalist Great War of the twentieth century had Christians and Moslems in the middle ages been blessed by universal compulsory military training, equipped with machine guns, hand grenades, Big Berthas, gasoline engines, and chlorine gas, and served by railways, steamships, cold storage, and "yellow" newspapers. Maybe so. It is one of those "ifs" which are ever the sport of publicists and the despair of historians. I am ready to grant that the greatest brutalities of which human beings were then capable were occasionally perpetrated in the middle ages in the name of Allah and his Prophet or in the name of the Man-God Christ. I am prepared to admit, moreover, that since the Industrial Revolution of the eighteenth and nineteenth centuries human beings have been enabled to practice brutality more elaborately, more scientifically, more subtly, and on a vaster scale. But I am personally of the opinion that, regardless of any mechanical aids, modern nationalism is a far more effective agency than Christianity or Mohammedanism for arousing and sustaining the war-spirit of human beings and for encouraging them to give free rein, in an idealistic orgy, to the worst brutalities of which at any given time they are capable.

Mohammedanism was propagated in great part by the sword, but once it became the dominant religion of large segments of the earth's surface it served as a bond of union among most diverse tribes and peoples and long promoted a more substantial and durable peace within its confines than had previously existed. Even minorities of dissentient faith, such as the Jews of Palestine and Mesopotamia, and the Armenian, Coptic, and Orthodox Christians of the Near East, were tolerated by triumphant Islam and accorded in most instances a considerable degree of political autonomy; these dissidents, until they adopted modern nationalism and so long as their overlords were primarily Mohammedans rather than nationalists, suffered no wholesale massacres.

Christianity was preached from the outset as a gospel of peace and human brotherhood, and its conquest of the ancient Roman Empire was almost wholly a work of "peaceful penetration"; subsequently, in the hands of barbarian kings, a Clovis or a Charlemagne, it seized the sword and slew Saxons and Saracens. But Christianity, once established, by whatever means, as the paramount faith of Europeans, surely did as much as the pagan Roman Emperors had done to assure a *Pax Romana* to the "civilised world," and the civilised world of the mediaeval Christians was larger in extent and more disparate in nationality than the civilised world of the ancient Romans. And, whatever may have been the practical shortcomings of individual Christians or the distortions and abuses to which Christian teachings were put by selfish and conceited persons who were Christian in name only, the Christian Church itself constantly pointed the masses toward the ideal of the Fatherhood of God and the brotherhood of man and toward the virtues of justice, charity, humility, and peace. Practical official efforts were made, directly by means of the Truce of God and the Peace of God and indirectly through arbitral devices, to diminish war and the threat of war. Nor could the individual Christian be totally and continually unmindful of the duty of loving one's neighbours as one's self, of forgiving one's enemies, of doing unto others as one would have done to one's self. The Christian saints were not, as a rule, warriors who battled with this world's weapons. A Saint Francis of Assisi, a Saint Francis Xavier, a Saint Catherine of Siena, a Saint Anthony of Padua did find in Christian idealism a moral substitute for war.

No moral substitute for war is popularly associated nowadays with any nationalist saint. On the contrary, the saints of nationalism almost invariably have been military heroes. In them is personified and idealised, for the masses of the present day, that sentiment, that religious faith—the faith and sentiment of modern nationalism—which has already produced great international wars and is almost certain, unless checked and controlled, to produce many more. Given the economic rivalries between capitalists and business-men of different nations, and a general situation now exists highly favourable to war. Given the great competitive armaments on land and sea, and the means are now at hand for prosecuting the most destructive kind of war. But the guns would not go off, and interested financiers could not precipitate war (even if they would), if the people of the several countries were not thoroughly imbued with the sentiment and creed of nationalism, with the conviction that therein they are the champions of a lofty and transcendent idealism. The masses, now as ever, must bear the brunt of fighting, and it is as improbable now as ever that the masses in any country, if they were appealed to only on economic grounds, could be persuaded to fight the masses of another country. Now as always, let us repeat, ordinary citizens do not lay down their lives for direct financial gain; they make the supreme sacrifice only for an ideal. Such an ideal, in its latest and most fearful form, is held up by nationalism.

Nationalism has latterly set before the ordinary citizen of every so-called civilised country on earth the ideal of fighting to secure any territory to which his nationality has ever had any sort of claim or on which his national flag has ever been hoisted, and to wreak vengeance on any land on which his fellow nationals have suffered in person or purse, an ideal which looks forward to the ultimate extension of one people's "mission" at the expense of the mission of all other peoples. Nationalism, unless it be rendered critical instead of ignorant, humble instead of proud, does not promise, despite its proved modernity, despite its admitted idealism, to promote real human progress. It promises not to unify, but to disintegrate, the world; not to preserve and create, but to destroy, civilisation.

3

Modern nationalism began its association with international war through popular attempts to realise the ideal of national self-determination. It should be recalled that in the eighteenth century, when nationalism as we know it had its rise, the political map of Europe, and of the whole world for that matter, was not drawn on national lines. At that time the polyglot dominions of Austrian archduke, Ottoman sultan, and Russian tsar and the rambling empires of China, India, Britain, Portugal, and Spain, bulked large on the map and blurred national boundaries. Italy and Germany were mere "geographical expressions," and Poland was obliterated in the eighteenth century. Only in western Europe did national states exist, and even here nationalism hardly had safe and sure footing: Spain comprised two nationalities (Castilians and Catalans) and remnants of two others (Basques and Galician Portuguese); France included a considerable German-speaking population in Alsace, a Celtic-speaking people in Brittany, and survivals of Catalan-Provençal and Basque nationalities in the south; Great Britain held three or four historic nationalities (English, Welsh, Scottish, and Irish); Norwegians and Icelanders were joined, along with fellow Scandinavians and with Germans of Schleswig-Holstein, to the crown of Denmark; Sweden still retained of her once great Baltic empire most of Finland and a bit of German soil; and the Dutch, in establishing a national state, had been obliged to leave the southern Netherlands, that is, Belgium (partly French and partly Flemish-Dutch), first to Spain and subsequently to Austria.

It was into such a political world and on such a political geography that, as we have previously noticed, the doctrine of popular sovereignty and its corollary the doctrine of national self-determination entered and found acceptance with intellectuals and then with the masses of one country after another. Obviously the old realities of world geography did not square with the new aspirations and aims of nationalism. If national self-determination were to prevail, the political map would have to be radically recast. But this was absolutely repugnant to persons and peoples who had vested interests in the existing order. The more a group clamoured for national self-determination and for national unity and independence, the more the emperors and potentates of non-national states strove to maintain the *status quo*. The more the revolutionaries sought to change the map, the more the conservatives laboured to preserve it. Both parties talked a good deal about civilisation and even about humanity. But it was evident, from the outset, that the issue would be settled only by resort to armed force, to war.

The very first wars of national self-determination were popular rebellions against an alleged tyrant, an "alien" king. Such, in essence, as early as the sixteenth and seventeenth centuries, were the successful revolt of the Dutch against Philip II of Spain and the unsuccessful rebellion of the Czechs against Ferdinand II of Austria. Such, too, in the eighteenth century, was the successful uprising of English-speaking Americans against George III of Great Britain. From the French Revolution, however, dated an almost uninterrupted succession of wars of subject peoples against "foreign" rulers and in behalf of the right of national self-determination. These numerous wars, as well as the few earlier wars of like nature, frequently extended beyond mere domestic insurrection and often gave rise to huge international conflicts, for the enthusiasm and fighting prowess which national idealism aroused in its devotees could be utilised, it was found, for other less national and more worldly purposes. Thus, the War of Dutch Independence was merged with the dynastic conflict between Spanish Habsburgs and French Bourbons, and with the general mercantilist struggles among the peoples of western Europe; the War of Czech Independence proved but a prelude to the vast international Thirty Years' War; the War of American Independence became part and parcel of the age-long contest for colonial and maritime supremacy between England on one side and France and Spain on the other; and the eagerness of the French Revolutionaries not only to "Frenchify" all inhabitants of France but also to incorporate into their national state all French-speaking lands, including Belgium, was perhaps the decisive factor in reopening the great international struggle between France and England and thereby in giving duration and virulence to the Revolutionary and Napoleonic Wars.

Merely to catalogue the modern wars of national self-determination is something of a task, and a task it would be both dull and idle were its assembled fruits not convincingly indicative of the force of nationalism in the nineteenth and twentieth centuries and positively redolent of gunpowder. Here is a partial list: the Irish Rebellion of 1798; the Haitian Rebellion of 1804; the Peninsular War of the Spaniards and Portuguese, aided by the British, against the French (1808-1813); the German War of Liberation against the French (1813-1814); the War of Greek Independence (1821-1829), culminating in the intervention of Great Britain, France, and Russia (1827), and the Russo-Turkish War of 1828-1829; the War of Serb Independence (1804-1830); the successful revolt of the Spanish colonists in South America, Central America, and Mexico (1810-1830); the revolt of the Belgians against their Dutch king (1830) and the consequent coercion of Holland by France and England; the unsuccessful revolts (1831) of Italians against Austria and of Poles against Russia; the Canadian Rebellion of 1837; the insurrection of Texas against Mexico (1835-1836) and the resulting war between Mexico and the

United States (1846-1848); the wave of nationalist wars in
Europe in 1848-1849—Italians against Austria, Czechs
against Austria, Magyars against Austria, Slavs against
Hungary, Germans against Denmark; the Crimean War
(1854-1856), waged by Russia against Turkey, France, and
Britain, and eventuating in the establishment of a united,
autonomous Rumania (1862); the French military occupation of Mexico and the War of Mexican Liberation (1862-
1867); the Polish uprising against Russia in 1863; the Wars
of Italian Unification—with France against Austria (1859),
with Prussia against Austria (1866), and against the Pope
(1870); the War for the preservation of the American
Union (1861-1865); the Wars of German Unification—
against Denmark (1864), against Austria (1866), and
against France (1870-1871); the Cuban Rebellion (1868-
1878); the Bosnian and Bulgarian revolts against Turkey
(1875-1876), leading to the Russo-Turkish War of 1877-
1878; the Chilean-Peruvian War (1879-1883); the Boer
revolt against the British (1881); the Serbo-Bulgarian War
of 1885-1886; the Sino-Japanese War over Korea (1894-
1895); the Cretan insurrection against Turkey (1895-1897),
producing the Graeco-Turkish War of 1897; the Cuban
revolt against Spain (1895-1898), terminating in the Spanish-American War (1898-1899); the Philippine insurrection
against the United States (1899-1901); the Jameson raid
in South Africa (1895), preliminary to the Boer War (1899-
1902); the protection of Korea against Russian aggression,
and the Russo-Japanese War (1904-1905); the Albanian
revolt against Turkey (1911-1912); the first Balkan War,
with Greeks, Yugoslavs, and Bulgarians in arms against
Turkey (1912-1913); the second Balkan War, with Greeks,
Yugoslavs, Rumanians, and Turks arrayed against Bulgaria
(1913); and the whole intricate series of struggles for national self-determination and for the assurance or comple-
tion of national unity and independence which attended and
constituted the outstanding achievement of the Great War
from 1914 to 1919—the final War of Yugoslav Unification,

the final War of Italian Unification, the final War of Rumanian Unification, the War of Czechoslovak Liberation, the War of Polish Restoration, the wars for the freedom of Finns, Esthonians, Letts, and Lithuanians from Russia, and of Arabs from Turkey, wars which returned Alsace-Lorraine to France and the Danish districts of Schleswig to Denmark, wars which contracted Austria, Hungary, Germany, Russia, and Turkey to the position of real national states. And in the same breath, for proceeding from the same spirit, may be added the Irish uprisings from 1916 to 1922 and the Graeco-Turkish War of 1920-1923.

If we were to take all these wars together and attempt to appraise their collective significance, we would doubtless be impressed by the fact that they have succeeded in their main purpose, that is, within a century and a half they have largely recast political geography on national lines. But we would also be struck by the staggering cost of such success. We would discover that, in order to establish and maintain a system of national states throughout the world, millions upon millions of human beings have been slain, many other millions have been maimed for life or rendered destitute, billions of treasure have been spent and incalculable havoc wrought. We might resign ourselves to these prodigious losses if we were convinced that they had been a sorry but strictly temporary incident in a more or less inevitable transition from an unjust and warlike stage of human society to a stage of society essentially peaceful, just, and humane. But a closer scrutiny of the nationalist wars of the nineteenth and twentieth centuries is hardly calculated to reassure us; it is more likely to engender in our minds serious doubts whether the recasting of political geography on national lines has actually promoted either humanity or justice and whether nationalism is a reliable harbinger of a quieter and better world in the immediate future.

We would have fewer doubts about the matter if modern nationalist wars had been simply and solely wars of national self-determination, if each nationality had beaten its swords into ploughshares so soon as it had secured the sovereign unity of lands in which it overwhelmingly predominated, and if it had thenceforth lived peacable in a mutually helpful concert of national states. Nationalist wars did begin, we have already remarked, as wars of national self-determination. The Spaniards fought in the Peninsular War and the Germans in the War of Liberation, the Spanish-Americans contended under Bolivar and the Serbs under Karageorge, the Greeks took arms in the 1820's, the Belgians and Poles in the 1830's, the Italians in the 1840's and 1850's, in every case not for conquest or domination abroad, but against alien tyranny at home. They struggled for human liberty and usually for political democracy as well as for national unity and national independence. Their fighting, though in some instances crude and even barbarous, prompted the most heroic deeds and invariably aroused the lively sympathy of humanitarians and liberals everywhere. Their leaders were unwontedly eloquent about "death to tyrants and peace to peoples." The right of self-determination, it was asserted, must be secured at any cost; once secured, it was alleged, the brotherhood of man would blossom from the brotherhood of peoples. The soulful outpourings and ecstatic visions of Mazzini reached the zenith of optimism about the nature and consequence of nationalist warfare; Mazzini lived fairly early in the nineteenth century, which is now past.

4

In fact, wars of national self-determination had not been waged long and the national recasting of political geography had not advanced far when complications arose, and these complications, which are still with us and which promise indefinitely to remain with us, have gradually altered the character, if not the reputation, of nationalist warfare. One such complication is commonly described by the word "irredentism." The word is of Italian origin and was first

employed in the 1870's to designate a nationalist agitation
in behalf of "Italia irredenta" (Italy unredeemed), the definite movement which aimed at the expansion of the united
and independent kingdom of Italy so as to include all the
lands in which resided any appreciable number of Italian-
speaking persons. What distinguished this Italian irredentism from the earlier form of national self-determination
was, first, that practically everyone in the unified Italy of
1870 was Italian in speech and feeling, and had been willing
if not anxious to become an Italian citizen, whereas in Italia
irredenta, that is, in Trieste, Fiume, Istria, and Dalmatia,
many Yugoslavs and some Germans were mingled with Italians, and were quite determined not to abandon their own
nationality, and, secondly, that Italy proper had been freed
from foreign rule and formed into a sovereign national state
as a result of enthusiastic popular uprisings and wars of
truly national self-determination, whereas the emancipation
of Italia irredenta and its incorporation with the Italian national state must involve not a popular insurrection but a
war of conquest, and must add to the new Italy regions not
exclusively Italian.

This was precisely an object and an outcome of the
Great War. Italia irredenta was finally, in 1919, annexed
to Italy, but it was annexed by conquest, and with it were
annexed Yugoslavs and Germans as well as Italians.
Thereby, in Istria, Dalmatia, and the Tyrol, what had been
an Italia irredenta became a Yugoslavia irredenta or an
Austria (Germania) irredenta. Italy justified her conquests
and annexations chiefly on the grounds that she was the
heir to the old Venetian empire and that the new frontiers were necessary for her military defence. But quite as
justifiably Yugoslavs may claim that they are heirs of the
mediaeval Serb empire of Stephen Dushan, or Germans that
they are the legatees of the mediaeval empire of the Habsburgs; and that the possession of the highest Alpine peaks is
requisite for military protection, is probably as valid a contention of Germans and Yugoslavs as of Italians. It will

be surprising if in the next generation, under the influence of nationalism, irredentists do not lift up their voices in Yugoslavia and Germany, demanding the "redemption" of their "lost provinces," and inciting to a retaliatory war of conquest. Such a war, if it comes, will be a nationalist war, an irredentist war, but it will not be, strictly speaking, a war of national self-determination.

The word "irredentism" originated in Italy, but the thing which it describes has not been narrowly Italian. It has almost universally attended the establishment of national states and has produced what may be termed the second degree of nationalist warfare. That is, nationalists first fight wars of national self-determination and erect a national state whose citizens are of the same nationality; they next fight irredentist wars and conquer adjacent territories whose inhabitants are only in part of common nationality. In other words, in some regions of the Earth's surface dwell fairly homogeneous nationalities whose political freedom and unity have been effected in first instance by wars of national self-determination, whereas, in other regions live peoples of divergent or doubtful nationality, who become, in second instance, bones of contention between neighbouring national states, objects of rival irredentist agitations, and sources of international irredentist wars. Thus, nationalist warfare, beginning as a struggle for human freedom, may soon lead on to a struggle for conquest and domination of dissident nationalities. And invariably such domination is excused on the grounds that the conquered regions were once inhabited wholly by persons of like nationality with the conquerors or that the conquerors represent a higher civilisation or that the regions are needful for the military safety or economic security of the conquering state. If nationalities were only fixed entities that occupied and always had occupied the same clearly marked territories, and had never been subjected at any time to foreign rule or foreign immigration, it would be an easy task to draw the political map of the world on national lines without recourse to irredentism. As it is, however, there must be wars of national self-determination not only, but also apparently wars of national irredentism.

Consider, for example, Alsace and Lorraine. These provinces in the middle ages had been German in speech and integral parts of the Holy Roman (German) Empire. Then, in the sixteenth and seventeenth centuries, they had been conquered by French kings who were not totally unmindful of the fact that the ancient northern and eastern boundary of Roman France—of Gaul—had been the Rhine. The French subjugation of Alsace-Lorraine occurred before the rise of modern nationalism, and consequently it did not produce a strong nationalist reaction in those provinces or in Germany as a whole; there was then no talk about a Germania irredenta. And with the lapse of time, the inhabitants of Alsace-Lorraine learned French as well as German, and, though bilingual, they developed a sense of belonging to France, a sense which the French Revolution and the Napoleonic Wars mightily enhanced. Eventually, however, the Germans in Germany became nationalist, and through wars of national self-determination—the wars of 1813-1814, 1848-1849, 1864, and 1866—established a powerful national state.

Then it was that German nationalism came into conflict with French nationalism; and the German conquest of Alsace-Lorraine in the War of 1870-1871, in an era of sharpening nationalism, produced results quite different from those which had attended the earlier French subjugation of the provinces. Patriotic Germans (and all Germans were now patriotic in the premises) insisted on having and holding Alsace-Lorraine because the territory had been German in the middle ages, because German *Kultur* was superior to French *civilisation* (which, they said, was frightfully decadent), and because their general staff assured them that the Vosges Mountains were a better defence than the River Rhine against future French aggression. On the other hand, patriotic Frenchmen (and all Frenchmen were now patriotic) longed and laboured for a favourable opportunity to regain the "lost provinces," because their inhabitants had protested in 1871 against incorporation in the German Empire, because German *Kultur* was brutal and barbarous, and because German armaments in Alsace-Lorraine were a constant menace to the safety and security of France. French irredentism finally found its favourable opportunity in the Great War, and by 1919 Alsace and Lorraine were reconquered and restored to France. It was not a war of national self-determination either on the part of the French in 1914 or on the part of the Germans in 1870; neither the Germans in 1871 nor the French in 1919 ventured to consult the wishes of the Alsatians and Lorrainers by a full and free plebiscite; both the Franco-German War of 1870-1871 and the Franco-German War of 1914-1918 were irredentist wars.

Irredentism has appeared at its worst within the confines of the former Ottoman Empire. Here, centuries of imperial domination, first Roman, then Greek, and latterly Turkish, and centuries of religious conflict, first between Christian orthodoxy and Christian heresy, and subsequently between Christendom and Islam, had conspired to create a hodgepodge of nationalities, many of whose members were strewn and scattered about like pieces on a crazy-quilt. In certain restricted regions lived fairly homogeneous populations— Rumanians north and near the mouth of the Danube, Serbs in and about Belgrade, Greeks in the Greek peninsula and on the Aegean islands, Bulgarians south of the Danube and east of the Serbs. But elsewhere confusion was worse confounded. In Macedonia and Thrace, Serb villages were interspersed with Bulgarian and Turkish villages, a Rumanian settlement was occasionally to be found, and the larger towns were Babels of Greek, Armenian, Jew (both Palestinian and Spanish), Turk, and Gipsy. Greeks predominated in many of the seaports of Asia Minor, but the immediate hinterland was largely Turkish. In parts (but only in parts) of certain provinces of Asia Minor, Armenians constituted a majority; in other parts they were a minority in the midst of a majority either Turkish or Kurdish. In Syria and Palestine, Arabs predominated, but there was a Jewish community as well as several Christian communities, and there were Turkish officials and Armenian and Greek traders everywhere.

Wars of national self-determination in the nineteenth century served to produce embryonic national states in those regions of the Ottoman Empire which possessed fairly homogeneous populations, and thus were born a little Greece, a little Serbia, a little Rumania, and a little Bulgaria. But every one of these little states was quickened from birth with an aspiration to become bigger and to embrace as soon as possible all the lands on which any of its real or fancied fellow nationals resided. It was an aspiration difficult to achieve, for by one and the same test Macedonia and Thrace must be Bulgarian, must be Serb, must be Greek, must be Turkish; if they were to be Bulgarian, then Serbs, Greeks, and Turks must be got rid of; if they were to be Serb, then Bulgarians, Greeks, and Turks must be expelled or slain; if they were to be Greek, then Bulgarians, Serbs, and Turks must be put out of the way; if they were to continue Turkish, in an age of acute nationalism, then the Turks must "Turkify" or destroy Bulgarians, Serbs, and Greeks; and still must endure the lesser problem of dissident groups of Jews, Armenians, Rumanians, Albanians, and Gipsies. But modern nationalism has never been daunted by the mere difficulty of a problem.

The attempted solution of the problem in the Balkans evoked most interesting expedients. At first more or less peaceful proselytism was tried. Not all the inhabitants of Macedonia and Thrace were certain of their nationality; some, not knowing, for instance, whether they were Serbs or Bulgarians, childishly referred to themselves simply as "Christians" or "peasants", and innocently spoke dialects which Bulgarian scholars declared to be Bulgarian, and Serb savants pronounced to be pure Serb: and such as these soon had the nationalist gospel preached unto them by Serbs, labouring to convince them that they were Serbs, by Bulgarians, toiling to persuade them that they had always been Bulgarians, and by Greeks who adroitly pointed out to them that since it was so extremely doubtful whether they were Serbs or Bulgarians, they must be Greeks (were they not Greek Orthodox Christians?).

Presently, and naturally, emerged those other interesting methods of idealistic irredentism which are denominated in vulgar parlance as terrorism and massacre. Not only in Asia Minor did Mohammedan Turks and Kurds massacre Christian Armenians, but in European Turkey Serbs massacred Bulgarians and Bulgarians massacred Serbs, whilst bands of both peoples massacred, and in turn were massacred by, bands of Christian Greeks. On occasion, an unique occasion, all these so-called Christian nationalities could and did agree (1912) upon an arbitrary allotment of the Macedonian and Thracian spoils and then together fell upon the Turks and decisively defeated them. But peace was not concluded with the Turks, when the Christian nationalities resumed their irredentist quarreling with one another, and the Greeks and Serbs proceeded in company with the Rumanians and the Turks (1913) forcefully to despoil Bulgaria of most of her allotment. Bulgaria fought in the Great War (1915-1918) a war of revenge, an irredentist war —and failed. The inhabitants of Macedonia and the greater part of Thrace must be either Serbs or Greeks; they cannot be Bulgarians. At least they cannot be Bulgarians until Bulgarian irredentism perceives a favourable opportunity to wage another irredentist war.

From the Graeco-Turkish War of 1920-1923, the latest irredentist conflict in the Near East, has resulted an experiment as amazing as it is novel. The war, it will be recalled, was fought primarily for the control of Asia Minor. Greece wished, for sentimental nationalist reasons, to annex Smyrna and other coast towns in which from time immemorial Greeks had constituted a large and influential element, and, for reasons of economic welfare and political prestige, to add a tract of the hinterland in which there were few Greeks and many Turks. On the other hand, Turkey, which had recently become a national state with its centre of gravity at Angora rather than at Constantinople, was resolved to prevent the loss not only of any territory in which Turks predominated but also of any port on which the economic prosperity and the military security of the Turkish national state directly depended. The war was vindictive and terrible as only an irredentist and Near Eastern war can be. There was organised massacre on both sides, arson, pillage, and rape, destruction and devastation. The Turks won, the Greeks were defeated. And then was provided by solemn treaty the revolutionary arrangement that all Greeks living in Turkey must give up practically all their property and possessions and remove themselves to Greece, and that all Turks residing in Greece must likewise leave their houses and lands and seek new homes and new livelihoods in Turkey. For two years after the signing of the agreement, the wholesale deportations went on. Hundreds of thousands of human beings were uprooted from soil which had been ancestrally theirs for centuries and planted anew in surroundings which were unfamiliar or in places that were waste; and pestilence and famine followed the refugees. Patriotism, the love of one's *native* land, was thus sacrificed on the altar of nationalism. Perhaps, in the long run, the Graeco-Turkish experiment will prove to be the best solution of the irredentist problem, perhaps it will be sanest to sacrifice literal patriotism to the national ideal, but as yet the remedy seems as distressing as the disease.

5

It is not altogether comforting that with the universal rise of national states in recent times irredentist problems have been increasing rather than decreasing. Directly or indirectly, the Great War, from 1914 to 1918, has brought many new national states into being and at the same time has created in political geography numerous "sore spots" which are the breeding places today of irredentist fevers and perhaps tomorrow of irredentist wars. The gentlemen who dictated the Peace of Paris in 1919-1920 honestly tried to recognise and validate the principle of nationality, but they represented, of course, the victors in the Great War and they were naturally disposed both to reward their own national states and to punish the vanquished. If a border-region was peopled in part by an enemy nationality and in part by a friendly nationality, the population-statistics supplied by the triumphant national state which claimed it, were usually preferred to the rival figures furnished by the defeated national state which had held it, and were henceforth cited as justification for its cession. If, too, a certain district—a mountain-pass or a coal field or a seaport—was deemed absolutely vital to the military security or economic prosperity of a friendly and allied national state, it was expropriated from the enemy, even though its population might be wholly or largely of the nationality of the state from which it was taken. In other words, the major irredentist claims of victorious national states—France, Italy, Rumania, Czechoslovakia, Poland, Yugoslavia, and Greece—were satisfied, in so far as the Allies could satisfy them at the expense of Germany, Austria, Hungary, Bulgaria, and Turkey.

Thereby a powerful stimulus was given to irredentism in the defeated countries. Germans were aggrieved by the French recovery of Alsace-Lorraine and the French military and economic occupation of the Saar Valley and by the Belgian annexation of Eupen and Malmédy; they were saddened by the incorporation of three millions of their fellow nationals in Czechoslovakia, by Italian possession of Bozen, and by the prescribed separation of German Austria from the German national state; and they were angered and outraged beyond words by the loss of valuable mineral resources (and some Germans) in Upper Silesia, by the loss of the historic German seaport of Danzig, by the loss of the fair agricultural province of Posen (in which resided many German landlords), and especially by the loss of the "corridor" from Posen to the Baltic (a "corridor," which was inhabited mainly by Germans, and the cession of which cut Germany in twain)—losses doubly outrageous and angering because they were gains to and for the Polish nationality that Germans had been patriotically taught to consider vastly inferior to themselves in culture and ability. The Magyars, who had become habituated to the flattering task of spreading their "higher" civilisation among the "inferior" peoples long subject to their sway, were now compelled to rest from their pleasant labours and to witness despised Yugoslavs, Rumanians, and Czechoslovaks lording it over persons of Magyar nationality. But these Magyars will not be mere witnesses, not so long as irredentism can be kept aflame in their hearts; they will strive some day to redeem the Hungary irredenta at the expense of Rumania, Yugoslavia, and Czechoslovakia.

Other "sore spots" are many. Bulgaria has an irredenta in Macedonia, in Thrace, and in Dobrudja. Greece has an irredenta in Cyprus and in the Dodecanese, and doubtless she will always have a supreme irredenta in Constantinople. Yugoslavia has an irredenta in Salonica as well as in Fiume, Istria, and Dalmatia. Lithuania and Poland have rival irredentas along their dubious dividing line. Ukrainia has an irredenta in Polish Galicia and in Rumanian Bukovina and Bessarabia. The Irish Free State has an irredenta in the six northeastern counties of Ulster. Peru has an irredenta in Tacna and Arica. The Arabs have an irredenta in Zionist-British Palestine and in French Syria. And by the time that nationalism produces the number of wars requisite for the establishment of the right of national self-determination throughout Asia and Africa and for the recasting of the political geography of these major continents on national lines, the number of irredentas on this little terrestrial globe of ours will be legion. Perhaps mutual and wholesale deportations and displacements of nationalities, as experimented with recently by Greece and Turkey, will increasingly be utilised in the future and will operate in the long run as an effective check upon irredentism. Perhaps so, though surely the run will be very long, and very deadly. The experiment in the case of Greece and Turkey was agreed to only as a last resort and only after the two countries had fought most fiercely and almost continuously for ten years.

Wars of national self-determination, to say nothing of irredendist wars, are scarcely finished. Perhaps they are hardly begun. Imperial dominion has been supplanted by national sovereignty in Europe and America, it is true, but not in the other continents, and the only way, apparently, by which Asiatics and Africans can assert and maintain national sovereignty is the self-same way by which Europeans and Americans have secured it—the warlike way of national self-determination. Just as subject nationalities in Europe rose in arms in the nineteenth and twentieth centuries against the dynastic empires of Ottoman, Habsburg, and Romanov, so in the future, if they will be true to nationalism, subject nationalities must revolt over a far wider area against the colonial empires of Britain, France, Italy, Portugal, Spain, Holland, Japan, and the United States. For these latter countries, vehemently nationalist at home, are quite as adamant as ever were divine-right dynasts against the national self-determination of subject and presumably inferior peoples abroad. Imperialism has always been a complicating factor in any national readjustment of political geography, and it probably always will be. How the complication is rendered more acute nowadays by the interrelations of imperialism and nationalism, we shall undertake later to suggest.[1]

6

In the meantime, let us consider briefly another complicating element in historic wars of national self-deter-

[1] See the next essay, on "Nationalism and Militarism," especially pp. 175-183.

mination and irredentism—the element of Pan-Slavism,
Pan-Teutonism, Pan-Latinism, Pan-Saxonism, *etc.* It is
hardly necessary to describe any of these "pan" movements
in detail. They are all products of the nineteenth century; all are fruits of the romantic youthful indiscretions
of philology and anthropology. Because several nationalities spoke kindred languages, it was assumed that they
were of the same race, that they were "brothers," that
they were destined to form a peculiarly sacred super-
nationality. Such an assumption might be quite fanciful,
but it was backed for a brief time by eminent scholars and
fronted for a long time by a host of publicists, and it has
found lodgement in the minds and hearts of a multitude of
Europeans and Americans, and has proved serviceable
sometimes to politicians and occasionally to warriors.
"Pan-nationalism" has never supplanted the fiercer and
more elementary nationalism of its constituent peoples,
but it has been sufficiently strong to affect international
politics and to complicate nationalist wars.

Napoleon III, for example, was fond of alluding to the
"Latin genius," which, he imagined, had come down in
unbroken racial descent from the ancient Romans and constituted the indelible common character of all peoples who
spoke a Romance language. The French Emperor, dreamy
mystic and splendid politician that he was, was thus cater-
ing to a sentiment which was already shared by numerous
nationalists, particularly by literary nationalists, in Spain,
Portugal, Italy, Rumania, and Latin America, as well as
in his own country. The French, as the foremost Romanic
nationality, were especially zealous both in the altruistic
promotion and in the selfish exploitation of Pan-Latinism.
It was with the enthusiastic support of French Pan-Latinists (and for French national interests) that France fought
with Austria in 1859 for the emancipation of the Italians,
that France secured in 1862 the union of the Rumanian
principalities, that France intervened in 1863 in Mexico,
that the French Government negotiated with Bismarck in

1867 for the annexation of Belgium to France and opposed
in 1870 the succession of a Teutonic Hohenzollern to the
Latin throne of Spain. Pan-Latinism, too, afforded a sentimental background for Garibaldi's participation in the
wars for the liberation of Latin America (1836-1846) and
in the Franco-German War (1870-1871). It was decisive
in the formation of the Latin Monetary Union (1865). It
was contributory to the later weakening of the alliances
of Italy and Rumania with Germany and Austria and the
eventual juncture of those Romanic nationalities with
France in the Great War. It has been of some emotional
significance in arousing popular feeling throughout South
America, Central America, and Mexico against any cultural,
economic, or political aggression on the part of the "Anglo-
Saxons" of North America.

Because a number of separate peoples spoke "Slavic"
languages, certain litterateurs and pseudo-scientists, especially among the Slavic nationalities of Austria-Hungary,
began in the first half of the nineteenth century to contend that all such peoples were closely related by blood
and should be welded into a cultural and political unit. Because the Russians were by far the most numerous of all
the Slavic peoples and because Russia was the only Slavic
Great Power, advocates of Pan-Slavism in Austria-Hungary, and in the Balkans too, turned naturally to Russia
for encouragement and leadership, and Russian nationalists were only too happy to utilise Pan-Slavism for their
own imperial ends. In the Balkan peninsula, where Russian Pan-Slavism was fortified by a community of religious
faith and observance, Russia stood forth as the stalwart
foe of the Ottoman Empire and the staunch friend of rebellious nationalities; in every war in that distracted part of
Europe, Russian armies or Russian intrigues were present.
Even among the Austro-Hungarian Slavs—Croats, Slovenes, Czechs, Slovaks, and Poles—who differed from the
Russians in religion and many other externals of culture,
Russian influence penetrated in the guise of Pan-Slavism

and with the aim of fostering a common Slavic consciousness and accustoming all Slavs to look upon Russia as
their guardian and big brother. In this way, Pan-Slavism
combined with the narrower and more intense nationalism
of the several Slavic peoples to threaten and finally to
destroy both the Ottoman Empire and the Austrian Empire.

A Pan-Teutonic movement appeared simultaneously
with Pan-Slavism, for German philologists, who were the
most original philologists in the whole world, could not be
behindhand in demonstrating the essential unity of the Teutonic languages, and, therefore [!], the racial oneness of
Germans, Scandinavians, Dutchmen, Flemings, and Englishmen. With the advent of the mighty German Empire
in 1871, Pan-Teutonism became a handle as convenient
for German nationalists (and imperialists) as Pan-Slavism
was for Russian enthusiasts or Pan-Latinism for French
patriots. To protect the Teutonic minority in the Austrian
Empire against Pan-Slavic plots and alarums, Germans
must do their utmost, must risk everything and every man,
to bolster up the Habsburgs and thwart national self-determination in Austria-Hungary. Furthermore, to forestall
any possible strengthening of Pan-Slavism, Pan-Teutons
must be as willing to die in defence of the Ottoman Empire as Russians were willing to perish in attacks upon it.
What had once been a sincere friendship between divine-
right monarchs of Prussia and Russia was gradually giving
way at the close of the nineteenth century and the opening of the twentieth, before the rising waves of Pan-Teutonism and Pan-Slavism, to a vindictive rivalry between the
peoples of Germany and Russia, the stakes of which were
primarily the preservation or destruction of the Austrian
Empire and secondarily the Teutonic or Slavic domination
of southeastern Europe. It was an indication of the complicating, paradoxical character of pan-nationalism that in
this rivalry the Russian Empire, which, strictly speaking,
was not a national state, should have sponsored the right
of national self-determination, whilst Germany, which had

been unified by wars of national self-determination, should have championed the integrity of non-national empires.

Pan-Teutonism came into conflict also with Pan-Latinism and exacerbated the rival nationalisms of Germany and France. German nationalists talked about the necessary cementing of the Scandinavians to Germany, about the desirable incorporation of Holland with Germany, about the bitter cry of the Flemish people for deliverance from Franco-Belgian bondage. French nationalists stressed the Latin element in the speech of Belgium and in the culture of Luxembourg and the Rhineland, and wept copiously over the sad enslavement of Alsace-Lorraine. The European stage was set for the Great War of 1914, and conspicuous among the stage-properties were Pan-Latinism, Pan-Teutonism, and Pan-Slavism. So ugly and so menacing were the mien and habilaments of Pan-Teutonism, that during the tragedy of the next four years Pan-Latinism was arrayed with Pan-Slavism in the grand design of making the world safe—for nationalism.

English, being a hybrid language, half Teutonic and half Romanic, and a language used not only in Great Britain and her self-governing dominions but also throughout the United States, was tempting though disconcerting bait for pan-nationalist fishermen. Pan-Teutonists made love to England, and Pan-Latinists flirted with her. For a long time in the nineteenth century, when Franco-English relations were spasmodically strained, and particularly after France had suffered defeat at the hands of Germany, many influential Englishmen and Americans lauded the Teutonic element in their speech and culture and flattered themselves that Anglo-Saxonism was an integral part of Pan-Teutonism. In the twentieth century, when Anglo-German relations neared the breaking-point, other equally influential Englishmen gloried in the Romanic element and boasted of the common "Celtic" blood (and soul) of Frenchmen and Britishers. This fluctuation, let us admit, was temporary and partial; what was enduring and more widespread, was an independent conviction among both Britishers and Americans that they were "Anglo-Saxons," distinct from Teutons, distinct from Latins, always the same, one in race and language and genius, with "hands across the sea," with "blood thicker than water," and, above all, with the "manifest destiny" of bearing "the white man's burden" by ruling the "lesser breeds without the law." Small wonder that when it came to assuring the freedom of the seas to Englishmen and Americans against German interlopers and to guaranteeing the integrity (and enlargement) of the far-flung British Empire, the Anglo-Saxons aligned themselves in the Great War with Pan-Latinism and Pan-Slavism against Pan-Teutonism and in defence of the right of national self-determination—for Belgians and other minor peoples in Europe.

Other "pan" movements are sometimes mentioned, such as Pan-Americanism, Pan-Islamism, Pan-Turanianism, *etc.*, but, with the exception of the last, which represents a most pedantic and trifling attempt to provide a sentimental tie for Magyars, Finns, Esths, and Turks, they can hardly be classed as pan-nationalist in the sense in which we have used this term. Pan-Americanism is a movement, fostered chiefly in the United States and redounding mainly to the advantage of the United States, to unite all the peoples of the two American continents—those who speak English and those who speak Spanish, Portuguese, or French—in a bond of peaceful coöperation and thus to offset the anti-Saxon tendencies of Pan-Latinism. Pan-Islamism is not linguistic at all; the word is employed by alarmist writers in Christendom to designate a supposititious solidarity of feeling and action on the part of all Mohammedan peoples which is actually as non-existent as that other bogey of nervous Westerners, the bogey of Pan-Mongolianism.

The significance of any or all of the truer and more real pan-nationalisms can, of course, be grossly overestimated. They have not directly caused any past international war, not even the recent Great War, and they are not likely to provide direct incitements to war in the immediate future despite the plea of an occasional sociologist that Europeans and Americans should put an end to their internecine nationalist wars by combining in Pan-Caucasian warfare against Pan-Mongols and Pan-Negroes.[1] Nationalism proper is a force in the world today far more compelling than any pan-nationalism, and the nationalist can be trusted every time, if the need arises, to sacrifice the interests of any larger group to the interests of his own national state. Moreover, the trend of contemporary events seems to set in the direction of smaller, rather than larger, national units; not the linguistic family group but the dialect, not the genus but the species, is becoming the goal of nationality and the *sanctum sanctorum* of nationalism. On the other hand, the importance of pan-nationalism should not be underestimated. Like irredentism, it has complicated many a past war of national self-determination and is qualified to continue its complicating function into the distant future. It can be utilised by Great Powers against lesser Powers. In a nationalist age it can admirably serve the purpose of imperialism.

Pan-nationalism and its sturdier brother irredentism have both been sired by that Mars who presides over wars of national self-determination and nursed by that modern Fury whose other name is nationalism. Mars is still presiding with unabated zest and his sons are still disporting themselves with unbounded vim; neither his presidency nor the playfulness of his brood is likely in the near future to end in dignified retirement or slumberous repose. For the Fury who is his latest handmaid and the mother of his wildest children is not a shy or restful creature; she is perpetually nagging him and the children too. These may fight most of the time, but fight she threatens all the time. For there is something about modern nationalism which not only brings its devotees to frequent war but keeps them always ready and prepared for war. From nationalism,

[1] C. C. Josey, *Race and National Solidarity* (1923).

militarism—the constant threat of war—is nowadays inseparable. It is also inseparable from modern imperialism. Militarism is a complex phenomenon and it deserves treatment as extended as we have here given to actual nationalist war.

VI

NATIONALISM AND MILITARISM

1

LET us suppose that a nationality has waged several wars of self-determination and finally established a sovereign national state. Let us suppose, further, that this state has been successful in irredentist struggles and has acquired every bit of territory inhabited by any considerable number of fellow nationals. Let us concede that the wars of national self-determination were of the nature of enthusiastic popular rebellions against intolerable abuses of alien tyranny and that they evoked from the rebels the noblest idealism and the most heroic deeds. Let us concede, too, even in respect of the subsequent irredentist conflicts, that they were precipitated by muddling attempts of a corrupt empire to restrict the liberties of its dissident nationalities and that they represented an honest and just effort to "redeem" a population, the large majority of whom truly yearned to become citizens of the emancipating national state. It is reasonable to infer from the circumstances that "liberals" and "radicals" and "humanitarians" and "progressives" in all countries acclaimed with one voice the spiritual grandeur of that nationality, that the wealthier among them contributed to relief funds in aid of its wounded and destitute and subscribed to the war-bonds of its government, and that the more romantic volunteered their lives in its military service and their pens in its journalistic propaganda.

We might imagine, if we knew no history and were incorrigible optimists, that such a nationality, that such a national state, would thenceforth be an exemplar of justice and charity to all other nationalities and national states and a pillar of world-peace. Unfortunately, however, the history of the nineteenth and twentieth centuries, whilst it gives ample support to our suppositions concerning the altruism and lofty purpose of wars of national self-determination and even of irredentist wars, affords little or no evidence that the attainment of national independence and unity is a sure preliminary to international peace and brotherhood.[1] On the contrary, it bears witness to the disquieting fact that nationalism does not exhaust its functions and resources when it unites a dismembered nationality and erects a national state; it shows that almost invariably nationalism is heightened rather than lessened by the attainment of national sovereignty and that a national state, so soon as it is solidly established, proceeds to evolve a "national policy," which is as bellicose as it is nationalist.

What this "national policy" is, has been nicely indicated in an illuminating essay by Mr. J. L. Stocks:[2] ". . . the 'national' policy of an established State . . . means, of course, a policy of national selfishness and aggrandisement, a 'sacred egoism,' made sacred, presumably, by the sentiment of nationality. Internally its effort is to strengthen and tighten the national bond by every means in its power; externally to make the nation feared or 'respected' by a bold and firm foreign policy, backed by a sufficiency of military force, and to obtain for it a share in the riches

---

[1] Certain apologists for nationalism, whose wishes outstrip their judgements and whose predilections pass muster for historical knowledge, have contended that the establishment of national states makes for peace. Even a distinguished historian, Dr. J. Holland Rose, has stated that "after the attainment of civic freedom and national solidarity, the national instinct, which strengthens with opposition and weakens after due satisfaction, ought to merge in the wider and nobler sentiment of human brotherhood in the attainment of which it is only a preparatory phase" (*Nationality in Modern History*, 1916, p. 202). Professor Rose, I suspect, was then speaking rather as an English nationalist in the midst of the emotionalism of the Great War than as an objective historian in the presence of facts. Though perhaps the national instinct "ought to merge . . . ," it obviously hasn't.

[2] *Patriotism and the Super-State* (1920), pp. 71-73.

of the undeveloped portions of the earth's surface. It appeals to the cruder forms of patriotism. Its love of country turns readily into hatred of the foreigner, its desire for prosperity into competition for territory; and the duty of service is interpreted as a duty to maintain national unity by unquestioning assent to every decision of government. The appropriate political ideas are instilled into the citizen by the machinery of public education and by compulsory military service; and direct inducement not to surrender these ideas in later life is easily supplied if the state keeps control over appointments in some of the main professions, especially the teaching profession, and is liberal in its rewards to right-thinking leaders of opinion. Such a policy is necessarily the antithesis of nineteenth-century liberalism. In the interest of national unity it will ruthlessly suppress dissentient groups within the nation, and will be prepared for whatever sacrifice may be necessary of the principle of free speech and thought. It will develop a national economy with all its machinery of tariffs, subsidies, and concessions. In every sphere it will tend to penalise the foreigner, in its colonies by frank preference for the trade and capital of the home country, at home by interposing obstacles to immigration and naturalisation. The rulers of Germany perceived further that a certain measure of what is called State Socialism is of assistance to the objects of this policy, which are to make nationality overwhelmingly important to the citizen and so strengthen the hands of government."

In other words, an established national state evolves, under nationalism, "national interests" at home and abroad; its citizens similarly develop "national rights," more national rights perhaps when they are abroad than when they are at home; and, above all, the aggregate of national state and its citizens come to possess a peculiarly precious "national honour." Now, to assure national interests and national rights and to preserve national honour, an established state, even more than a would-be nation, must be prepared to use force and to wage war. Militarism thus becomes an abiding characteristic of nationalism and the chief means to nationalist ends. Militarism is not merely a temporary instrument thrust by a fortuitous Providence into the hands of oppressed nationalities and idyllic irredentists and enabling them to recast political geography on reasonable national lines. Militarism, with its displays of might and threats of force, is a permanent feature of triumphant nationalism in a world in which non-national empires have largely been replaced by national states.

Because present-day militarism exists primarily for the sake of national honour, national rights, and national interests, it will be apposite to our study to investigate the import of these phrases. Let us begin with "national interests."

2

"Interests" chiefly connote advantages of an economic sort, and they are basically individual. Everyone of us has an interest in living and in securing enough wealth to enable us to live in that degree of comfort to which we are accustomed or to which we aspire. At the same time everyone of us must admit that we cannot secure our economic interests by purely individual methods; we must rely upon coöperation with our fellows, upon public sanction for our private profit, in last analysis upon the police-power of the state. Certain philosophical anarchists, I know, have urged that individual interests would be promoted more generally if there were no authoritarian state whatsoever, but their urgency is obviously contrary to human experience in the past and repugnant to human sentiment today. Always, from the dawn of recorded history, human beings have joined in, or submitted to, the corporate entity known as the state in order to safeguard and advance their interests.

Individuals do not invariably recognise their true interests; they seldom foresee what in the long run will be most conducive to their real interests. But—and this is what matters—they *think* they know their interests and the vast bulk of them believe, and always have believed, that the state is the surest, though a rather mysterious, giver of all good gifts for themselves and for their posterity. Undoubtedly the state, whether it be the imperial state of ancient Romans or the city-state of antique Greeks, the tribal state of primitive American Indians or the feudal state of mediaeval Europeans or Asiatics, has conferred economic benefits upon certain individuals and certain groups, particularly upon those individuals and groups who have been most influential in the state. And other individuals and other groups, who have received very little, perhaps less than nothing, have always been inclined to perceive in the guaranteed interests of some the assured interests of all and in the prosperity of its leaders the prosperity of the state and therefore the vicarious prosperity of the whole state's citizenry.

Now the national state is a far more efficient promoter of individual interests than any other kind of state which the world has ever known. Political democracy and the Industrial Revolution, which alike attended the rise and propagation of nationalism, have conspired to exalt the national state as the custodian of the economic interests of all its citizens and thus to endow nationalism with a mission which if half cultural is half economic. The Industrial Revolution has created a multitude of new interests and given new direction to the host of old interests. Political democracy has enlisted all the people in attempts to make the state serve their economic interests. The Industrial Revolution began in a national state, and the profound changes which it effected in man's ways of working and travelling and living have, under democratic influence, been organised on national bases and appropriated to national ends.

A group of industrialists in a given country may feel

that their interests will be furthered if their state removes all restrictions on the importation of foodstuffs and raw materials and on the exportation of every commodity. A group of industrialists in another country may think that their interests will be fostered if their state aids them in competition with the industrialists of the first country by granting bounties or levying protective tariffs. Groups of agriculturists may believe that their interests will be safeguarded if their respective states similarly grant bounties to native agriculture or levy protective tariffs against foreign live-stock and farm-produce. Groups of commerce-carriers may imagine that their interests will be promoted if their state subsidises a merchant marine or a railway system. Groups of workingmen may reason that their interests will be defended if their state enacts labour legislation and restricts the immigration of alien workingmen.

Such group interests and group convictions are not peculiar to recent times or to national states, but the methods of securing them possess nowadays, thanks to the Industrial Revolution and to political democracy, a novel and nationalist character. Economic groups, as a rule, have wide and deeply ramifying interests. Rarely can one economic group promote its interests without affecting the interests of other groups. Industrialists, to secure their interests, must obtain assistance from farmers, workingmen, or commercial men, and these groups, in turn, to promote their interests, must have popular support. And so it transpires that every group, when it appeals to the democratic national state, talks little about its own specific (and possibly selfish) interests and much about the general (and presumably altruistic) national interests. Interests of groups are represented as national interests. Industrialists ask individual favours because favours accorded them, they say, redound to the wealth and well-being of the whole nation. Farmers seek individual advantages because, they allege, such advantages makes the whole nation self-sufficing. Traders and artisans and day-labourers request special concessions because, they affirm, the whole nation must suffer if they suffer.

Inasmuch as most citizens are nationalist, they understand and heed these appeals. They come naturally to believe that the wealth of individuals is truly national wealth, that the manufactures, agriculture, commerce, and labour, of special groups, are in reality the nation's manufactures, the nation's agriculture, the nation's commerce, and the nation's labour. The most poverty-stricken patriot in the East End of London is apt to swell out his chest when he thinks of England's industry and wealth, for is not England's wealth his? Whence it follows that every citizen in a national state is expected to approve of and work for the economic interests of his fellow citizens; no matter what his own occupation or profession may be he should be prepared to accept as his own the interests of groups who plead earnestly and eloquently that their interests are national interests; he can thus speak with pride, be he bookkeeper or bricklayer, of his natural resources, his factories his ships and railways, his farms, his industrial man-power. Surely, the concept of national interests is most comforting and exhilarating; the least among the citizens of a national state, if he will but entertain the concept, can instantly tower in his own estimation into a very big and great and happy personage.

Of course in every national state there are conflicts among the various economic groups and few of them secure all that they desire. But out of the conflicts emerge compromises which receive democratic sanction and thereby become cardinal points in a public policy of national economy, a democratic policy of national neo-mercantilism. In the name of the nation and for the avowed purpose of national prosperity, a tariff may be enacted which attempts at once to protect "infant" industries, to give surer and better paid employment to workingmen, and to encourage domestic production of foodstuffs, or subventions may be granted simultaneously to a merchant-marine and to agricultural coöperative societies, or workingmen may be insured against accident, sickness, or unemployment at the same time as protective tariffs are enacted and subsidies are voted. More and more the national state assumes the function of arbiter and controller of group interests, more and more it aims to hold an even balance between conflicting group interests and to foster all of them. This very fact tends more and more to confirm the popular belief that group interests are national interests, which must be advanced at all hazards.

Nationalism has thus an economic aspect. It moves the masses in every national state to exalt particular economic interests and economic policies into national interests and national policies. By means of nationalism a minority whose ambitions have been popularly identified with national ambitions can be assured of the ardent and active support of the majority. The ordinary individual will not risk his life in furtherance of his own selfish interests, but the ordinary nationalist is ready to do battle in behalf of national interests. To prosaic economics nationalism now supplies the needful poetry and idealism.

So soon as a nationality develops nationalism and achieves political unity and independence, it begins to prosecute its national interests. For example, German manufacturers shortly after the establishment of the German Empire demanded the protection of their "infant industries" against foreign competition, especially British, on the ground that it would make Germany stronger and more self-sufficient, and protection they obtained; simultaneously German farmers and landlords demanded protection against the importation of cheap Russian and American foodstuffs, and protection they too obtained. Again, American manufacturers and American farmers, for like reasons, demanded tariff-protection, and tariff-protection they obtained; American workingmen and American farmers demanded protection against the cheap labour of foreign immigrants, and protection they eventually secured through the total prohibition of Chinese and Japanese immigration and the rigid restriction of all other immigration. Such public policies as tariff-protection and restriction of immigration may originate with a relatively small group and may actually serve only group interests, but under nationalist influence they come to be popularly thought of as serving national interests and they soon partake of the almost sacred character of national traditions. Thenceforth any domestic critic of this or that "national policy" is likely to be considered by his fellow countrymen as lacking in patriotism if not in sense.

The prosecution of national interests by an established national state may be desirable and praiseworthy; it is certainly, in a nationalist era, natural. But it is also dangerous, for it gives rise to international difficulties. Apparently no national state can promote all its national interests without impairing the national interests of other national states and without endangering its peaceful relations with them. Once upon a time there was the friendliest possible feeling between the dynasties and governing classes of Russia and Germany; once upon a time there was the utmost reciprocity of sentimental regard between the governments and peoples of Japan and the United States. Doubtless many factors have operated in both instances to change the feeling and sentiment, but conspicuous among such factors has been the prosecution of national interests. The German farmers and landlords, in order to obtain popular support for their policy of tariff-protection against Russian competition, led a nationalist campaign in Germany against Russia, instilling into the minds of the German people the idea that they were defenceless against Russian attack and the notion that Russians were barbarous and uncouth Asiatics rather than refined Europeans, evil slinking Slavs rather than fine upstanding Teutons. Russian landlords, on the other hand, angered by the consequent German tariff against their own economic interests (which were generally interpreted as Russian interests), proceeded to retaliate; they aided Russian industrialists to secure tariff-protection for their "infant industries" against the cheaper products of German factories; and all sorts of Russians, stung by German abuse of themselves, assailed the Germans in kind and gave hearty thanks to the Tsar for his championship of national interests. To remove from American farmers and workingmen, especially those on the Pacific Coast, the increasingly strenuous competition of Japanese immigrants who were accustomed to a lower standard of living, the whole American people must be stirred up against the Japanese "menace"; and so Japanese were depicted as wily and desperately wicked men of the Yellow Race totally unqualified for the blessings of American liberty and American civilisation; and with such success that anti-Japanese activity became an American national interest and national policy and, as usually happens in these premises, anti-American feeling became a trait of the Japanese.

Tariffs and resulting "tariff-wars" have not led inevitably to armed combat. Usually national states have been able to agree in time to some compromise, to some *modus vivendi,* whereby national interests are still served but international peace is formally maintained. Tariffs and rumours of tariffs and "tariff-wars," however, have not tended during the last three or four decades to promote sympathetic and cordial relations between the Governments and peoples of Germany and Russia, or, for that matter, between those of Germany and Great Britain or those of Germany and the United States or between other national states. It is memorable that just preceding the Great War of 1914 the relations between Serbia and Austria-Hungary, already strained by soaring nationalism of the idealistic type, were aggravated by a tariff-war over pigs, for pigs were national interests alike of Serbia and of Hungary. And though, over national policies of emigration and immigration, actual war has not eventuated between Japan and the United States, the national psychology in both countries has been brought to a warlike mood.

The outstanding difficulties about national interests are these. First, they are prosecuted so intensely by every national state that broader international and world interests are obscured. Secondly, their pursuit is attended less by competent individual reason than by popular nationalist emotion. Thirdly, they are backed up not by an international conscience and an international tribunal, which might regulate and harmonise them, but by the several national states infinitely proud and jealous of their ultimate and absolute sovereignty. It is as much a national interest of Japan, and of Italy also, to encourage emigration as it is a national interest of the United States to discourage immigration. But not one of these nationalist countries can tolerate foreign or international interference with its domestic affairs; each of them must back up its national interests, so far as physically possible, by forceful display of its lustful sovereignty. And the mass of Americans, Italians, and Japanese are so imbued with faith in their respective sovereign states and so devoted to their respective national interests that they are utterly unfitted to envisage the problem of emigration as a world problem or to deal with it in a sane and sensible way.

There is another difficulty about national interests. They frequently collide with the principle of national self-determination and complicate irredentist problems. Of this difficulty, there are many contemporary illustrations. Polish national interests have required a seaport, and so the German city of Danzig and a "corridor" of German territory from Poland to the Baltic have been taken from Germany; Poland has obtained outright ownership of the latter and special privileges in the former. Italian national interests have required hegemony of the Adriatic, and so Austria and Hungary have been deprived of seaports, and Yugoslavia has been obliged to content herself with inferior ports. French national interests have required more coal as well as more iron, and so not only has France reannexed Alsace-Lorraine, with its valuable iron mines, but she has obtained the right to exploit the rich coal fields of the German valley of the Saar. The United States has national interests in the Caribbean, and so Americans protect their interests by flouting from time to time the right of self-determination in Haiti or Santo Domingo or Nicaragua.

But such a description tells only half the tale. For in every instance here mentioned military force has been the means of securing national interests. Besides, if it is a national interest of Poles to possess a port on the Baltic, it is a national interest of Germans to recover their Baltic ports. If it is a national interest of Italians to dominate the Adriatic, it is a national interest of Magyars and Yugoslavs to obtain maritime outlets at least as serviceable as Italy's. If "Anglo-Saxon" Americans have national interests in the Caribbean and serve them by the agency of militarism, then surely Latin Americans have national interests there too and may safeguard them, if they think they can, by resort to force and violence. Economic interests acquire from nationalism a character almost sacred and quite belligerent.

3

"National rights" are corollaries to "national interests." First and foremost, every national state has the right, according to nationalist precept and practice, to pursue its national interests in whatever way and by whatever method seems meet and right to itself alone. It is a basic part of the nationalist creed, in which every citizen of a national state is now educated, that absolute sovereignty is a right inherent in his national state and that any impairment or threatened impairment of such sovereignty is a wrong which cries to Heaven—and to himself—for vengeance. It is a part of the same creed, and a part almost as basic, that the prosecution of national interests is a right of national sovereignty, and that any alien interference with this right is an unpardonable sin.

A national state has not only the right to a theoretical

sovereignty but also the right to such activities as are calculated to make its sovereignty real and practical. It has
the right to determine and to change at will its form of
government. It has the right to make laws regulatory of
the conduct of all persons within its territories. It has the
right to maintain armaments and to wage war. It has the
right to enforce its laws and to repress domestic insurrection. It has the right likewise to defend itself against foreign aggression and even to attack other sovereign states
for redress of its grievances against them.

National rights, like national interests, may be needful
and highly desirable, but they are fraught with certain
dangers to the peace of the world. One such danger arises
from the fact that a national state, in the undoubted exercise of its national rights, may enact domestic legislation
which satisfies national opinion at home but creates ill-
feeling abroad. For much legislation that is purely domestic in appearance has in effect far-reaching foreign implications. For example, the United States has acted quite
within its national rights when it has levied a protective
tariff or restricted immigration or adopted an eighteenth
amendment to its Constitution. But American refusal to
receive alcoholic beverages at its ports has undoubtedly
injured the national interests of France; American refusal
to admit immigrants from the Far East has certainly run
counter to the national interests of Japan; and American
discrimination against numerous categories of foreign im-
ports, whilst it has served the national interests of American producers, has been costly to American consumers not
only, but very costly to many foreign countries. It should
occasion no surprise if Frenchmen, Japanese, and other
affected nationalists were to urge their respective governments to press for a vindication of their national rights.
If a nationality felt it was strong enough in a military way,
it would probably vindicate its national rights fully. The
boundary between domestic and foreign questions is kept

distinct only in the glare of cannon-blaze and battleship searchlight.

Another danger arises from the presence of aliens on the territory of a national state. Human beings have always used their legs for purposes of locomotion, and since the Industrial Revolution their natural legs have been potently supplemented by the artificial devices of steamship and railway, motor car and airplane. Nowadays it is easy to travel, and the incentive for travel has not decreased with the rise of nationalism. It is still as natural as ever for an adventurous person to seek his fortune in a strange country. What the rise of nationalism has done, in this connection, is, on the one hand, to strengthen the sentimental bond between the emigrant and his native land, and, on the other hand, to establish a curious and dubious relationship between the immigrant and the country of his adoption. As a rule national states desire that all their inhabitants shall be citizens of the same nationality and consequently that immigrants shall be naturalised as speedily and as completely as possible; and, whether naturalised or not, aliens are expected to obey the laws of the national state in whose territory they dwell. At the same time national states desire that such of their citizens as remove themselves to foreign parts shall retain their original nationality and citizenship and shall not be naturalised; some emigrants do not become naturalised, and over these as well as over citizens at home the national state of their birth claims some jurisdiction, at least the assurance of their national rights. One and the same national state may resent foreign interference with any of its inhabitants and paradoxically be eager to interfere in behalf of its own citizens who live in foreign countries.

Whence proceed conflicts over national rights of citizenship. Great Britain, for example, long insisted that "once an Englishman always an Englishman"; her refusal to recognise the validity of American naturalisation of British subjects justified her during the Napoleonic Wars in the impressment of sailors who were of English nativity but of American residence; thereby she was asserting her national rights, but by the same token she was assailing the national rights of Americans, for these impressed seamen had duly been naturalised as American citizens; it was patently the duty of the United States to defend the national rights of all her citizens, those who were naturalised quite as much as those who were native-born; and the War of 1812 was fought between the United States and Great Britain. That was more than a century ago, but the War of 1812 did not solve the problem. Under nationalism it can hardly be solved. Great Britain and the United States, it is true, have gradually arrived at an amicable understanding, and the British no longer impress American seamen, but the peoples of the United States and Great Britain possess almost a common nationality and the United States is nowadays too much of a Great Power to have its citizenship openly denied and defied. But between other national states the problem is still an annoyance. Both France and Germany, for instance, define citizenship in terms inconsistent with the laws governing naturalisation in the United States, so that a person of German or French birth who is naturalised an American may be simultaneously an American citizen, according to American law, and a German or French citizen according to the law of his native land.

Precise determination of citizenship is important, because, as we have just remarked, every national state claims the right to protect all its citizens—those abroad as well as those at home—and to protect those abroad alike in person and in purse. When, in 1891, an American sailor was killed in a brawl in a drinking den in Valparaiso, the United States Government branded the affair as an outrage, refused peremptorily to listen to any explanations, and demanded and obtained from Chile an indemnity of $75,000. When in the same year, a mob in New Orleans lynched eleven Italians accused (but not convicted) of crime, the Italian Government protested vehemently, demanded ample satisfaction, and finally accepted a financial indemnity of $25,000. Such episodes, which are countless, do not tend to foster the most friendly relations between national states, especially as it becomes strikingly obvious to every nationalist the world over that the United States got $75,000 from Chile for one American life, whilst Italy got only $25,000 for eleven Italian lives, chiefly because the United States could put more military force behind its demands of Chile than Italy could put behind its demands of the United States.

Nor are these frequent ultimata for indemnities mere routine communications from the Government of one national state to the Government of another. They are always accompanied, in our modern nationalist society, by journalistic jingoism and popular excitement. All Americans are stirred by what they imagine must be the barbarous cruelty of the Chileans, and overnight a common sailor leaps into fame as a national hero and martyr; simultaneously all Chileans are disgusted by an unseemly disturbance of their domestic peace and public morals and are angered by the brusque and brutal behaviour of a swinish "gringo" people far to the north of them. All Italians are aroused by the horribly anarchistic actions of Americans and immediately a few ignorant fellow citizens are raised to the altars of Italian nationalism, whilst Americans denounce the attempts of foreign "dagoes" to dictate to them about a band of hardened criminals.

As between national states of historic Christendom—between national states in much the same stage of development and with much the same customs and civilisation—the assurance of national rights of citizenship occasions many governmental threats and considerable ugliness of popular temper, but it seldom leads directly to armed conflict. "Civilised" national states generally have the same laws for alien inhabitants as for resident citizens, and they administer justice in their courts almost, if not quite, as

impartially for the one category as for the other. The
consequence is that normally a "civilised" national state
suffers its citizens in another "civilised" national state to
subject themselves to the latter's laws and discipline and
even to pay the prescribed penalties, contenting itself with
a general supervision (which at best is galling to the sovereign state so supervised) and, in emergency, if its citizens
are discriminated against or in any exceptional manner
abused, with solemn protests and finally with such demands
for indemnity as its just cause and its military might may
appear to warrant. Of course, a national state which is a
Great Power expects more and gets more than a national
state which is so unfortunate as to be a Lesser Power. In
1914 Austria-Hungary made demands on Serbia such as
Serbia would never have thought of making on Austria-
Hungary. In 1923 Italy delivered an ultimatum to Greece
such as Greece would never think of delivering to Italy.
Of course, too, Austria-Hungary made her demands in high
hope that no country would come to Serbia's assistance,
and Serbia refused full compliance only because she was
reasonably certain of Russian support; Greece was subsequently sure of no foreign aid, and so she complied
promptly with the Italian ultimatum.

No gloves are employed by "civilised" national states in
handling "backward" states. It has been assumed by the
former, sometimes correctly, that their wandering citizens
under the native laws and in the native courts of the latter
would not receive the same kind of justice or the same degree of consideration as they would receive at home or in
another "civilised" community. Wherefore one national
state after another in Europe and America, "civilised" presumably not so much by Christianity as by nationalism and
the Industrial Revolution, has followed its citizens with
its protecting aegis to the uttermost parts of Asia and
Africa, and, ever in defence of national rights, has wrested
now from the Ottoman Empire, now from Persia, now from
China, and Japan, and Siam, special concessions and fa-

vours in the form of "capitulations" or rights of "extra-territoriality." Under these forms, citizens of a "civilised" national state obtain a highly privileged position in the territories of a "backward" state; they may reside and travel wheresoever they wish; they may freely engage in commerce; they may obsence and propagate their religion without let or hindrance; they are exempt from local law and local judgement and subject only to the jurisdiction of ambassador, consul, or other official representative of their own national state; in fine, they constitute an *imperium in imperio*, an alien group independent of the country in which they dwell. The growth of this system of capitulations and extraterritoriality has been quickened by the development of nationalism and its maintenance has been assured by the agency of militarism. Undoubtedly it has operated to enlarge the national interests and to enhance the national rights of forceful national states, but it has also served to chafe backward peoples, to elicit from them protests and acts of violence, and eventually to prove a most powerful stimulant for the development of a nationalism of their own.

With the lapse of time, the spread of nationalism, as we have seen, has not been confined to the peoples of Europe and America, to the "civilised" peoples of historic Christendom; of late it has penetrated among the populations of the "backward" East and Far East. And from the West the peoples of the East have derived not only the new nationalism, but its seemingly inevitable concomitant, the new militarism. The result is that every nationality, so soon as it becomes nationalist and builds a nationalist state, is determined to proclaim and to exercise to the full its national rights and to get rid of any capitulations or alien rights of extraterritoriality to which perforce in less favoured (and less nationalist) days it may have been obliged to submit. Then, so soon as it evolves sufficient military strength, it proceeds to give effect to its determination. Japan proved herself by the close of the nineteenth century a nationalist Great Power, and the extraterritorial chains with which she had been bound were snapped with as good grace as the European Powers could summon for the occasion. Recently, as a consummation of a series of victorious national wars, Turkey has freed herself from capitulations, and China is now ardently aspiring to the same end. So far as Japan and Turkey are concerned, it is apparent that these states are no longer to be regarded as "backward," for in nationalism and in militarism they have given ample proof of possessing that final lofty civilisation for the advancement of which Europeans and Americans have been wont to deny to others what they have claimed for themselves. Japan is not least among those "civilised" national states that seek to forward their national interests and guarantee their national rights at the expense of China's national but "backward" sovereignty.

Some "backward" states have not been so fortunate as Turkey and Japan. Either they have not accepted the blessings of nationalism for themselves or they have been unable to make their nationalism immediately effective in a military way. In any event their national rights have fallen prey bit by bit to the exigencies of mighty national states intent upon the assurance of their own national rights. Such "backard" states, such unhappy far-off countries, may first have agreed to some measure of extraterritoriality and then signed capitulations; next, under pressure, they may have granted certain embarrassing concessions of an economic nature; finally they may have been forced, in the midst of riots or rebellions or other undignified performances, to accept the financial tutelage and the political control of an alien government representing a little group of resident aliens. And thus in modern times, always and forever in pursuit of national interests and in defence of national rights, have national states by means of spheres of influence and veiled protectorates and outright annexations, blotted out the national rights of peoples who were weak as well as "backward."

National rights, when asserted by a powerful national state and backed by the eager nationalism of its people, brook no infringement at home or abroad. Abroad, particularly as against "backward" peoples, they brook even less infringement than at home. But this thought carries us into a special category of national rights and national interests—interests and rights that link nationalism with modern imperialism—and it is a category which requires our special attention.

4

Imperialism—the extension of the sway of a people or government over alien peoples or alien lands—has been a constantly recurring phenomenon in human history. Sometimes, as in the cases of Assyrian, Roman, Chinese, Arab, and Austrian, it has taken the form of military conquest of widely divergent nationalities. At other times, notably with ancient Greek and Phoenician and with Western European of the sixteenth and seventeenth centuries, it has partaken of the nature of a colonial expansion overseas. But whether it has eventuated in the establishment of distant colonies of common nationality or in the creation of a political union of diverse nationalities, it has always involved the use of force, and has invariably carried the cultural influence of the conquering or expanding nationality far beyond its original habitat.

With the rise of nationalism in modern times it might appear that imperialism was doomed. Certainly, before the buffeting waves of nationalist wars of self-determination and irredentism in the nineteenth and twentieth centuries, one military empire after another went to pieces—the Holy Roman Empire, the Napoleonic Empire, the Ottoman Empire, the Austrian Empire, the Russian Empire. Even overseas colonial empires were rocked to their foundations, and transplanted Europeans broke away from their mother-countries and set up national states of their own—Portuguese in Brazil, Spaniards in a group of republics in the New World, Britishers in the United States. What still remains of the Portuguese, Spanish, and Dutch empires of yesterday is a mere anachronistic survival, and the contemporary British Empire, in so far as it comprises European emigrants, is not so much an empire as a league, or commonwealth, of self-governing and essentially national Dominions—Canada, Australia, New Zealand, and South Africa. Imperialism of the older kinds was proved to be incompatible with nationalism.

In fact, however, imperialism is still with us, and paradoxically, it is a keener, subtler, and more ubiquitous imperialism in the present age of intense nationalism than ever before. Why? Because, simply, the prosecution of national interests and national rights by forceful national states, imbued with nationalism, has produced, in conjunction with the Industrial Revolution, a mighty revival and re-orientation of imperialism. Nationalism itself, the destroyer of old imperialism, has been the begetter and inspirer of a great new imperialism.

To the Industrial Revolution have properly been ascribed the predisposing economic conditions and needs. The Industrial Revolution created a demand on the part of manufacturers for greatly augmented supplies of raw materials and foodstuffs, and for vastly extended markets in which the large surplus of manufactured commodities could profitably be disposed of. The Industrial Revolution also, by creating surplus capital, created a demand on the part of capitalists for wider opportunities for its lucrative investment. But these demands could hardly have produced the precise type of nationalist imperialism with which nowadays we are familiar, had not the Industrial Revolution, from the outset, been associated with rising nationalism. The Industrial Revolution, as we have elsewhere indicated, began in a national state, and mainly by national states it was subsequently exploited. As nationalism came to inspire and dominate these states, it was but natural that their whole citizenry, with negligible exceptions, should conceive of the economic interests of manufacturers and capitalists as being national interests, and should permit if not encourage the adoption and furtherance of public policies in aid of private profits. Wherefore the governments of most industrialised national states, in answer to the entreaties of the manufacturing and capitalist classes, and with the patriotic support of the masses, not only levied protective tariffs and granted financial subsidies in behalf of "infant industries" (and the "full dinner-pail"), but also did everything in their power to promote close commercial relations with "backward" peoples. For many of the raw materials and most of the foodstuffs which were needed in an industrialised community were grown in countries that were industrially backward, and, on the other hand, such "backward" countries afforded peculiarly promising markets for the sale of manufactured goods and most favourable fields for the investment of surplus capital. And as the competition among industrialised national states grew sharper and tariff barriers grew higher, it became all the more a national interest of each to secure free entrance for its traders into "backward" regions.

The traders from an industralised national state, and their colleagues, the prospectors and investors, who entered a "backward" region, frequently encountered difficulties. Perhaps the natives didn't quite appreciate all the goods brought to them. Perhaps they were chary of granting "concessions" for the development of their natural resources. More than likely they were averse from the steady disciplined toil requisite for supplying all the rubber or oil or cotton which their visitors demanded of them. Then, too, they usually seemed to have only a rudimentary knowledge of law and order of the European and American variety. They didn't always respect the concessions that had solemnly been accorded to foreigners by a susceptible chieftain

or sultan; sometimes they wilfully destroyed foreign property and maliciously killed foreign superintendents; chron-
ically they engaged in feuds and brigandage and other fes-
tive occupations, from the pursuit of which their foreign
guests, more or less innocent bystanders, often suffered in
pocket and dignity. They were sadly lacking in personal
efficiency and business acumen—at least for others than
themselves. They were singularly blind to "national
interests" and obtuse about "national rights."

National rights and national interests, however, the foreign guest had and knew how to use. Confronted by difficulties with natives in backward regions, he could appeal
for assistance to the government and people of his national
state in the almost certain knowledge that his own interests
would be interpreted as national interests and that their
enforcement, so far as possible, would be effected as a
national right. If the government were slow to act, it could
be jogged by the judicious goading of nationalist newspapers
and patriotic societies, and, before long, in any event, a
battleship from home would arrive off the coast of the backward country, marines would be landed, perhaps some backward persons would be shot, and at the point of the bayonet
additional concessions would be obtained, a degree of order
would be restored, and the civilising march of the Industrial
Revolution—and nationalism—would go forward. It might
not be an obligation of a national state to guarantee the
financial profits of every citizen at home, but it became a
commonplace of nationalist philosophy and practice that the
profits of citizens abroad, at least in backward regions, were
matters of national interest and must be guaranteed, as
matters of national right, at all hazards, by the full political,
diplomatic, military, and naval resources of the national
government.

Difficulties with natives were not the only difficulties
which faced the trader or prospector or investor from an
industrialised national state. He was almost sure, sooner
or later, to encounter a rival from another industrialised na-

tional state, who was likewise having his troubles with the natives and invoking aid from his government and people. Economic rivalries between different foreigners complicated the relations of both with the natives, and, of course, led to conflicts between their respective national interests and national rights. In this manner many backward regions became what Mr. Walter Lippmann has described as "arenas of friction." [1]

Under the circumstances, it is not surprising that such industralised national states as possessed adequate nationalism and militarism undertook to secure specially favoured positions in backward regions, whether by way of outright annexation or through the more delicate and adroit devices of protectorate and sphere of influence. Beginning in the latter half of the nineteenth century, this kind of imperialism advanced by leaps and bounds. Disraeli and Salisbury in Great Britain, Ferry and Hanotaux and Delcassé in France, Bismarck and William II in Germany, Crispi in Italy, McKinley and Roosevelt and Wilson in the United States, were prominent among statesmen who, heeding the demands of national interest and national right in backward regions, conducted their respective national states along the pathways of the new nationalist imperialism.

The people of these states followed, and followed gladly, not simply because the sordid financial interests of a few of them were at stake, but rather because the vast majority of them were prompted by the glorious and compelling ideals of nationalism. From nationalist training in the public schools, in the military services, and in "yellow" journalism, the average citizen of a national state had learned that there was something peculiarly sacrosanct about his nationality, and that this something, like a halo, accompanied and surrounded every one of his fellow citizens whenever and wherever they went among savages and barbarians and other "backward" peoples, or, for that matter, among "civilised" foreigners. He might denounce the politics and religion,

[1] Walter Lippman, *The Stakes of Diplomacy* (1917), ch. vii.

the morals and manners of some of his fellow citizens at home, and even when they went abroad he might still entertain mental reservations about their common sense and interior holiness, but he was estopped by the faith within him from doubting their general superiority to foreigners and from denying the paramount right and duty of his national state to protect their lives and property abroad.

This popular nationalist conviction covered not only traders and prospectors and investors in "backward" regions, but also missionaries and explorers and scientists—all fellow nationals, in fact, whether they were exploiting the Industrial Revolution or the Gospel of Jesus or the endowments of Messrs. Carnegie and Rockefeller. If a Christian missionary was slain in Africa or Asia, his fellow nationals viewed him less as a martyr to Christianity than as a martyr to the national state of his birth and citizenship, and, not content to allow his blood to become merely the affair of his God and the seed of his Church, they cried for vengeance to the military arm of their state and frequently utilised the opportunity to assert national rights and extend national interests. No matter how critical ultra-nationalists might be of certain forms of Christianity at home, they were of one mind in espousing the interests and rights of Christians of their own nationality abroad. It lacks not an element of humour—and perhaps of pathos—that the Government of the Third French Republic, at the very time when in France it was assailing the Catholic Church and expelling the religious Orders and suppressing Catholic schools, was valiantly defending Catholic missions and Catholic schools in Turkey, in China, and in Africa, or that the Imperial German Government, fresh from a *Kulturkampf* with the Catholic Church in Germany, promptly avenged the murder of two German Catholic priests in China by despatching a naval expedition to the Far East and wresting from the Chinese Empire a strategic port and valuable economic concessions, or that the Government of the United States, most vocally insistent upon the absolute separation of Church and State, employed its diplomatic offices and the decks of its gunboats for the physical salvation of Protestant and Catholic missionaries of American nationality.

Imperialism of the new nationalist type has been fostered among the Great Powers of Europe and America almost as much by the nationalising of Christian missions as by the nationalising of the Industrial Revolution. Christian missionaries have usually preceded and paved the way for traders and investors in "backward" countries. The myriad societies which exist in Christian lands for the raising of funds for the spread and maintenance of foreign missions and the countless publications which they issue, have served to emphasise to the masses of people in every national state of Christian antecedents the "backwardness" of other peoples and the crying need of the latter for the abundant blessings of Christian civilisation, and such emphasis has carried general conviction, if not in its Christian aspects, at any rate in its nationalist implications. Some sincere Christians may have a fleeting doubt now and again concerning the effect upon the Christian missions of entangling them with national rights and national interests, but the great bulk of professed Christians in nationalist Great Powers seldom fail to egg on their respective Governments to imperial enterprise, even to bloody reprisals, in avowed support of Christian civilisation. Whether they do so because of Christianity or because of nationalism, they could hardly say themselves; probably their motive springs from a curious compounding of the two. Be that as it may, Christian missions, along with trade and investment, have become, alike in popular opinion and in governmental policy, fit subjects of national interest and national right and, as such, convenient stepping-stones to the modern imperialism of nationalist states.

Outside of narrowly economic and ecclesiastical considerations, modern nationalists come honestly by their imperialist impulse. Nationalism involves an implicit and explicit faith in the superiority of one's own nationality to all other nationalities in virtue and valour, in civilisation and "mission." To the ardent nationalist the attainment of unity and independence by his nationality appears as the culmination and acme of aeons of human history, but who is he that he should stay the onward and upward progress of the human mind and the human spirit? If his nationality has been guided by Providence through innumerable centuries and untold suffering and led on to emerge at length as the contented chosen people *par excellence* among all the tribes of the Earth, may it then stop short with a glorious and powerful national state all its own? Why thenceforth should it hide its light under a bushel? Is it not clearly designed to be throughout all ages a light to lighten the Gentiles? Has it not a stern duty to forego its own selfish and exclusive contentment of the moment and to gird itself for the forceful discharge of the difficult obligations of its manifest destiny? Should it not communicate some of its own inherent valour and virtue to less fortunate nationalities? Should it not extend its beneficent sway and civilising influence over backward peoples? Obviously!

And suppose that such a fortunate and high-minded national state is a bit overpopulated, so that every year a considerable number of its citizens leave the Fatherland and settle in foreign lands where they are gradually corrupted and brought down from that higher plane to which their original heritage had raised them. Cynics there have been, suggesting that emigration might be lessened and other ills of overpopulation remedied if the Fatherland were less smugly content and more disposed to recognise the basic requirement of assuring to its citizens at home an equitable distribution of wealth. Enthusiastic nationalists, however, have little patience with cynics and scant ear for suggestions of radical domestic reform. They prefer to champion the acquisition of sparsely inhabited regions whither the surplus population may go and continue, without interruption or deterioration, to live under the grand old national flag, to speak the grand old national language, and to cherish the grand old national traditions and faith.

The future welfare of the race—the call of the higher civilisation—the cultural mission—the white man's burden—manifest destiny—the need of providing for surplus population of the homeland—the need of "cleaning up" a foreign land—these are shibboleths not only, but sincere expressions of a widespread and deep-seated conviction which has rendered nationalism a most devoted helpmate to imperialism and has enabled Britain and France, Germany and Italy, Russia and the United States, Belgium and Japan, within the last half-century to subject to their sway millions of square miles of territory and millions of human beings in the "backward" regions of the Earth. The original prompting to this imperialism may come mainly from small groups of capitalists and business-men, to whom its financial profits may chiefly accrue, but its strength and persistence are derived from popular nationalism, which, in turn, it nourishes. And, as contemporary imperialism depends for its necessary idealism upon nationalism, so it depends both for the subjugation of backward peoples and for protection against other imperial nationalist Powers upon militarism. And as imperialism exalts nationalism, so, too, from the very nature of the thing, it exalts militarism.

5

Then there is "national honour"—something transcending concrete national interests and pecuniary rights, something intangible and immaterial, something ethereal and spiritual, something beyond price—the ultimate concept of nationalism. The phrase is used by nationalists most glibly to cover a multitude of exigencies and eventualities, but the lowest common denominator of all these is, in plain English, national prestige. The patriotic citizens of a national state, convinced that they of all earthly nationalities possess the highest civilisation and the greatest destiny, are determined that their state and their nationality shall be treated by other states and peoples with due deference. They are insistent that others shall regard them as they regard themselves. This is not to say that they expect others to be altogether sincere in such regard, for others may imagine—vainly and foolishly imagine—that they possess an even higher civilisation and an even greater destiny. It is to say, however, that others must play a game of make-believe with the utmost seriousness. To Haitian nationalism it is vital that an Haitian admiral be regarded by Americans and Britishers with as much outward courtesy and respect as these nationalities expect to be shewn their admirals by the Haitians; otherwise there is a stain upon the national honour of Haiti, and the sovereign national state of Haiti loses prestige.

If a citizen of a national state suffers insult or injury in a foreign country, "civilised" or "backward," it at once becomes for his state not only a matter of national interest and national right to seek redress, but also an object of national prestige, an affair of national honour, to secure redress. With the injection of the concept of national honour, the situation forthwith assumes the sportsmanlike character of duelling. The aggrieved party demands "satisfaction," that is, ceremonious apology and ample reparation, and, failing satisfaction, swords must be drawn, shots must be fired, blood must be shed. It is no longer incumbent upon the challenger, or upon the challenged (if the challenged is a nationalist Great Power), to reckon the risk or to calculate the proportion which the cost of remedy or retaliation may bear to the material gains at stake. The motivation in the case promptly shifts from the ground of material interest and legal right to the spiritual ground of national honour. And national honour does not always carry connotations of honesty, veracity, equity, liberality, and unselfishness. It does carry nations into war or threats of war.

Many examples might be cited to shew that in our

nationalist era an offense against the national honour commands a profounder and more unreserved popular resentment than a simple infraction of the rights of person or property. To mention but one, the United States went to war with Germany in 1917 less to protect American lives and possessions than to assure national prestige and to avenge national honour. From the outbreak of the Great War in 1914 the two coalitions of European belligerents vied with each other in attempts to enlist American aid; both tried intimidation and cajolery; both interfered with American rights of property and persons; but whereas Germany had recourse to effrontery and ostentatious use of threats and acts of violence against American travellers and traders, Great Britain and France, even while engaged in the persistent infraction of American commercial rights, constantly observed a deferential attitude towards American self-esteem and self-respect. Eventually, as everyone knows, America in war spent vastly more money and sacrificed vastly more lives than had been jeopardised in neutrality, but she vindicated her national honour.

National honour "is subject to injury in divers ways, and so may yield a fruitful grievance even apart from offences against the person or property of the nation's business-men; as, *e.g.*, through neglect or disregard of the conventional punctilios governing diplomatic intercourse, or by disrespect or contumelious speech touching the Flag, or the persons of national officials, particularly of such officials as have only a decorative use, or the costumes worn by such officials, or, again, by failure to observe the ritual prescribed for parading the national honour on stated occasions. When duly violated the national honour may duly be made whole again by similarly immaterial instrumentalities; as, *e.g.*, by recital of an appropriate formula of words, by formal consumption of a stated quantity of ammunition in the way of a salute, by 'dipping' an insign, and the like,—procedure which can, of course, have none but a magical efficacy. The national honour, in short, moves in the realm of magic, and touches the frontiers of religion." [1]

Though in essence national honour has little or nothing to do with economics, in substance it is likely to supplement national interests and national rights of an economic nature and to provide in the popular mind a spiritual justification for the securing of financial advantages by certain classes and even for the extension of the new imperialism, which, we have remarked, is half economic and half nationalist. Any event, no matter how trifling or fortuitous, when clothed in the righteous armour of national honour, is apt to produce prodigious consequences. In 1827 negotiations were proceeding fairly amicably between the French Government and the dey of Algiers for the settlement of a debt which a former French Government owed two Algerian Jews, when in momentary anger the thoughtless dey tapped the French consul on the head with a fan-like fly-slapper; now this was obviously a slap at the national honour of France, and so Frenchmen, who had been quite unmoved by the financial bickerings, flew to arms, Algiers was blockaded by a French squadron, a goodly number of Algerians were killed, the dey was transported to a cooler and quieter place where fly-slappers were less fashionable, and eventually the whole country was subdued and annexed to France. Thereby French national honour was repaired and a rich field opened to French bankers and business-men. In 1898, in the midst of promising negotiations between Spain and the United States for the pacific settlement of Cuban difficulties, an American battleship was blown up in the harbour of Havana; this was plainly an affront to national honour so outrageous that peaceful negotiations could go no farther, not even to seek an impartial determination of how or why the ship had been destroyed, but must give way to an ordeal

---

[1] This quotation and other thoughts and phrases in this section are taken from chapter i of Mr. Thorstein Veblen's thoughtful *Inquiry into the Nature of Peace and the Terms of its Perpetuation* (1917). On the subject, too, the book by Mr. Leo Perla, *What is National Honour?* (1917), may be read with profit.

by battle. And so America, to vindicate her national honour (and to promote civilisation), sacrificed the lives of about 2,500 of her citizens in a war with Spain and obtained in Porto Rico, the Philippines, and Guam an imperial domain for her national interests.

If national honour, as Mr. Thorstein Veblen has said, "touches the frontiers of religion," [1] it also reaches back over the sea of natural rights and national interests to touch the frontiers of military science. It is, in fact, the bridge between nationalism as a religion and militarism as an art. Whenever the god of sectarian nationalism is blasphemed by foreigners or sacrilege is committed by them against any of the god's symbols or ministers or sacred vessels, the ardent nationalist recoils instantly and seizes sticks and stones and any other available instruments of physical force; he stands ready in ecstasy and by violence to avenge the national honour and to maintain the national prestige. National interests may sometimes be submitted to international arbitration, and national rights may occasionally be compromised by international agreement, but national honour never!

6

Militarism, the maintenance of large armaments on land and sea, has been an outstanding characteristic of national states in modern times, and it is more so now than ever before. Apparently, the more progressive and "civilised" (and nationalist) a nationality is, the more militarist it must be. In a very recent year—a year of international "peace"—a year subsequent to the Great War which was "to end war"—twenty national states spent together more than twenty-five hundred million dollars upon their armies and navies, and, judging by their comparative expenditures, Great Britain is the most civilised and progressive (and nationalist), the United States is next, France is third, and then follow in order Italy, Germany, Russia, Poland, Spain,

[1] *Op. cit.*, p. 29.

Mexico, Netherlands, Greece, Sweden, Argentina, Yugoslavia, Brazil, Belgium, Turkey, Japan, Rumania, and Chile.[1]
Why all this expenditure? Why all this militarism? Because, say some persons, interested and influential capitalists
and business-men demand and obtain it for their own economic purposes. And doubtless there is a substratum of truth
in such allegations. In every industrialised national state
there are economic backers of militarism: those who ask
and receive from their national Government "protection"
for their foreign trade, whether in the form of a fancied "in-
surance" or in the nature of grandiloquent "advertising";
those who beg and obtain from their national Government
"protection" for their foreign investments, especially in
"backward" regions; those who, having loaned money to
their national Government, think that their debtor will be
in a better position to pay it if it is stabilised and
strengthened by armaments; those who call for military
force to repress internal disorders and unrest, both political
dissent and economic strikes; and those who manufacture
munitions of war and materials for army and navy. One
can hardly expect an enthusiastic advocacy of reduced militarism to proceed from the Krupps in Germany, the Creu-
sot works in France, the Armstrongs in England, or even
the Du Ponts and Maxims in the United States, and one
may scarcely censure honourable gentlemen because they
have had the foresight and genius to build up such great
and gainful industries.

Nor may one lightly condemn American citizens who
have, or hope to have, extensive property-rights in Mexico

[1]Great Britain spent $652,696,789 (exclusive of India and the self-gov-
erning Dominions), or $835,196,789 (including India); the United States,
$554,372,018 ($257,274,768 for the army and $297,097,250 for the navy);
France, $220,403,601; Italy, $117,093,411; Germany, $107,100,000; Russia,
$105,752,070; Poland, $85,102,964; Spain, $76,601,243; Mexico, $63,238,095;
etc. These figures are for a fiscal year 1923-1924 and have been com-
piled by the Statistics Branch of the War Department of the United States
Government, translated into dollars by officials of J. P. Morgan & Co.,
of New York, and published by the Information Service of the Department of Research and Education of the Federal Council of the Churches
of Christ in America, July 18, 1925.

and South America or in the Far East or in Turkey simply
because they rejoice once in a while to see an American gun-
boat or a detachment of American marines. As Mr. Allan
Westcott of the United States Naval Academy has admirably pointed out, the increase in value of American exports
to Turkey from $3,300,000 in 1913 to $42,200,000 in 1920
"was brought about in large measure through skillful coöperation with business interests on the part of the American
High Commissioner in Turkey, Rear-Admiral Bristol. . . .
A short time ago there was much opposition to a bill in Congress to put commercial agents on men-of-war. Now de-
stroyers are entering Turkish ports with 'drummers' as reg-
ular passengers, and their fantails piled with American sam-
ples. An American destroyer has made a special trip at
thirty knots to get American oil prospectors into a newly
opened field." [1]

But with militarism in times of "peace" as with militarism in times of war, it is extremely doubtful whether the
masses of any country would concern themselves merely for
the pecuniary advantage of oil prospectors or "drummers,"
What gives vogue to contemporary militarism with the
masses is not the economics of big business or imperialism
—not economics at all—but the sentiment of nationalism.
Nationalism is woven and inextricably interwoven with militarism. According to nationalist theory, every national
state is absolutely independent and sovereign and fully
equal to every other national state, and though in fact national states are very unequal and even the strongest among
them is not strong enough to maintain its independence
should the others unite against it, nevertheless each proceeds to act in most cases as though it were self-sufficient and
as though its own self-interest were its supreme guide. In
other words, nationalist society is anarchial society. Sovereign national states accept no law-giver and admit no law
superior to their several choosings and devisings, and, al-

[1] "The Struggle for the Mediterranean," *Our World,* vol. ii. no. 5 (February, 1923), p. 17.

though they profess to conduct their relations with one another in accordance with traditional usages of "international law" and international diplomacy and in consonance with dictates of "civilisation" and "humanity," it inevitably falls out in nationalist society, as in any anarchial society, that indirectly if not directly force and power are the final arbitrament among them. It is no euphemism that every such state is styled a "Power" and that a few national states by reason of the thickness and weight of their armour-plate and the prestige which customarily attends their shows of might are classed as "Great Powers." The very fact that nationalism presupposes a group of mutually exclusive national states tends to cause the people of every national state to rely ultimately upon militarism for the attainment of its selfish (and altruistic) ends.

In militarism, too, as we have observed in another connection, nationalism has had a pragmatic test. National self-determination has usually been secured by militarism, and by militarism national irredentas have been redeemed. Besides, how, without militarism, could national rights be guarded, national interests promoted, and national honour vindicated? The property-rights and financial interests of individuals may not, as such, be worth arming for and fighting about, but, once raised to the sentimental and emotional plane of national rights and national interests, they justify every nationalist in his whole-souled endeavours to add weight and strength to his "Power," and, if perchance they are carried still higher into the nebulous heavens of national honour, they impel him to hurry to the nearest recruiting station, not stopping "to reason why," but eager only "to do and die."

For the nationalist appeal of militarism is all powerful. There is nationalist pride in the uniform of soldier and sailor, in the spectacle of military parade or naval review, in the very thought of bursting bomb and screeching shell. The most revered historic traditions of every nationality on earth are traditions of war; the most heroic figures of the past are military or naval heroes; the greatness of nations is measured chiefly by their fighting prowess. It was the military ideal of the ancient imperial Romans of which Virgil sang:

> "Let others better mould the running mass
> Of metals, and inform the breathing brass,
> And soften into flesh a marble face;
> Plead better at the bar; describe the skies,
> And when the stars descend, and when they rise,
> But, Rome! 'tis thine alone, with awful sway,
> To rule mankind, and make the world obey,
> Disposing peace and war thy own majestic way;
> To tame the proud, the fetter'd slave to free:—
> These are imperial arts; and worthy thee." [1]

But Kipling or Barrès or any other nationalist litterateur of our age could sing much the same song and strike an even more responsive chord in the popular heart than Virgil struck nineteen hundred years ago. To modern nationalism the ancient Roman spirit has been bequeathed with compound interest. As Professor David S. Muzzey has said, "Beneath all the art and letters, all the industry and commerce, all the advance in humanity throughout European history, that Roman ideal remains. When the . . . nations speak of patriotism they mean the memory of their glorious wars. . . . It is not alone Germany, with the celebration of its men of blood and iron from Otto the Great to Otto von Bismarck. The French, too, rejoice in the Napoleonic legend. They have their glorious wars of the *Grand Monarque*. They bow before the white plume of Henry of Navarre, and thrill to the echo of Roland's horn at Roncesvalles. The English have their proud memories of Agincourt and Blenheim and Crécy and Waterloo, and celebrate their Napiers and Nelsons and little 'Bobs.' All these nations . . . have their glorious traditions of war, and each one can find enough victories in the uninterrupted course of slaughter through the Christian ages to justify its belief

[1] Dryden's translation.

in its own invincible prowess—nay, even in its divine mission to rule the rest."[1]

What makes militarism even more popular in our day than in Virgil's is the fact that glorious military traditions and ideals are now sedulously extolled by nationalists among all civilised peoples. Not in one empire only, but in a large number of independent and sovereign national states, are these traditions and ideals inculcated in the masses, and they are inculcated nowadays almost universally by the novel and potent means of compulsory state-education, extensive military training, and "yellow" journalism. Militarism has been made an integral part of nationalism, and it is but natural that peoples who are indoctrinated with nationalism should be imbued with militarism.

And when one thinks of the widespread popularity of militarism and then recalls the anarchial character of modern nationalist society, with its fifty-odd sovereign "Powers," one can easily understand that modern militarism is competitive to a degree unknown to the ancient Romans. It is a nationalist conviction that a national state, to maintain its independence and sovereignty, must always have an army and usually a navy, and, to enhance its prestige, must from time to time, with growth of population and commerce, expand its armaments. Its citizens who urge an increase of armaments are praised for their patriotism, whilst citizens who suggest any decrease are denounced as lacking in patriotism and as being deficient in red corpuscles, in a word, are called "pacifists" (with all the evil connotations which this word has for nationalists).

But an increase of armaments in one national state is likely to alarm the patriotic citizens of another national state, who may imagine that the increase is directed against them and their interests and rights, and so these must prove the redness of their blood and the quality of their national faith by increasing their armed forces. Thereupon it is the

[1] *The Menace of Patriotism,* Society for Ethical Culture (New York, 1916), pp. 4-5.

turn of the red-blooded nationalists of the first state to quake in their beds and see in wild nightmares the invasion and devastation of their land, the rape of their women, the slaughter of their infants, and the enslavement of their whole nationality, unless promptly several new regiments are added to their army and several new battleships to their navy. But if the citizens of the second national state were alarmed by the original increase of the armed strength of the first state, they are certain to be terrified by its subsequent additions, and so for a moment—only a moment—they gain a fancied security by augmenting their army and their navy. Of course, if guns are piled too high, they have a tendency in recent times to go off. The guns of Germany, for example, were piled mountain-high in 1914, and off they went, without noticeably increasing Germany's security, or the security of the world.

Every national state arms ostensibly for "defence." It is not a tenet of popular nationalism that one's own national state should prepare for, or wage, wars of offence. One's own nationality is too pure of heart and too upright in conduct to give real offence to anyone. But it is a curious obsession of the nationalist mind that whilst one's own national state arms only for defence, all other national states arm for offence. Consequently, if a given nationality has won political independence and unity, its members feel that they cannot afford to disarm; if formerly they had to fight for freedom against an imperial Power, henceforth they must be doubly prepared, morally and physically, to defend their freedom against the almost certain onslaughts of envious national Powers. Pride in the loftiness of the aims of one's nationality and boastfulness about the ability of one's nationality to realise those aims usually beget among other nationalities a fear and a dread which create an irresistible popular demand for "defensive" preparedness, that is, for national militarism.

Every national state has a class of professional militarists, who constantly play upon the nationalist emotions of their

fellow citizens, particularly upon national fear and dread
of the foreigner, and who perennially emphasise the competitive nature of national militarism. This class includes
numerous officers of the army and navy, especially such as
have retired from active service and are possessed of an
abundance of leisure and zeal,—these are "experts" whose
function it is now to lament the woeful unpreparedness of
their country and again to laud its military destiny. The
class includes likewise many fiery civilians who organise
themselves into Army Leagues, Navy Leagues, National Security Leagues, *etc.*, and employ speakers and writers to
prod the Government and the people to effect that preparedness and that destiny which the "experts" advise. It is
obvious that the larger a military establishment is, the larger
and more influential will be the class of professional militarists. It is obvious, also, that the more influential this class
is, the more pressing and successful will be the popular demand for additional militarism. Professional militarists
are invariably rampant nationalists. Their vocation is preparedness for war and their avocation is a search for national
injuries or national wrongs. In appealing to the masses
they usually argue for "defence," but their arguments are
apt to be so punctuated with boasts and threats that what is
taken for "defence" at home is interpreted abroad
as "offence."

And in all the international differences and disputes which
arise concerning national interests, national rights, and national honour, it is well-nigh impossible for nationalists the
world over to distinguish impartially and objectively between offence and defence, for what is defence to the nationalists of one country is offence to the nationalists of
another. In international disputes, nationalists ordinarily
limit themselves to assertion of the justice of their own
country's cause and to demands for greater truculence—a
heavier show of force—on the part of their own government
in championing its cause.

Thus in diplomacy and in international intercourse of all

sorts, a world that is nationalist must seemingly be governed ultimately by militarism, and by militarism which is competitive. This is why nationalities after achieving political unity and independence do not always become exemplars of justice and charity to all other nationalities, and pillars of world-peace. It is why, on the contrary, they continue to nourish and cherish militarism, why they seek by war or by threat of war to satisfy their immediate selfish ambitions sometimes at the expense of the health and happiness of the world.

VII

NATIONALISM AND INTOLERANCE

1

TOLERANCE—the spirit of "live and let live"—has not been, we must confess, a chronic attribute and ideal of all human beings. Whenever it has been in evidence, it has been associated either with a sweet reasonableness of rare and choice souls or, more often, with an indifference, scepticism, or doubt on the part of groups. In the latter instances, groups may be tolerant about something in which they have lost interest, but this is not to say that therefore they have become tolerant in general and on principle; they may simultaneously be very intolerant about something else in which they have acquired a vital interest. The tolerance which springs from indifference is a specific tolerance which has only a distant and poor relationship to the generic tolerance begotten of reasoned conviction.

It would be comforting to believe what we are told so frequently that tolerance—generic principled tolerance— is a part of the "swift ice-run of progress" into which "the toboggan of human affairs" [1] is led ever faster and faster, extra fast in our days, towards the goal of perfect health, happiness, and sanity. But a little reflection, a little sweet reasonableness of our own, may suffice to make us cautious about accepting such a belief, however comforting it may appear. Perfect health, happiness, and sanity are certainly an attractive goal for humanity—they always have been

[1] The phrases are Mr. H. G. Wells's, and the work in which they appear (*The Outline of History,* vol. ii, page 391) leaves as a whole a perplexing doubt in the mind of at least one reader whether Mr. Wells is pointing his "toboggan" on toward the millennial goal or back in the direction of his fearful cavemen and their "hot red eyes" (*cf.* vol. i, p. 377).

alluring—but are we sure that we are appreciably nearer them than were the ancient Greeks? Haven't they always been a bit utopian? If so, isn't the "toboggan run of progress" a mere rhetorical flourish? In any event, we can afford to pause in honest doubt before we affirm that there has been a steady progressive growth of true tolerance.

The current notion that there is more tolerance in the world today than ever before is the outcome of a mixture of facts and fancies. It is a fact that optimism about tolerance, as about almost everything, is a characteristic of modern times, but it is a fancy, to our way of thinking, that all such optimism is justifiable. It is probably a fact that some progress has actually occurred in the refinement of penalties and punishments dispensed to victims of intolerance. It is assuredly a fact that certain specific intolerances have sensibly diminished. Pagans no longer make a sport of throwing Christians to the lions. Catholics no longer burn heretics at the stake. Protestants no longer hang Catholics from Tyburn tree or set their gory heads upon poles at city-gates. But it is fanciful to suppose that persons, grown tolerant about Paganism, or about Christianity, either Protestant or Catholic, have become tolerant about other things, especially about those things in which nowadays they are vitally and emotionally interested. The objects of intolerance have changed, but intolerance *per se* remains, so that, though Christians and Pagans as such may have made some real progress towards tolerance, innumerable other humans and even Christians and Pagans in their non-Christian or non-Pagan aspects have progressed very little or not at all.

Nationalism is nowadays a vital interest of vast masses of mankind, and it is an interest richly emotional and moving. Taught in school, indoctrinated by military training, preached by press and from rostrum, personified in the national state, symbolised by the flag, it touches the life of the modern man from cradle to grave. It is a creed believed by multitudes and a cult exercised by multitudes. It is a

novel expression of human idealism. It inspires noble deeds
and heroic sacrifice. What more natural than that it should
sometimes prove to be intolerant of doubt and dissent?

That nationalism has produced a whole crop of wars—
wars of self-determination and wars of irredentism and wars
of imperialism—and that it has fostered a new and peculiarly persistent type of militarism, we have already been led
to see. Now national militarism and nationalist wars are
themselves closely articulated with intolerance. They are
caused in large part by an intolerant attitude of one nationality towards another; by their course and in their
results they usually confirm and strengthen international
intolerance. Altogether they indicate a desire and impulse
of one human group to destroy another human group, and
however justifiable the desire may be, however idealistic
the impulse, they betoken a contemporary and popular intolerance essentially one with the intolerance of an Henry
VIII, a Torquemada, or a Nero.[1] And certainly international intolerance of modern times already has far more
victims to its credit (or debit) than inter-religious intolerance of antiquity or of the middle ages. Pagan or Christian (or Moslem) intolerance may have come, or be coming,
to a timely and unregretted end, but the end of international intolerance is not in sight, and, if it were, nationalists
would probably mourn.

So glorious and beneficent, to nationalists, is the systematic, wholesale destruction of foreigners that any diminu-
tion of this supreme form of international intolerance must
occasion the most poignant regrets. As a rather sombre but
very eloquent nationalist professor has said, "In war and
the right of war man has a possession which he values
above religion, above industry, and above social comforts;
in war man values the power which it affords to life of
rising above life, the power which the spirit of man possesses

---

[1] It should be remembered that these gentlemen, in their several ways,
were idealists and that each of them could justify his intolerance to his
own satisfaction and to the satisfaction of the majority of his immediate
contemporaries.

to pursue the Ideal. . . . The friendship of nations is an empty name; peace is at best a truce on the battlefield of Time." [1] Or, as another equally gifted philosopher and professor has testified, "A victorious war may bring to a nation a complete regeneration—the moral energies awake; vice is repressed; life is protected; education flourishes; hygiene spreads; science rebuilds the land; prosperity grows; temperance and self-discipline prevail; family life can expand in the new abundance." [2] And to preserve all the happy fruits which the professors have plucked from international war, no less a nationalist authority than Admiral Mahan has left us as almost his last literary legacy a solemn warning against any lessening of international intolerance. "It is of the first importance," he writes, "that the European family of states retain in full the power of national self-assertion, of which the sentiment of nationality [nationalism] is the spirit and armaments the embodiment, for so only, by the national force of the several states in active competition with one another, can the force of the whole be depended upon for maintaining itself, and thus ultimately reducing by assimilation the opposing external forces." [3]

So, then, if we heed the admonitions of those most competent to speak in behalf of nationalism, we shall go on forever heightening our national militarism, waging nationalist wars, and necessarily becoming ever more intolerant of foreigners. It is barely possible that in that direction lies the path of human progress, the very toboggan run towards perfect health, happiness, and sanity. Only, if we take that direction, let us not regale ourselves with self-congratulations upon our growing tolerance.

The intolerance which attends international war and national militarism is, however, only one, though perhaps the supreme, aspect of nationalist intolerance. Other aspects appear in connection with the internal concerns of every

---

[1] J. A. Cramb, *Germany and England* (1914), pp. 67, 147.
[2] Hugo Münsterberg, *The War and America* (1914), p. 195.
[3] A. T. Mahan, *Armaments and Arbitration* (1912), pp. 9-10.

national state. If nationalism, in times of international tension, encourages a whole nationality or the entire citizenry of a national state to present a united front and to evince a collective intolerance towards an alien nationality or a foreign state, nationalism at all times actuates certain individuals or groups within a nationality to assume that they are the standard, one-hundred-per-cent. patriots of that nationality and to adopt an appropriate degree of specialised intolerance in coping with their less endowed fellow countrymen. The specialised domestic intolerances of nationalism are not nearly so deadly in effect as its collective foreign intolerance, but they are of such great and varied importance, of such mounting proportions, as to call for some examination. It will suit our convenience, in dealing with them, to distinguish the intolerant tendencies of nationalism in domestic affairs, in respect of (1) devotees of international religions, (2) disciples of social and economic movements of foreign origin, (3) members of alien or "inferior" races, and (4) dissentient national minorities.

2

It is not to be wondered at that there is conflict between nationalism and "world" religions. Every great international religion—Buddhism, Christianity, Mohammedanism—teaches the equality and brotherhood of human beings regardless of their nationality; nationalism, on the contrary, invariably inculcates a sense of superiority of and in a particular nationality. Again, world religions have delimited wide cultural areas, such as those of the West, the Near East, the Middle East, and the Far East, in each of which a community of customs and usages overlaps national boundaries; on the other hand, nationalism seeks to provide for each nationality a distinctive culture and to exalt it above the culture of the broader religious area.

Then, too, international religions have some central authority, possessing greater or less actual power and influence over all their respective adherents, and operating usually outside of any given nationality, whilst nationalism is jealous of any real or fancied infringement upon the absolute and final sovereignty of each separate national state. In the case of an international religion, the central authority may be that of a book, a Bible or a Koran, or it may be the authority of a person, a pope, a patriarch, a dalai-lama, or a caliph. The personal head of an international religion has seldom been able or anxious to divorce his priestly functions and spiritual ministrations from secular concerns, and most sacred books of such a religion contain not religious precepts exclusively, but political, social, and even economic directions which may contravene the practices and enactments of a national state. To the devotees of a world religion, the dictates of conscience, as sanctioned by religious authority, must be followed, whether they violate the laws of the land or not. To the nationalist, the laws of the national state must be obeyed whether or not they conform with the precepts of a sacred book or with the admonitions of a sacred person.

Nationalists do not take kindly to the divided allegiance of fellow citizens who sometimes obey the state and sometimes obey a "foreign" church, and who reserve to themselves the right of private judgement whenever it is a question of reconciling the two. Wherefore, zealous nationalists strive to subordinate the church to the state, to transfer to the latter as many of the functions of the former as possible. In every country influenced by nationalism there has been a marked tendency on the part of the national state to take over from the local agencies of an international religion the custody of vital statistics, the regulation of family relations, and the conduct of public charities and education, and in some instances to deny these agencies full freedom of organisation and propaganda and to supervise, if not to cut off, their intercourse with their fellow religionists, even with their head, in other countries. "Laicising" or "secularising," this process is euphemistically termed; in plainer English, it is "nationalising." Especially over education has con-

flict raged during the past hundred years between nationalists and devotees of international religions. Shall education remain within the scope and under the control of an international organisation, or shall it be nationalised and
dominated by the national state? Both parties to the dispute know that the future of their faiths depends principally
upon a suitable indoctrination of the young.

On the whole, nationalists have made noteworthy progress
in their struggle to lessen the menace of world religions.
They have been greatly assisted by the compulsory character
of the national state as over against the voluntary character of the church. People nowadays are not forced to belong to a church or to pay tithes for its support; if they
were, nationalists would complain bitterly of religious intolerance. But people have to belong to the state and have
to pay taxes for its maintenance; they have to obey its
laws or be fined, imprisoned, or put to death; and therein
no nationalist perceives any intolerance. Nationalists have
been immeasurably aided, moreover, by every success they
have won. As one secular function after another has been
transferred from church to state, the masses have come step
by step to look upon the state, rather than upon the church,
as the guardian of the family, the dispenser of charity, and
the promoter of education and culture. Finally, with the
gradual actual process of extending the functions of the
state and of establishing what the French call *étatisme*,
has gone the persistent and highly effective propaganda of
nationalism as an emotional force, as a spiritual "mission,"
as a substitute for other religion if not as a religion itself,
with the result that citizens of a modern national state imbibe nationalism with the air they breathe and that many
a nominal adherent of an international religion is really a
devotee of nationalism. This development has enormously
lightened the labours of professed and convinced nationalists, who repeatedly have derived aid and comfort from
their "enemies."

It would be possible to describe in some detail the nature

of the conflict between nationalism and Buddhism or between nationalism and Mohammedanism and to give specific illustrations of the intolerance of ultra-nationalists in Japan and Turkey in respect of fellow citizens who happen to be disciples of Buddha or Mohammed—or Christ. For the sake of brevity and point, however, it seems preferable to restrict ourselves here to a brief description and a few illustrations of nationalist intolerance in Europe and America as it affects, first, Christians, and, secondly, Jews.

Christianity has always been haunted by the spirit and teaching of Jesus. Equality and brotherhood of all races, all nationalities, and all men, justice and charity to all, peace on earth to all men of good will, humility and self-sacrifice and meekness and long suffering—these are concepts and precepts that occur and recur as a constant *motif* in the four Gospels, in the epistles of St. Paul, in the apologetics of the Fathers, in the treatises of St. Thomas of Aquin, in the poems of Il Poverello. How diametrically opposed they are to the spirit of extreme nationalism, of the nationalism which lives by the sword, may best be gathered from a paraphrasing of the message of one of the most brilliant writers of the nineteenth century: "Ye have heard how in old times it was said, Blessed are the meek, for they shall inherit the earth; but I say unto you, Blessed are the valiant, for they shall make the earth their throne. And ye have heard men say, Blessed are the poor in spirit; but I say unto you, Blessed are the great in soul and the free in spirit, for they shall enter into Valhalla. And ye have heard men say, Blessed are the peacemakers; but I say unto you, Blessed are the war-makers, for they shall be called, if not the children of Yahweh, the children of Odin, who is greater than Yahweh." [1] Nietzsche himself was not a nationalist, and mild and humane nationalists there be who repudiate his loud praise of might and valour. On the other hand, numerous nominal Christians behave as though they agreed with

---

[1] *Cf.* F. W. Nietzsche, *Also sprach Zarathustra* and *Der Antichrist*. The paraphrase is Professor J. A. Cramb's, *Germany and England* (1914), p. 130.

Zarathustra rather than with the Sermon on the Mount.
Yet between extreme and literal Christianity and extreme
and literal nationalism there can be no compromise. The
devotees of the one cannot make terms with the devotees
of the other. It is a fight to the finish, and such a fight must
involve persecution and intolerance.

Christianity is not, like Confucianism, a mere tissue of
ethical teaching. It is, and always has been, an organised
society, with bishops, priests, and deacons, with a mission
to go and teach all nations to observe whatsoever its
Founder has commanded, and with a special injunction to
render unto Caesar the things which are Caesar's and unto
God the things that are God's. And in distinguishing between what is God's and what is Caesar's, in executing its
own mission, and in assuring the unity and independence
of its own visible society, Christianity is provided with
manifold opportunities to fall foul of modern nationalism.

As has been pointed out elsewhere, Christianity has always recognised the principle of nationality and has frequently made minor concessions to it. In some instances
the Christian liturgy has been celebrated in national languages; certain Christian saints have been honoured more
by one nationality than by another; each Christian nationality has ordinarily been accorded a subordinate ecclesiastical organisation of its own, with a primate, a national
episcopacy, and national synods. Sometimes what a united
Christianity refused to concede for the sake of nationality
has been secured by means of rebellion against ecclesiastical
authority and at the expense of the continued unity and
complete independence of Christianity. In this way, long
before the advent of modern nationalism, national Christian Churches had come into existence among Armenians,
Copts, Greeks, Serbs, Bulgars, and Russians. In this way,
too, at the beginning of modern times, national Christian
Churches arose among Germans, Scandinavians, Dutch,
English, and Scots, and even within the remaining domain
of the Universal Christian Church additional concessions

were granted to the several nationalities—French, Spanish, Portuguese, Italians, *etc.* And, as we have also pointed out elsewhere, this progressive nationalising of organised Christianity, whether by the Orthodox schism of eastern Europe or by the Protestant revolt of northern Europe or by the Catholic reformation in southern Europe, was a contributing factor of no small significance to the rise of nationalism in modern times. National Churches made very great concessions to the principle of nationality; in turn, national patriots exalted them, in contradistinction to a foreign or an universal church, and used them more and more as agencies for the propagation of nationalism.

Doubtless all national Churches, both Orthodox and Protestant, in expounding the Christian Gospel nowadays, tend to counteract the extremes of nationalism and to exert some influence upon their followers in the direction of a Christian interpretation of nationalism. Therefore, they are liable to incur the displeasure or to arouse the antagonism of ultra-nationalists bent upon the haughty, selfish, and bellicose aggrandisement of their several nationalities or national states. Such sects as the Quakers, among Protestants, and the Doukhobors, among Orthodox, for example, are so emphatic in their devotion to Christian ideals of peace and love and forgiveness that they refuse to bear arms or engage in war, and both Quakers and Doukhobors have been denounced and cruelly persecuted by nationalist compatriots. The Doukhobors, in particular, have suffered grievously; victimised in innumerable ways by Russian nationalists under the Tsar Nicholas II, many emigrated to Canada only to evoke during the Great War suspicion, dislike, and persecution from Canadian nationalists. However, despite these exceptions, it may be affirmed that in the main Protestant and Orthodox Churches have not encountered very serious difficulties with modern nationalism. The origin of these Churches is too closely associated in the popular mind with the beginnings of nationalism; their organisation is predominantly national; and the syn-

cretism of their religion with the religion of nationalism
is likely to be far advanced. Neither Protestantism nor
Eastern Orthodoxy appears dangerous to the average
nationalist.

3

It is different with Catholicism. Catholicism, in spite
of its traditional respect for the principle of nationality and
its later concessions to national sensibilities, is still an international religion, with an international organisation, and
with an authoritative manner of speaking its mind—and its
mind is frequently out of harmony with the nationalist
mind. Nationalists, however indifferent or friendly they
may be to Protestantism, are never indifferent and seldom
friendly to Catholicism. They perceive in Catholic Christianity not merely a more or less utopian preaching of
brotherhood and equality, not merely a more or less per-
functory teaching of international peace and justice and
charity, but a very real and very effective international
organisation, and a very vital international influence which
radiates from a central person, a bishop of Rome, the pope,
out across national frontiers, and into the domain of national policy and national education. "Divided allegiance"
is not a common taunt against the Protestant or the Orthodox Christian; it is an everyday reproach of the rabid
nationalist against the Catholic Christian.

With the ubiquitous rise of nationalism in the nineteenth
and twentieth centuries, an anti-Catholic movement styled
anti-clericalism has appeared in every country which is
traditionally Catholic. This omnipresent anti-clericalism
has roots other than nationalist, roots in general scepticism
concerning the truth of the Christian revelation, in doubts
touching the divinity of Jesus and the holiness of the
Church, in imaginary conflicts between science and theology,
and in reasoned opposition or emotional repugnance to
specific doings and sayings of ecclesiastics; and a considerable number of persons who think that Catholicism is

superstitious and untrue or that it is unprogressive and un-
enlightened and who would welcome its dissolution and
early demise, are far removed in thought or intention from
nationalism. But it hardly admits of question that anti-
clericalism has been exploited by nationalists and has gained
popular headway through its appeal to the rising nationalism of the masses. To date, non-nationalist anti-clericals
have succeeded not so much in stamping out "superstition"
or in starting a new "illumination" as in helping nationalists
to pull their chestnuts out of the fire. Wittingly or unwittingly, all anti-clericals have had a hand in assaults upon
the Catholic Church which have often been attended by
nationalist intolerance and which have eventuated most
noticeably in an access of nationalism.

The French Revolution assailed and then practically proscribed Catholic Christianity, and Catholicism was reëstab-
lished in France under Napoleon Bonaparte only when the
pope agreed that ecclesiastical property which had been
confiscated should not be restored, that priests should be
salaried officials of the state, and that bishops should be
appointed on the nomination of the French Government.
Throughout the nineteenth century the national Government steadily encroached upon the functions and liberties
of the Catholic Church in France, especially upon the freedom of religious education. In 1901 it banned numerous
religious associations and expelled their members from the
country. In 1905 it abrogated Napoleon's concordat with
the papacy, withdrew financial support from the clergy, and
confiscated all the property which the Church had acquired
since the Revolution. In taking these measures, the French
Government has been applauded by a large number of
anti-clericals of various shades of opinion: some thought
the measures needful for political reasons; others thought
them desirable for intellectual or cultural ends; still others
thought them useful for social and economic purposes. But
it is a fact that the outstanding protagonists of anti-clerical
legislation in France have been sterling French nationalists,

such as the revolutionary patriots themselves and, subsequently, MM. Guizot, Gambetta, Ferry, Buisson, Combes, Viviani, and Clemenceau. It is also a fact, though perhaps only a coincidence, that every weakening of the Catholic Church in France has been accompanied and followed by a strengthening of French nationalism.

In all traditionally Catholic countries, a similar anticlerical movement has produced similar results. As in France, during the past hundred years, so in Italy, in Spain, in Portugal, in Belgium, in Austria, and in the republics of Latin America, sometimes more and sometimes less, the Catholic Church has been deprived of rights and privileges, relations with the papacy have been interrupted or censored, ecclesiastical property has been declared to be the property of the nation, monks and nuns have been expelled, Catholic citizens have been discriminated against in election or appointment to public office and otherwise subjected to petty annoyance if not to persecution. That some of these evidences of intolerance have been justified by new needs of the several peoples, admits of little doubt. That in large part they have been both cause and result of rising nationalism, admits of no doubt. Certainly in Italy the papacy was attacked primarily as the foe of national unity, and Italian anti-clericalism since the days of Mazzini, Garibaldi, and Cavour down to the period of Sonnino, Orlando, D'Annunzio, and Mussolini, has been the vanguard of Italian nationalism.

In most Catholic countries Catholicism has been a national tradition too long and still has a hold too strong upon the masses to be routed immediately and utterly. In fact, groups of patriots have sought in all these countries to identify Catholicism with their particular brand of nationalism and to make it serve their political interests. Thus, in France, the Royalists of the last fifty years, who as a group have not been surpassed in nationalism by their Republican compatriots, have been staunch patrons of the Catholic Church, but, it must be added, the Catholic Church of their patronage is less the Universal Church than the Catholic Church of the French nation, the Gallican Church. In Italy, too, Signor Mussolini has latterly displayed a tendency to reckon the Catholic Church in Italy and the presence of the pope in Rome as assets rather than as liabilities of Italian nationalism. But here as elsewhere the favours extended by nationalists to the Catholic Church have much the same source and effect as the more prevalent intolerance; they spring from nationalist, rather than from Christian, conviction, and they are more advantageous and fruitful to nationalism than to Catholicism.

In a country such as Czechoslovakia, where the population is traditionally Catholic but where also there are traditions of a great though unsuccessful revolt against the papacy, nationalists never miss an opportunity to appreciate the old "martyred" heresy as a sacred national legacy and to deprecate the Catholic Church as an alien institution. The Honourable Thomas Masaryk, the first president and the "grand old man" of the Czechoslovakian Republic, has been an ardent nationalist and a determined exponent of *étatisme,* and, though an agnostic and "freethinker" in respect of Christianity and an avowed anticlerical, he has always expressed the utmost respect and veneration for Jan Hus and has lent the full strength of his Government and his personal prestige to the erection and fostering of a national Christian Church independent of Rome. The mere fact that the large majority of Czechs and Slovaks have remained in communion with Rome and have refused to join the national Church has not deterred the government from persevering in a campaign of persecution and intolerance against the Catholic Church.

In a country of which the population are fairly evenly divided in allegiance between Catholicism and some other form of Christianity, it is usually Catholicism which bears the brunt of nationalist intolerance. For example, although at least half of the German nationality and more than a third of the inhabitants of the German Empire are Catholic in faith and tradition, and although Catholic Germans have not been lacking in German patriotism, German unification was effected between 1866 and 1871 under a Government whose nationalism was of the Protestant persuasion. At once Bismarck and his colleagues, anxious to maintain and solidify national unity, took steps to subordinate the Catholic Church in Germany to the state. The so-called *Kulturkampf* resulted. The Government, with the aid of Protestants, anti-clericals, and nationalists, enacted a series of laws providing that no one should be appointed to office in the Catholic Church except a German citizen who had received his elementary and secondary education in a German public school, had studied for three years in a state university, and had passed a state examination in German history and German literature; ecclesiastical seminaries for boys were abolished, and all other training schools for priests were placed under the control of the state. The Catholic bishops in Germany, with the approval of the pope, condemned these laws and urged German Catholics not to obey them. Then the Government retaliated with sterner measures: any ecclesiastic guilty of disobeying the laws of the land might be deprived of his rights of citizenship and might be ordered to live in a particular district or be fined, imprisoned, or exiled; official relations with the papacy were broken off; no one might exercise ecclesiastical functions without governmental authorisation; certain religious orders, notably the Jesuits, were expelled; and, in case of continued recalcitrancy, financial support of the Catholic clergy was to be withheld. So drastic was the enforcement of these measures that within a single year six Catholic bishops were imprisoned and in over thirteen hundred parishes Catholic worship ceased. The bulk of German Catholics, however, rallied to the defence of the Church, and eventually the intolerant enactments of the *Kulturkampf* were repealed or allowed to fall into abeyance.

Nevertheless German Catholics continue to the present day to have ample proofs of an intolerant attitude towards them on the part of many of their fellow citizens and of intolerant activities on the part of various nationalist societies. Though German Catholics shared the patriotic emotion which swept all Germans into the Great War and though they did their bit in that herculean struggle, they have latterly been accused by no less a nationalist than General Ludendorff himself of being traitors to Germany and responsible for her defeat. The murder of the Catholic statesman, Herr Erzberger, was the crowning achievement of youthful nationalists inspired with an anti-Catholicism which equalled their anti-pacifism. In the electoral campaign between Dr. Marx and General Hindenburg for the presidency of the German Republic, Catholicism was as injurious to the one as nationalism was helpful to the other.

As Germany has witnessed the intolerance of Protestant nationalists toward their Catholic fellow citizens, so Yugoslavia today is witnessing the intolerance of Orthodox nationalists toward their Catholic compatriots. The present Yugoslavia is in reality an expansion of the kingdom of Serbia, which traditionally is Orthodox and which has long possessed a national Church, so as to include the whole Yugoslav nationality, large numbers of whom, in the former Austrian Empire, are Catholics. It is natural therefore that Serb nationalists should view their national Church as a monument and bulwark of the nationalism which must distinguish all Yugoslavs and that they should cooperate with such Slovenes and Croats as are more nationalist than Catholic to weaken the Catholic Church in Yugoslavia. Even now a *Kulturkampf* is impending in the Kingdom of the Serbs, Croats, and Slovenes.

However, it is in countries which are largely non-Catholic in religious affiliation or tradition but which have a considerable Catholic minority, that Catholics have suffered most from nationalist intolerance. In the Russia of the Tsars and in the Russia of the Bolshevists, Catholicism has been assailed as foreign and alien, as "Polish" or "Austrian," as the mask of "western" liberalism and democracy or as the tool of "western" capitalism and imperialism, and against Catholicism an endless succession of discriminatory and persecuting decrees have been promulgated. In the Rumania of the present day, the Orthodox Government and popular majority are displaying a marked intolerance in their treatment of the Protestant and especially of the Catholic minority of Transylvania; they are determined to "Rumanise" these minorities thoroughly, and "Rumanisation" involves logically the adoption of one faith for one people, the general acceptance of the national Orthodox Church of the majority of Rumanians.

In English-speaking countries, anti-Catholicism has long been a conspicuous plank in the platform of a particularly prevalent type of nationalism. Since the days of Queen Elisabeth it has been the feeling and inmost conviction of generation after generation of Englishmen, Scotsmen, and Americans that Catholics cannot be good citizens, and this feeling has found repeated expression not only in the penal laws of the seventeenth and eighteenth centuries but in the Gordon riots, the "no-popery" demonstrations, the activities of the British Kensitites, and the propaganda of a horde of American societies—the Know-Nothing Party, the American Protective Association, the Ku Klux Klan, *etc.* It is difficult, indeed impossible, for a fair-minded scholar to find in the history of the last three hundred years any occasion on which the Catholic minority among these nationalities have lagged behind their fellow citizens in the discharge of civic obligations; invariably they have willingly borne their proportionate part of losses of blood and treasure in the national wars of their respective countries. Yet today Catholics in England, Scotland, and the United States, though they are legally tolerated, are objects of popular suspicion, sometimes victims of social ostracism and political and educational discrimination, and always targets for vilification by professional itinerant lecturers and by cheap and widely circulated publications. Just as Britishers still think it important to retain the legal pre-

scription that their king, who has no power, shall be a
"faithful Protestant," so a sufficient number of Americans
can be counted on to unite at a moment's notice to prevent
the great powers of the presidency of the United States
from being wielded by a Catholic American.

Referring specially to anti-Catholic intolerance in the
United States, Professor Mecklin has recently observed:
"There are of course surface irritants such as the petty
jealousy and fear . . . for the power and prestige of the
Church of Rome, the reputed clannishness of the Catholics,
the charge of collusion between priest and politician to get
social control, and the alleged hostility of Catholics to the
public school. But deeper than all this lies the vague feeling that the centre of authority of the Roman Catholic
Church, as opposed to Protestantism, lies outside of and
superior to the American society . . . " [1] It is nationalism and nationalist dread of "divided allegiance" which
focus all the currents of anti-Catholic feeling and sentiment in the United States and Great Britain. It is iden-
tification of Protestantism with nationalism which makes
many a British and American Protestant the agent of an
intolerance which is anti-Catholic and above all nationalist.

4

Judaism, like certain forms of Christianity, has been an
object of nationalist intolerance in recent times. But the
explanation of the nationalist intolerance toward Jews is
somewhat different from that of the corresponding intolerance toward Christians. Judaism, unlike Christianity, is
essentially not a world religion; it is, in creed and code, in
origin and historic development, a tribal religion of the
Hebrew nationality. If most Hebrews had remained in
Palestine and there continued to the present day to constitute a fairly homogeneous population, speaking the
Hebrew language and adhering to Judaism, their tribal religion would fit in admirably with the contemporary nation-

[1] J. M. Mecklin, *The Ku Klux Klan* (1924), p. 158.

alist scheme of things throughout the world; by nationalists everywhere Judaism would today be recognised as
the national religion of the Hebrews in the same way and
with as little fuss as Shinto is recognised as the national
religion of the Japanese. The Hebrews, however, have
long since almost ceased to be a nationality; the vast majority have emigrated from Palestine, have found homes in
divers distant lands, have neglected or forgotten the Hebrew
language, and have learned the language and accepted the
nationality of the peoples with whom they have settled.
One thing and one thing only they have carried with them
whithersoever they have gone, and this thing is an attachment to, or at least a sentimental regard for, the religious
traditions of Judaism. Thus it has transpired, through the
dispersion of the Hebrews, that Judaism, whilst not strictly
a world religion, has become an international religion in
the sense that it provides a religious, cultural, and moral
background for influential minorities in a large number of
nationalities and national states.

Community of religion among widely dispersed Hebrews
long served to promote a peculiar clannishness among them
and to mark them off from neighbouring Christians and
Moslems. So long as the peoples among whom Jews formed
a religious minority, were fanatically Christian or Moslem,
the Jews, despite the preaching of tolerance in their behalf
by Catholic popes and Mohammedan caliphs, frequently
endured various kinds of popular persecution in the name
of religion, and therefore they chose or were obliged to in-
tensify their peculiar clannishness and to exist as a nationality within, but apart from, other nationalities. But with
the growth of religious tolerance, especially with the progress of the "enlightenment" and "humanitarianism" of the
eighteenth century, the persecution of Jews lessened. Hebrews came out of their ghettos and basked in the sun-
shine of "emancipation"; they entered into the public and
private life of the nationalities which emancipated and
adopted them. Gradually, in most instances, they ceased

to be "Hebrews" and became "Frenchmen," "Italians," "Englishmen," "Germans," even "Poles," "Russians," or "Americans." Most of them remained Jews in religion, at least formally, but in the days of the enlightenment religion was held to be a personal and very private affair.

Why shouldn't a Jew be just as good a citizen, just as much a patriot, of France, Italy, England, or Germany, as a Christian or an atheist? As a matter of fact his Jewish ancestors had resided in some of these countries longer than Christian ancestors of fellow citizens, and if patriotism meant love of native land then assuredly the Jew had every right in nature to be more patriotic about the land in which he was born than about the land in which his religion had its origin. Christians thought of Palestine as the Holy Land, but that didn't prevent them from paying superior homage to the sacred soil of their respective Fatherlands, of their several *Patries*.

So, in the nineteenth and twentieth centuries, Jews, as a rule, have become free citizens of the countries in which they live, indistinguishable in most respects from their fellow citizens. They are now nationals, sharing in national rights, intent upon national interests, and alert to national honour. Nor should it occasion surprise that prominent Jews have been prominent nationalists in France, Italy, England, Germany, the United States, and elsewhere. Jews, equally with other citizens of national states, have been subjected to the nationalist training of public schools, national armies, and "yellow" journals; their very emancipation has quickened their responsiveness to national stimuli of all sorts; and many of them have perceived in moderate nationalism a useful foil to earlier religious intolerance and in the national state the best and safest guarantee of their continuing emancipation. Time and again, in the past hundred years, Jews have coöperated actively with anticlerical Frenchmen and Italians or with Protestant Germans in combatting Catholicism and in strengthening the national state—and nationalism.

As Jews more and more have become integral parts of various modern nationalities, their international solidarity and clannishness have decreased. Nowadays they differ from one another enormously. Among them, as among other human beings, there are extremes of poverty and opulence, conservatism and radicalism, virtue and vice, literacy and illiteracy, genius and stupidity. They reflect the diverse environments in which they live, intellectually, culturally, and nationally. Among themselves, Spanish and Portuguese Jews patronise German Jews, and German Jews despise the Jews of Russia and Poland. They certainly have no racial unity; according to the most reliable anthropological evidence, they differ widely in physical type and tend in this respect, as in others, to approach the several peoples among whom they reside and of whom nationally they form a part.[1] Even in their religion they have no single central authority and differ among themselves all the way from Judaism of the orthodox synagogue and strict observance of the Mosaic law, through innumerable varieties of "reformed" Judaism, to "ethical culture" or the most advanced scepticism; a few have embraced Christian Science or Christian Unitarianism. From all of which it would appear that Jews are a mere religious sect, or congeries of sects, within the several organisations of modern nationalism, that there are Jewish Frenchmen or Jewish Germans in exactly the same way as there are Calvinist Frenchmen or Lutheran Germans.

[1] See especially the treatment of this subject by Professor Roland B. Dixon of Harvard University in his *Racial History of Man* (1923), pp. 162-175. Professor Dixon finds that the peculiar form of nose which is popularly denominated "Jewish" or "Semitic" is most prevalent among Spanish and Portuguese Jews, though it occurs among only about a third of these. He concludes: "If, as is possible, the northern Arabs or Bedouin of today are to be regarded as the best modern representatives, from the racial point of view, of the very early Semitic-speaking peoples of whom the original Hebrews were a part, then the great majority of all Jews today are 'Semites' only in speech, and their true ancestry goes back not so much to Palestine and Arabia as to the uplands of Anatolia and Armenia, the Caucasus and the steppes of Central Asia, and their nearest relatives are still to be found in those areas today."

Yet many a contemporary nationalist will not have it so. The Jews, despite their own disparities, despite their almost universal adoption of the nationality of their Gentile neighbours, despite their obvious devotion in many cases to nationalism, are still thought of as dissentient minorities, as a nationality scattered among other nationalities, as an impediment to complete and perfect nationalism. The rise of nationalism with its attendant intolerance has wrought this paradox. It has freed them in large degree from religious persecution but it has visited them with its own persecuting spirit. For the average nationalist is eager to safeguard his national state against any foreign influence whatsoever and to promote among its citizens uniformity not only of language but also of customs and ideas. Now the average Jew, whether he is "orthodox" or "reformed," "conservative" or "radical," is apt to associate with fellow Jews more than with other fellow citizens, to hold ideas and observe customs which have been transmitted to him from his Jewish ancestors and which are at variance with the customs and ideas of the dominant majority of any given nationality, and to entertain at least a sentimental regard for Hebrew traditions and for other Jews in different parts of the world. Consequently the average Jew is looked upon askance by the average nationalist, who sees in him an internationalist, a "foreigner," a discordant element in the national life and national economy.

Many are the charges which nationalists have brought against the Jews: that they are clannish; that they are cosmopolitan; that they are peculiarly unscrupulous capitalists; that they are particularly violent socialists; that they are cunning; that they are cowardly; that they serve in armies only to betray one country to another; that they are arch conspirators for the overthrow of modern civilisation; that, above all, they are not and cannot be sincere patriots or good citizens. Nationalists have also done much to give currency to popular notions that the Jews are a distinct and

separate "race"—the Semitic "race,"—that they possess
great international cohesion and solidarity, that they speak
a common semi-secret language, that they act as a unit
under the direction of some central authority, in a word,
that they are a nationality firmly resolved by fair means
or foul to build their national state upon the ruins of all
others. In pressing such charges and vulgarising such notions, nationalists have often found favour with persons
who were not rabidly nationalist but who for religious or
economic reasons had grievances real or fancied against
particular Jews. In France and Austria, for example, anti-
Jewish (anti-Semitic) movements have represented a temporary alliance of nationalism and Catholicism; in Prussia,
England, and the United States they have represented a
juncture of nationalism and Protestantism, and in Russia
and Rumania a working union of nationalism and Orthodoxy. In all these countries, too, economic considerations
have played a part in nationalist anti-Semitism.

Actual nationalist intolerance in respect of Jews has been
conspicuous during the past fifty years. In Russia and
Rumania it has taken the form of popular massacres—
pogroms—and of governmental action disqualifying them
from national citizenship, requiring them to live in special
areas, restricting their opportunities for education, forbid-
ding them to engage in certain occupations, and harassing
them in ways too numerous to recount. Generally it has
taken some form of social ostracism, discriminating against
them in business, in public office, in the teaching profession, in colleges and universities, in clubs and vacation-
resorts. Definite nationalist campaigns have been under-
taken against them, such as that in France associated with
the name of M. Édouard Drumont and with the Dreyfus
affair, or that in Austria patronised by Herr Lueger, the
late mayor of Vienna, and promoted by the "Christian
Socialists," or that in Germany presided over by Herr
Stöcker, the Evangelical court preacher to their gracious
Majesties, the First and Second Williams.

The spread of anti-Semitism in the latter part of the nineteenth century caused some Jews to grow sceptical of the possibility or desirability of Jewish assimilation in Gentile nationalities and to evolve a political nationalism for the Hebrew people. If their fellow citizens in existing national states were resolved to treat all Jews as a distinct and separate nationality, then they might as well accept the situation, confess that they were a nationality and not merely a religious sect, cease to seek absorption in other nationalities, and, by reviving the Hebrew language and Hebrew traditions, strive to foster among all Jews a consciousness of common Hebrew nationality, which should in time inspire a general exodus to Palestine and the erection there of a Hebrew national state. This was Zionism, which as a definite movement was founded by Dr. Theodore Herzl of Vienna in 1896, speedily championed by such distinguished Jewish litterateurs as Dr. Max Nordau and Mr. Israel Zangwill, and adhered to (in 1910) by over 300,000 Jews throughout Europe and America.

Zionism won a triumph in the midst of the Great War by securing from the British Government a formal declaration [1] that they "view with favour the establishment in Palestine of a National Home for the Jewish people and will use their best endeavours to facilitate the achievement of this object," and, with the aid of Arab blood and Jewish treasure, a British general did succeed in wresting Palestine from the Ottoman Empire. But the increasing immigration of Jews into Palestine after the war and the favours accorded them by the British Government through the Jewish High Commissioner aroused resentment among Arabs, who comprised the large majority of the inhabitants of Palestine and who were now becoming nationalist themselves, and elicited criticism from Christians and Moslems alike.

Only a small proportion of Jews throughout the world were vitally interested in Zionism, and the vast majority

[1] The so-called "Balfour Declaration," November 2, 1917.

showed no disposition to abandon the several countries of
which they were citizens and undertake an exodus to Palestine. Nevertheless, thanks to growing anti-Semitism and
resultant Zionism, Jews everywhere were developing a national consciousness of their own and thereby providing
some foundation for continued anti-Semitism. It would
appear as if Zionism, in its anxiety to counteract nationalist intolerance of anti-Semitism, was preaching ever more
zealously a Hebrew nationalism, which, in turn, would
prove to be intolerant itself and might accentuate the
intolerance of non-Hebrew nationalism in respect of the
Jews.

In any event, with the access of nationalism since the
Great War, anti-Semitism has become more pronounced
than ever. There have been popular outbreaks against
Jews in the newly unified national states of Rumania, Poland, Czechoslovakia, and Yugoslavia. General Ludendorff has recently coupled Jews with Catholics as authors
of Germany's misfortunes, and the Jewish statesman Rath-
enau was murdered by youthful German nationalists in
the same year as the Catholic Erzberger. The Fascisti
have lately linked Jews with Socialists as the would-be
subverters of Italy's national soul. In the United States,
Mr. Henry Ford and his *Dearborn Independent* have broken
loose against the Jews, and the Ku Klux Klan has made
heroic and extended efforts to save America from Jews as
well as from Catholics. Even in England, the reputed
haven of tolerance, the *London Post* has circulated most
virulent and inflammatory propaganda against the Jews.
To belong to a religious minority who have international
affiliations is likely to be disquieting in these days of rampant nationalism.

5

International religions have been by no means the only
objects of nationalist intolerance. Certain movements of
a social or economic nature, especially when they originate

in a foreign country and are embraced by minorities, have been pronounced unpatriotic and subversive of nationalism, and their followers have frequently been treated accordingly. Socialism, anarchism, and various other widespread manifestations of labour unrest in recent times have doubtless been opposed by great capitalists and a multitude of middle-class property owners primarily on economic grounds. But persons who have much to lose financially through the triumph of socialism or syndicalism have been able, by emphasising the alien and anti-national character of these movements, to enlist in their own defensive cause a very large number of fellow citizens who are stirred less by economics than by nationalism.

The sources of conflict between nationalism on the one hand and such social and economic movements as Marxian Socialism and Revolutionary Syndicalism on the other, are deep. These movements, so long as they are minority movements within a given nationality, are hypercritical of economic and social conditions within the nationality and are therefore hostile to the feeling of superiority inculcated by nationalism. To the nationalist it is axiomatic that his nationality has already attained to the utmost felicity compatible with human nature; he boasts of the economic conditions under which he lives as a necessary part of a highly beneficent system of national welfare; he rejoices that his country, as it is, is the country *par excellence* of golden opportunity for all; and he naturally resents the aspersions which radical orators and pamphleteers cast upon his country and his nationality and seeks to combat their insidious propaganda of social discontent.

Then, too, these movements, so long as they are minority movements, are inclined to oppose the existing political order, that is, the existing Government and the nationalist policies of the existing Government. It may, or it may not, be in accordance with Socialist principle for a national state to maintain armaments and to promote imperialism, but it has been characteristic of Socialist tactics for a Socialist minority to oppose the specific armaments and the specific imperialism of a Government which they were labouring to supplant. No wonder that nationalists charge Socialists with lack of patriotism; almost invariably during the past fifty years Socialist deputies in the legislative body of every national state have voted against increase of armies, against colonial enterprise, against tariffs and bounties and subsidies, against all those policies which to the nationalist are requisite for national interests, national rights, and national honour.

Besides, these radical social and economic movements are usually international in the sense that they have minority followings in several nationalities, some form of international organisation and coöperation, and some international programme of principles and ideals and tactics. Their members hold international congresses, help and encourage each other by advice and money across national frontiers, and, in general, speak and act outside of and above nationality. Their propaganda, moreover, is frequently carried forward among immigrants by persons who are themselves of alien birth or dissentient nationality; the prominence of migratory Jews among the founders and leaders as well as among the rank and file of Marxian Socialism has strengthened nationalist intolerance alike of Jew and of Socialist. Worst of all, their propaganda is directed chiefly at a particular class—the working class—throughout the world, regardless of nationality; both Socialists and Syndicalists preach social cleavage within every national state, and both employ the formulas of the Communist Manifesto of 1848—"workingmen have no country," "workingmen of all countries, unite!" No wonder that nationalists are scandalised and alarmed; no wonder that they perceive in the advance of these movements a grinding of nationalism between the upper and nether millstones of cosmopolitanism and class-warfare. The nationalist says that nationality is the unit of human society; the Socialist, that class is the unit. The nationalist affirms that the individual members of all classes within each nationality must work together in harmony; the Socialist, that the individual members of a single class in all nationalities must coöperate. The nationalist insists that international conflict is normal, and that the whole citizenry of every national state should be equally prepared for it; the Socialist, that normal conflict is inter-class, and that the workingmen of all national states must be exceptionally educated. The one would break the solidarity of the world's workingmen; the other would destroy the solidarity of every nationality and every national state. Between them there may be forced truces, but no real peace—and no real tolerance.

To guard itself against subversion every national state under nationalist influence has sought to curb Marxian Socialism, Revolutionary Syndicalism, and other radical economic and social movements. Everywhere laws have been enacted against revolutionary violence or threats of violence, and as a rule Socialists and Syndicalists and their kind have received harsher treatment than other criminals both from the populace and from national courts of justice. Frequently, too, even when violence has not been involved, national states have enacted laws restricting the activities and propaganda of radicals and directing the public teaching of principles and policies of a nationalist character in contradistinction to those of a Socialist or Syndicalist nature. Aside from positive governmental enactments, so strong is the nationalist popular reaction against the "reds" that few economic radicals, even if they are of the faintest shade of "pink," are tolerated as teachers in national schools or state universities, as officers in national armies or navies, or as writers for the national press.

In some countries especially active popular campaigns have been conducted by professional nationalists against "the radicals," and especially stringent legislation has sometimes resulted. In Tsarist Russia, nationalists were in the forefront of the foes of Bolshevism and other radical eco-

nomic movements, and the Government, with nationalist
backing, long employed its secret police and its terrorist
methods to ferret out and punish the apostles and disciples of Socialism and Anarchism.   In Bismarckian Germany, the nationalist *Kulturkampf* against the Catholic
Church was followed closely by the nationalist struggle
against Marxian Socialism; the anti-Socialist law of 1878
prohibited Socialist propaganda by means of books, newspapers, or public meetings, empowered the police to break
up meetings and suppress publications, and authorised the
arbitrary arrest and punishment of Socialist offenders.   In
certain of the United States, notably in the Empire
State of New York, not only has Socialist propaganda been
forbidden, but, more drastically than in Germany, duly
elected Socialists have been deprived of their seats in the
democratic legislature.

In some instances nationalists have sought to counteract
radical movements by making the welfare of the working
class a special concern of the national state.   This was
palpably the case in Imperial Germany; and much of the
social legislation which has been enacted by national states
during the past fifty years has been motivated by the nationalist ambition not only to establish the supremacy of
the national state in the economic and social sphere but
also to confound the Socialists and lessen the effectiveness
of their popular propaganda.

It must be said, in respect of economic radicals as in
respect of devotees of international religions, that their
conflict with nationalism has not been strikingly successful.   Nationalists enjoy several advantages over radicals:
membership in the national state is compulsory, whereas
membership in a Socialist Party or in the I. W. W. is voluntary; nationalism is more emotional and therefore more
widely influential than economics; the ordinary individual,
who for his own financial gain will shoulder a rifle with
reluctance, will fight with enthusiasm and to the last ditch
in behalf of a spiritual ideal; and, though many radicals

make of their radicalism a veritable religion and find in Marxian Socialism or in Revolutionary Syndicalism not so much a reasoned programme of economics as an emotional gospel and an idealistic "mission" quite as compelling as the mission and gospel of nationalism, numerous other radicals have been prone in times of stress and strain to hear the call of their nation above the call of their class and to sacrifice a more or less platonic internationalism to a very serviceable nationalism. In the last Great War, Socialists were hopelessly divided; only a minority, a pitifully small minority, remained absolutely true to their principles and refused to fight against their comrades in other countries; the Socialists, and all economic radicals, split mainly along national lines, and in most countries the large majority loyally supported their respective national Governments and dutifully participated in the slaughter of the national enemy. And individuals who lapsed from emotional radicalism to more emotional nationalism were not least among the nationalists who evinced intolerance in respect of pacifists and other radicals.

It is to be expected, moreover, that a radical social and economic movement, so soon as it ceases to be a mere minority opposition and becomes officially identified with a national state, will thenceforth adopt a nationalist spirit and win popular support by branding previous social and economic conditions as alien. Whatever may have been the decisive factors in bringing about the Russian Revolution of 1917 and setting up the Soviet Socialist Republic of Russia, there can be little doubt that the Bolshevists have remained in power because, *inter alia,* they have convinced the masses of the Russian people that Bolshevism is now a defence against foreign capitalism, alien imperialism, and "Western" exploitation. Certainly, the Bolshevists in power have shown themselves to be as intolerant of domestic dissent as were their Tsarist predecessors, as intolerantly devoted to what they conceive to be national rights, national interests, and national honour as are any nationalists in any country in the world. The effigies in the national pantheon have been changed—Lenin has supplanted Peter—but the Russian pantheon, under the Bolshevists as under the Tsars, is still nationalist. And, if anything, the intolerance of nationalism in Russia is more pronounced now than formerly.

Outside of Russia Bolshevists are not in power, and therefore outside of Russia the forces of nationalism have been mobilised against Bolshevism. In the United States, for example, sixty-one national organisations accepted in the spring of 1924 the invitation of the American Legion to be represented in an "All-American Conference" for "an aggressive fight to exterminate revolutionary and destructive radicalism." The conference met in Washington in the auditorium of the Interior Department of the National Government, and, according to a press despatch, its delegates, representing more than twenty million American patriots, adopted the following resolutions:

"1. Opposition to all forms of Soviet propaganda, whether in politics, in labour unions, in civic and social groups, in Government, or in schools and churches;

"2. Opposition to recognition of Soviet Russia by the United States Government;

"3. Congratulation of the American Federation of Labour upon its reaffirmation of opposition to anti-democratic and destructive radicalism;

"4. Refusal to regard America's entry into and conduct of the war as a debatable question, but sustaining that course as vigorously now as during the war, striking directly at such utterances as those contained in Congressman Berger's House resolution and Senator Shipstead's recent speech;

"5. Demand for unadulterated and undiluted American history in American schools, as opposed to the emasculated history which has been introduced so generally [!], robbing Americanism of much of its significance and robbing democracy of its most precious heritage;

"6. Rebuking the diplomatic representative of a friendly Power for a recent intrusion in a purely American political issue;

"7. Denouncing Senator Borah for abandoning the hearing on his resolution for recognition of the so-called Soviet Government and demanding that he continue the hearing indefinitely;

"8. Demand for immigration restriction in order to protect American institutions."

The list of organisations accrediting delegates to this "All-American" Soviet and presumably endorsing these resolutions is lengthy, but it is indicative of the various elements which can be brought together under the banner of nationalism to do battle with an "alien" movement of social and economic nature. Here is the list: "American Legion, American Federation of Labour, American Defense Society, American Library Association, American Women's Legion, Association of Newspaper Advertising Executives, Association of Military Surgeons of the United States, Better America Federation, Benevolent Protective Order of Elks, Descendants of the Signers of the Declaration [of Independence], Fraternal Order of Eagles, General Federation of Women's Clubs, Grand Army of the Republic, Hebrew Sheltering and Immigrant Aid Society, Knights of Columbus, League of Foreign-Born Citizens, Modern Woodmen of America, Motion Picture Producers and Distributers of America, National American Council, National American War Mothers, National Catholic Welfare Council, National Civic Federation, National Congress of Mothers and Parent-Teacher Associations, National Council of Catholic Women, National Education Association, National Geographic, National Grange, National League of Women Voters, National Society of Colonial Dames of America, National Society Daughters of the American Revolution, National Society of United States Daughters of 1812, National Women's Christian Temperance Union, Order of the Eastern Star, Disabled American Veterans, International

Committee of Young Men's Christian Associations, United
Confederate Veterans Association, United Daughters of the
Confederacy, and United States Chamber of Commerce." [1]

It is no purpose of the present study to apologise for
Bolshevism or to suggest that there were no rational
grounds for the action of the "All-American Conference."
We may grant that Bolshevism and Marxian Socialism and
Revolutionary Syndicalism possess the gravest defects, that
they lead to an enslaving rather than a freeing of the
human mind, that they represent a "progress" which is
backward rather than forward. Yet it is extremely doubtful whether the average nationalist, with his intense emotionalism, his tendency to substitute shibboleths for definitions, and his susceptibility to gusts of intolerance, is
markedly competent to understand all the movements
which are labelled "anti-national," to discriminate among
them, or to meet evil ones with reasoned arguments and
reasoned action. The suspicion lurks in our mind that
many an American nationalist who denounces Bolshevism
knows little or nothing about it and is only too ready to
classify as "Bolshevist" any person whom he detests or
any thing which he abhors. We may be pardoned for
harbouring another suspicion in this connection, that there
is something about nationalism which not only renders
its devotees very gullible about "alien" phenomena such
as Bolshevism but also insulates them most successfully
against any current of information or logic which might
enlighten them and render them less gullible. For example, they are told that Bolshevism is bad (which it may
be), that it is Socialism (which it is only in part), and
that it is spreading rapidly in the United States (which
lacks proof), and then, when they are told that Socialism
is un-American (which depends upon one's definition of
"Socialist" and of "American") and that a proposed child-
labour law is Socialist (which again depends upon definition), they jump to the conclusion that the law in ques-

[1] *New York Times,* May 17, 1924, p. 2, col. 2.

tion must be opposed because [!] America must be saved from Bolshevism. This they do with a noble enthusiasm and with a total disregard of "undistributed middles" and other *bêtes noirs* of the severe logician. And any American who ventures to explain exactly what Bolshevism is, to suggest reasons for its vogue in Russia, or to express doubt about its being a menace to the United States, is liable to be accused by nationalist fellow citizens of being a Bolshevist himself and as such of being an advocate of the immediate violent overthrow of the American nation, the American Government, and the American home.

Socialism, Anarchism, Bolshevism—these are three terrifying menaces to the average nationalist in most countries today. But there is another social movement, at least there is another word, which to the fanatical nationalist is as detestable, if not as dangerous, as the movements which aim at economic revolution. We mean pacifism, not so much the thing itself (for the mass of mankind, even the large majority of nationalists, say they desire peace) as the word. To the hundred per cent. nationalist the word pacifist sounds very sinister; it connotes a fellow citizen who criticises national interests and belittles national rights, who is strangely insensitive to national honour, who urges reduction of national armaments, and who, *terribile dictu,* excuses foreigners and even praises them. The word is constantly employed, moreover, for when one citizen calls another a "pacifist" he establishes forthright with nationalists his own reputation as a sane and sterling patriot and that of his adversary as a criminal, a lunatic, or a fool.

A similar type of intolerance is displayed occasionally by groups of nationalists here and there in respect of adherents to any international movement. International trade-unionism, international feminism, even international Freemasonry, have been objects of nationalist suspicion and denunciation. In the United States, advocates of the League of Nations have been accused of a desire to create a world organisation which will impair American sovereignty and prevent America from fulfilling her manifest destiny in Latin America and in the Far East; they have variously been denounced as "internationalists" and "pacifists."

6

Much has been said and written of late concerning "race." Some of it has scientific value, but a good deal of it, especially that part which has greatest vogue among ardent nationalists, is chiefly rubbish. We do know that there are hereditary physical differences between white men (Caucasians) and black men (Negroes) and yellow men (Mongolians), but no one knows positively what, if any, are the differences between these races in mental or spiritual capacity. We do know that Caucasians can be divided into round heads (Alpines), long-headed blonds (Nordics), and long-headed brunets (Mediterraneans), but no one can be certain that these "races" are "pure" or that one is superior to another in intellectual endowment. We do know that every nationality represents some degree of racial admixture, but it is an hypothesis rather than a proved fact that a particular racial mixture produces bigger and better brains than a different mixture. It is a mere assumption that the intelligence of a nationality is proportionate to its relative purity of race.

Now the nationalist who devours pseudo-scientific "racial" literature—which, at any rate in America, is put forth as profusely as breakfast-foods—finds that he and his nationality are suffering from a fearful kind of indigestion; and he usually accepts both the diagnosis and the prescription of his quack doctors. If he is advised that the majority of his fellow nationals are long-headed blonds, and particularly if he is a long-headed blond himself, he is favourably disposed to receive with the utmost composure the gratifying preliminary news that long-headed blonds are vastly superior, the world over, to all other humans in courage, in intelligence, in nobility of character, in body, mind, and soul. Then comes the blow. He is given the harrowing information that his ancestors in some past time, when they were blissfully ignorant of the indigestibility of "inferior races," admitted to his nationality and to his national state groups of blond or brunet round-heads and brunet long-heads, who, breeding like rabbits whilst the superior blond long-heads have been breeding like gentlemen, are now in a fair way to become a majority, to dilute hopelessly all the rich red blood of him and his kind, and thereby to reduce to the vanishing point the intelligence and courage of the whole nationality. What shall he do to save himself and to restore his nationality to health? Obviously, he must act on the advice of his doctors, and act quickly. He must first arouse to a full realisation of their awful plight all his fellow nationals who are lucky enough still to possess long heads and blond complexions, and then in conjunction with them he must take steps to expel the poisonous foreign bodies from the national organism, or, if it is too late to superinduce such drastic relief, at least to go on a diet, abstain from receiving other members of "inferior races," isolate those already with him, and abandon all attempts to digest them. The doctors, quacks though they may be about "race," are good psychologists; they gravely shake their heads, darkly hint at "only a fighting chance," and hold out almost no hope for a complete recovery; consequently, their services are in great demand and their patients, with gamblers' desperation, are resolved to stake everything upon winning the long uphill battle against national dyspepsia and that "run-down feeling."

Something can be said in defense of round-heads and brunets, and much has been said—especially by themselves. The average nationalist among a people who are predominantly Alpine, such as the Czechoslovaks, or among a people who are overwhelmingly Mediterranean, such as the Greeks, is not going to admit that his fellow countrymen are inferior to Nordic Swedes or Nordic Scots, no matter what pseudo-scientists may say or what Nordics may do.

He is going to evince some "pride of race" himself and to
maintain that his people have lived their glorious past
and arrived at their enviable present without the help of
any large quantity of Nordic blood. And when, as frequently occurs, a nationality is part Nordic and part Alpine
and Mediterranean, the latter elements are not inclined to
take kindly to Nordic assumptions or to Nordic demands
for national discrimination against them. In fact, they
show collectively no tendency to commit suicide or to emi-
grate; on the contrary, they are apt to go about their business, replenishing the land in their own way, and making
more and more inroads upon Nordic purity. Which excites
Nordic nationalists all the more.

Racial intolerance has been displayed by nationalists in
many places and under many guises. "Nordicism," under
one name or another, has been in evidence continuously
since the publication, in 1853-1855, of the Comte de Gobineau's fanciful work on "The Inequality of Human Races."
A prophet, as is well known, is not without honour save in
his own country, and to his fellow Frenchmen, who per-
versely came rather to like the idea that they were not
largely Nordic, the Comte's theory proved less acceptable
than to his neighbourly Germans, who were grateful to him
for providing them with a satisfactory racial basis for their
self-acknowledged supremacy. Many of the British, too,
fell gradually under the spell of the Teutonic, Nordic myth;
they explained away the dark hair and dark eyes of some of
their number and insisted that in themselves as a whole the
"Great Race" had flowered and fruited. Wherever Nordic
Britishers went, they carried with them the gospel of their
anointed race, to Australia, South Africa, Canada, and the
United States. But whereas in Britain the Nordicists assumed that the entire population was so predominantly
Nordic that it needed no legal protection against "inferior"
races, in English-speaking countries beyond the seas they
demanded and secured discriminatory legislation against
"lesser" breeds. As Mr. Madison Grant testifies in the pref-

ace to the fourth edition of his twentieth-century version of the Comte de Gobineau's Nordicism: " 'The Passing of the Great Race,' in its original form, was designed by the author to rouse his fellow Americans to the overwhelming importance of race and to the folly of the 'Melting Pot' theory, even at the expense of bitter controversy. This purpose has been accomplished thoroughly, and one of the most far-reaching effects of the doctrines enunciated in this volume and in the discussions that followed its publication was the decision of the Congress of the United States to adopt discriminatory and restrictive measures against the immigration of undesirable races and peoples." [1]

The measures to which Mr. Grant points with pride are the recent laws of the United States for the restriction of foreign immigration. These laws have been enacted for a variety of reasons, economic as well as nationalist and "racial"; and in so far as they provide that immigration from all foreign countries shall be restricted alike to a particular percentage or quota of the actual number of immigrants formerly coming from the several countries, they can hardly be termed discriminatory or inequitable. But the latest of these laws directs that the several quotas shall be computed not on the basis of the latest American census, that of 1920, but upon the census of 1890, and this is both discriminatory and in accordance with the intolerant preconceptions of certain American nationalists of "Nordic race." For the bulk of foreign immigrants into the United States prior to 1890 were from Britain, Germany, and Scandinavia—presumably Nordic countries—whereas the bulk of immigrants since 1890 have been from southern and eastern Europe, regions peopled mainly by Mediterraneans and Alpines; and thus, by taking the census of 1890 as the basis for the computation of quotas, the United States is now officially discriminating against "Alpines" and "Mediterraneans" and in favour of "Nordics." Australia, also, in response to "Nordic" nationalism, has similar restrictions on foreign immigration.

[1] *The Passing of the Great Race* (1921), p. xxviii.

Now it may be desirable and even needful for Australia, the United States, or any other national state to discriminate against one white foreigner in behalf of another, but to do so on "racial" grounds is bound to foster the pride of one "race" and to arouse the resentment of another "race."

The subject of race, moreover, is complicated by the popular tendency to think of every nationality as being a distinct "race." In common parlance the Germans as a whole are a "race," and so are the English, the Irish, the Italians, the Poles, and the Jews. This ignorant manner of speaking and thinking of modern nationalities produces many curious results, not least among which is a "racial" stimulation of nationalist intolerance. For example, because Jewish Americans or Italian Americans have some customs and manners which are different from those of Americans of British extraction, it is inferred by certain nationalists among the latter that Jewish or Italian peculiarities are racial peculiarities, that is, strictly hereditary, and, therefore, indelible, and that any attempt to "Americanise" Jews or Italians must inevitably fail. Sometimes it is explained that colorful fiestas, vengeful vendettas, and fondness for macaroni and chianti—attributes supposedly of all Italians —are the inevitable outcome of "Mediterranean" blood, predestined behaviour of long-headed brunets; more often, it is imagined merely that they are perennial marks of the Italian "race." Sometimes it is alleged that abstinence from pork and attendance at synagogue, sharpness in business dealings, and much show of jewelry and furs—imputed characteristics of all Jews—are irremediable consequences of "Semite" blood, necessary accompaniments of large noses; more often, it is said simply that they are inherent qualities of the Jewish "race." In other words, to certain American nationalists it appears that there is a taint in the blood of Italian and Jew, of "Mediterranean" and "Semite"; otherwise, these people would behave at once and altogether in conformity with the predilections of New England Puritans or Virginia planters.

No human being, at least in modern times, likes to have his ancestry impugned, and yet what many a "racial" nationalist does nowadays is to impugn the ancestry of a whole nationality or of an entire religious or linguistic group. Magyar nationalists have long proclaimed that they as members of a superior "race" were more or less divinely commissioned to dominate inferior Slav "races." German nationalists have called the French a decadent "race" and now style the Poles an infantile, irresponsible "race." English nationalists have expressed pity that among the Irish there should be a most degrading "Neanderthal" survival. The result of this calling of "racial" names is an intensification of nationalist intolerance in two directions. On the one hand, it increases international intolerance of one national state towards another, of Hungary towards Czechoslovakia and Yugoslavia, of Germany towards Poland, of England towards Ireland, and thereby helps to create a state of mind favourable to international war. On the other hand it increases domestic intolerance in any country which has dissentient national minorities, say the United States, where long settled peoples evince a hostile attitude towards more recent immigrants, and thereby create a situation conducive to civil strife.

If nationalists of one group of the white race show intolerance towards another group of the white race, how much the more will they show intolerance towards groups of the black and yellow races! If "Nordic" nationalists feel that their nationality cannot comfortably assimilate "Mediterraneans" and "Alpines," "Semites" and "Slavs," how much the less will they undertake to digest Japanese and Chinese and negroes! It is nothing new for an European to think of yellow and black men as being different from himself and to have some prejudice against them; but prior to the advent of modern nationalism obvious physical differences were generally viewed as interesting results of climate or curious freaks of nature, and the popular prejudice was not so great as to prevent in the New World a very considerable fusion of white emigrants, especially those from the traditionally Catholic countries of Portugal, Spain, and France, with red Indians, and even with blacks. The Dutch and English were a bit more fastidious throughout modern times, but it was only the nineteenth century—the century of rising, raging nationalism—which universally magnified racial prejudices and racial intolerances.

To this end, the institution of slavery unwittingly contributed, especially in respect of negroes. Human slavery is, of course, an extremely ancient phenomenon, and, historically, it has not necessarily involved an assumption on the part of slave-owners that they were superior to their slaves in body, mind, or soul. In ancient times white men were frequently enslaved by white men, and in Greece and Rome, for example, a slave class existed side by side with a free class of the same race and nationality. Slavery was then deemed a convenient economic outcome of victorious war rather than a mark of racial inferiority. In the middle ages, under Christian influence, white slavery practically disappeared from Europe; and in the eighteenth and nineteenth centuries many Europeans—and Americans— moved by humanitarian and ethical considerations, demanded the abolition of all forms and types of slavery. Then it was that owners of negro slaves fell back upon the arguments that even if a man might not enslave his brother-man, he was fully justified in enslaving men who were not his brothers, and that negroes were not brothers of white men; negroes were a race totally different from, and quite inferior to, the Caucasian race. Negro slavery was actually abolished by legislative means in most countries, by military means in the United States. But the arguments originally advanced by pseudo-anthropologists and appropriated by slave-owners in the first half of the nineteenth century, were seized upon by groups of nationalists and thereafter utilised as the basis for discrimination against negroes within a nationality.

Negroes in the West Indies and in the United States are

not "African" in nationality; they are "French" or "British" or "American," as the case may be, in the language they speak, in the religion and culture they know, and in the traditions they cherish. The ordinary negro of Virginia or Jamaica, quite as much as the white Virginian or the white Jamaican, would recognise at once that he was an "alien" in Timbuktu or on the Congo. For it must be remembered that American negroes as a whole are among the "oldest families" of the New World; no recent immigrants are they; they are now nothing if not American, and they have as good a title to America as most white men. But white nationalists in the United States, for instance, are determined to assure white supremacy within the American nationality, and so by means of political and civil discrimination, social ostracism, and occasional terrorism, black Americans are kept more or less distinct from white Americans, and the single American nationality is broken into two racial parts, the one white and superior, and the other black and inferior. Any mixture of white and black becomes instantly black and inferior. And any obstreperousness on the part of the "inferior" is usually visited by the "superior" with that kind of mob massacre described in America as lynching. It is extremely doubtful whether the number of Jews who suffered from mob violence during all the centuries of the middle age equals the number of American negroes who have been lynched by their fellow Americans of white race during the last half century.

Intolerance toward negroes in the United States is perhaps the acme of the racial intolerance of modern nationalism. But intolerance toward negroes is not so dangerous, at least in its international aspects, as intolerance of white nationalists toward Mongolians. The latter have certainly developed great cultures and civilisations, and they now possess in Japan a nationalist Great Power and in China a huge reservoir of numbers and resources. The "Yellow Peril," it is true, has been largely conjured up by white nationalists in Europe and America, but it may become something more than a bogey if white nationalists continue in America and in Australia to invoke it as an excuse for racial discrimination and intolerance. For a nationalism which has been communicated from the West to the Far East may carry in its train to the Far East the racial intolerance as well as the international war which have characterised it in the West.

7

There are few national states in the nationalist world of today which comprise one and only one homogeneous nationality. The presence of a dissentient nationality within the political orbit of a dominant nationality is attributable to one of three historical processes: (1) military conquest, the process by which long ago the Welsh were incorporated in the English national state, or that by which recently Germans of the Tyrol and Yugoslavs of Istria and Dalmatia have been brought under Italian sway; (2) protracted political connection, the process by which Bretons have become a part of France, or Catalans, of Spain; and (3) immigration and colonisation, the process best illustrated in the United States.

Now, regardless of how it originally came under alien sway, the tendency has been marked in recent times for a subject or dissident nationality to retain and develop some national consciousness of its own. In extreme cases, particularly in cases which are the result of military conquest, this tendency may lead to irredentism and rebellion. In such cases, national feeling begets nationalism, conscious solidarity is quickened, and discontent grows rife. Then it usually happens that ardent patriots among the majority nationality, frightened by the growth of dissident nationalism and fearful of irredentism, adopt an intolerant attitude toward the minority and endeavour by social pressure and legislative enactment to destroy its solidarity and stamp out its discontent. As a rule, however, such patriots by their intolerance succeed only in fanning the discontent and confirming the solidarity of the dissentient nationality. Thus is described in many instances a vicious widening circle of irredentism, intolerance, more intense irredentism, more intense intolerance, still more intense irredentism, *etc.*

Where immigrants of one nationality settle voluntarily among another nationality, as in the United States, the immigrants bring with them, of course, their own language and their national traditions and customs, which for a time may distinguish them sharply from the majority nationality among whom they have settled. In such a case, it has been observed that, so long as legal compulsion is not employed, dissident nationalities show a natural tendency to adopt the national language, traditions, and customs of the majority and, whilst retaining some vague sentimental attachment to the land of their origin, to become eager nationalists in support of the country of their adoption. In recent times, nevertheless, many nationalists of the dominant majority have been tempted by the burning faith within them to use compulsion on a dissident minority. They perceive the immediate advantages of a single language and a single tradition for commerce, industry, and journalism, for the public school system, for democratic uniformity, for the realisation of the ideal of complete national unity, and hence they grow impatient with the slow simmering of a mere social melting-pot. They suspect either that the melting-pot won't really melt or that the fine meat which they themselves put into it will be contaminated and spoilt by the refuse contributed by others. The outcome is likely to be, on the side of the majority nationality, an intolerant attitude toward "foreigners," almost invariably attended by legislative restrictions on immigration and naturalisation, and, on the side of the dissident nationality, an exaggerated clannishness, which, in turn, has a baneful influence upon the conduct of democratic politics.

Many have been the attempts to compel dissident nationalities to conform to the nationalism of the dominant majority. Germans between 1871 and 1914 pursued fairly systematically a policy of Germanising dissentient Poles, Danes, and Alsatians: they forced the use of the German language in the schools and even in religious instruction; they expropriated agricultural land from dissident nationals and assigned it to German colonists; they discriminated in favour of Germans in civil and military services. This "Germanisation" or "Prussianisation" was paralleled in other countries by a "Magyarisation," by a "Russification," by an "Ottomanisation," *etc.*; and the "Americanisation" which has recently been much in evidence in the United States, if not employing all the methods of "Prussianisa-tion," sets itself a similar goal. At its best, it may produce beneficent results; at its worst, it is fanatical nationalist intolerance whose ultimate fruits are domestic strife and foreign war.

8

There are many shades and degrees of nationalist intol-erance. In times of great international war, in times of mod-ern nationalist crusading, the populace of one belligerent national state vies as a whole with the populace of another in mutual intolerance. In times of "peace," the educa-tional processes of the several national states serve to imbue entire nationalities with at least a latent hostility to everything that is "foreign" or "alien."

But while most citizens of a national state, regardless of politics, economics, race, and religion, are patriotic, while they think of themselves as "good citizens," express will-ingness to defend their country to the last drop of their blood, and on occasion evince a collective intolerance toward citizens of other national states, a certain select num-ber of citizens commonly claim for themselves a superior patriotism, a paramount nationalism. These citizens are not content with unity of national action in time of war; they must secure in time of peace unity of national word and thought and usage, and the unity at which they aim involves, of course, the adoption of their particular and peculiar brand of nationalism by all their fellow citizens. If the adoption is not voluntary, then it must be compulsory, for to the minds of these "hundred per cent." patriots no latitude is allowable within a nation for differences of language, religion, race, or historic traditions; all must be one as they are one. This is the nationalist intolerance which gathers up all other intolerances of modern times and provokes domestic discord and strife. And against it, true patriotism—as patriotism has ordinarily been defined—is no proof.

In Germany, for instance, there are groups of citizens who are convinced not only that High German is the national language and that the German Empire is the national state, but also that the Nordic race is the national race, Protestantism the national religion, and individualism the basis of national economics, and who cannot understand how a round-headed person or a Catholic or a Jew or a Socialist can possibly be a real German and patriotic fellow citizen. It doesn't matter at all that German Socialists and German Jews and German Catholics and German "Alpines" love their native land, proclaim their patriotism to the Fatherland, and fight and die in Germany's battles. Hardly is the Great War over, when General Ludendorff becomes the mouthpiece of an influential nationalist sect in Germany and delivers philippics not only against all Frenchmen and all Poles, but also against such fellow Germans as differ a bit from the General in head-shape, dogmatic theology, or political economy.

A similar nationalist sect flourishes in the United States. Its members do not specialise in intolerance; they are broadly and comprehensively intolerant of all fellow Americans who dissent from them in economics, theology, tradition, and race. These American sectarians are, or think they are, the exclusive heirs and divinely designated custodians of particular traditions of the white Nordic race, of the British stock, of evangelical Protestantism, of Plymouth Rock, of the Declaration of Independence, of individual

liberty, of the public schools, and of "manifest destiny."
They are always vocal and sometimes violent. They speak
from pulpit and platform. They publish innumerable
pamphlets and periodicals. They form secret societies. They
penetrate American life, public and private. They invade
politics, the army, and education. They are resolved to
make of America a white country, a Nordic country, an
English-speaking country, a Protestant country. They
inveigh unceasingly and indiscriminately against negroes,
Catholics, Jews, Socialists, Italians, Slavs, Japanese, Chinese, and any other category, foreign or domestic, that
they deem to be different in any respect from themselves and, therefore, inimical to their conception of
American nationalism.

Examples of the intemperance and intolerance of ultra-
nationalists in any modern national state may be cited *ad
nauseam*. One will be quite sufficient for us. It is a single
issue of a semi-monthly publication widely circulated in the
United States, containing, among much else of a similar
nature, the following statements:

"The essential Nordic, Anglo-Saxon origin of American
ideals and institutions today compels recognition. Lief
Ericson, the Discoverer, in 1000; the Pilgrim Fathers and
Mothers, of 1620; the Colonial Founders, of 1776, were
Nordics. Latinism, Romanism, Columbianism, is an alien
enemy invader."

"Japanese do not belong here, cannot dictate our laws,
can never become part of us, must be excluded entirely and
those here must be deported."

"We declare, in Christ's name, that under our American
law no Roman Catholic can hold office in America or exercise the rights of American citizenship, because of his allegiance to a foreign potentate—the pope of Rome."

"Because America is today *the only truly Christian* nation, whose standards shall eventually govern all of Anglo-
Saxondom; because real Americans hunger after righteous-
ness; because America is the place where prophecy is
being fulfilled, through Christ's second coming—for these
reasons, the Jews . . . and the Roman Catholics . . . can

no longer remain here. The defenders of America know that this is Christ's land, and that he, through his people, will drive all aliens from our shores." [1]

Let us grant quickly that such propaganda makes little headway among intelligent and well-informed persons in America or elsewhere. The fact remains, however, that in the present age in every national state there are large numbers of persons who, because they have learned to read but not to think, are potential dupes of any propaganda, especially of propaganda in the name of patriotism and nationalism. The unthinking masses who are told only fine things about their own country and are largely kept in ignorance of fine things about other countries and other peoples, are likely to be as proud and boastful—and as intolerant—as they are ignorant. And it is relatively easy to sway intolerant and boastful and ignorant persons to the support of that type of extreme nationalism which is advocated and propagated by self-styled "hundred per cent." patriots.

Such propaganda within each national state is a natural outcome of boastful, intolerant nationalism in general, but it frequently has the curious effect of defeating its own object. Instead of inculcating in all citizens of a given country a common respect for all good and fruitful elements of national life and national aspiration, it exaggerates differences and gives rise to an amazing and alarming growth of special group-loyalties, not only among the original assailants, but contrariwise among those assailed. For example, in the United States, the group who sponsor "white, Gentile, Protestant" Americanism, are stirring up several other Americanisms—a negro Americanism, a Jewish Americanism, a Catholic Americanism, an Italian Americanism, an Irish Americanism, *etc.* Growing intolerance towards negroes has done much of late to evoke something resembling a negro nationalism. Mounting intolerance toward Jews and Catholics and toward minority nationalities, promises to strengthen, rather than to weaken, the solidarity and

[1] *The American Standard,* vol. i, no. 8, April 15, 1924.

clannishness of each of these groups. And each of these groups in the United States is becoming more and more insistent that it stands for the purest, best Americanism. Anyone who knows aught of the school-system of the United States knows with what pertinacity every religious group and every racial group and every sub-national group contends with others for official recognition of its distinctive status as "American." The time may come when, by the spirited stirrings of ultra-nationalists, the American melting-pot will be a seething cauldron of fiery nonfusible nationalisms.

If nationalism proceeds unchecked and proud and intolerant, it is bound to produce ever uglier domestic strife. It is already clear that individual liberty and the tolerance which springs from humility and sweet reasonableness are rapidly declining in every country that nourishes nationalism.

VIII

NATIONALISM—CURSE OR BLESSING?

1

IT MAY appear to some who have followed the argument of the preceding essays that the present title is superfluous, that from what has already been said the conclusion must now be drawn that nationalism is to the human race a curse, and nothing but a curse. On the other hand, it may seem to some critically minded persons that the nationalism hereby cursed is merely a fanciful caricature of a true and real nationalism which to humanity in its present stage of development is not a curse but a blessing.

Regarding the latter point, let us frankly acknowledge that much depends upon the definition of terms. We are fully conscious that despite an earnest effort to speak with precision and to avoid ambiguity we ourselves have been using the word nationalism to indicate two quite different things. We have employed it to denote an actual historical process, the process of establishing nationalities as political units, of building out of tribes and empires the modern institution of the national state. We have also employed the same word to describe a contemporary popular belief, the belief that one's own nationality or national state has such intrinsic worth and excellence as to require one to be loyal to it above every other thing and particularly to bestow upon it what amounts to supreme religious worship.

Whether nationalism *as a process* is a curse or a blessing, we have no stomach to declare. We have read enough history to make us timid, if not humble, about passing moral judgement or basing philosophic speculation on great and long continued historic processes. Nationalism as an his-

toric process has been great and long continued, and to regret and condemn it would be for us purely academic di-
versions; we couldn't undo it if we would; we certainly
couldn't refashion all those multitudinous factors, personal
and social, economic and political, religious and cultural,
which during many centuries now past recall have transformed city-states and feudal states and imperial states
into national states. Nationalism of this sort is not a proper
subject of praise or blame; it is simply a fact, and a fact as
little deserving of benediction or anathema as the fact that
man has two legs or the fact that the earth revolves about
the sun.

But nationalism *as a belief* belongs to another category.
To every thoughtful person, save only the unqualified fatalist, it is as fitting to criticise nationalism of this kind as to
criticise any other popular creed, say Christianity or Socialism or Liberalism; it is important for our generation and
for that which follows us that we should judge all living
growing trees by their fruit, and that if to our taste any
tree brings forth evil fruit we should attempt to cut down
or at least to engraft good fruit upon that tree. It is nationalism as a popular contemporary belief concerning which
we would put the question, is it curse or is it blessing? And,
reverting to the first sentence of this essay, we would unhesitatingly affirm that, judged by its fruitage of intolerance, militarism, and war, nationalism as the belief which
we have indicated is evil and should be cursed—and cured.

It is possible, of course, to use the word nationalism, as
some writers have used it, to indicate "wholesome national
patriotism" and to describe certain precepts and practices of
national life which do not incite to war or militarism or
intolerance. But let us not dodge the issue by verbal quib-
bling. Grant that there is a rampant, blatant nationalism
which produces evil fruitage and which is a curse, and it will
gladly be conceded that there may be a sweet amiable nationalism which will bring forth good fruit in abundance
and will be to all men a solace and a blessing.

Though we shall persistently plead "not guilty," and always with a clear conscience, to any charge that we have "caricatured" nationalism, we are ready to admit that in our exposition of the faith and works of nationalism we have hitherto been concerned almost exclusively with its evil side. It is only fair and just that before bringing our study to a close we should ask ourselves if nationalism has, or can acquire, a good side? Even if the nationalism hitherto discussed is a curse, may it not be reformed and rendered a blessing?

2

Whether we like it or not, some form of nationalism is likely to continue indefinitely. Present-day nationalism, as we have been at some pains to explain, is a novel and recent phenomenon, but its roots reach far back into the past. One vital element in it—the element of nationality—is coextensive with man's habitat and is older than any written records. Primitive tribes were nationalities; ancient city-states developed within nationalities; ancient empires included nationalities; mediaeval cultural areas embraced nationalities; modern states have been built of nationalities. Nationality and some degree of national consciousness have been, in man's experience, ubiquitous and universal, and, having been so, they will in all probability continue so to be. For nationality and national consciousness are aspects of gregariousness, an instinct or complex of instincts natural to man and continuously efficacious with him. Gregariousness, like any instinct, can be controlled and directed, but it cannot be suppressed; and though gregariousness by nationality might conceivably be transmuted into gregariousness by class or by race, such an event is highly improbable.

Nationality has been for centuries upon centuries too constant and consistent an expression of man's gregariousness to make us optimistic about our chances of substituting for it in the twentieth century *anno Domini* some other

form of gregariousness. It is freighted with too precious a
cargo of popular feeling and desires and sentiments. "The
fact remains," as Professor van Gennep has indicated, "that
in our days a certain combination of ideas, sentiments, and
wishes constitutes a special phenomenon which we call
nationality and that this phenomenon cannot be eliminated
by any argument whatsoever or by any procedure whatsoever, not even by economic pleas and achievements. Direct
observation proves that, free choice being assured and material conditions being normal, economic interest is subordinated to sentiment. It is true of nationality as of love;
sentiment comes first, and it is only after a blow that one
tries to reason about it. . . . It is only on the excrescences
of nationality that conscious control can be exerted." [1]

According to most contemporary students of the subject,
national consciousness is not only natural and instinctive
but valuable and useful, and should be fostered rather than
repressed. We shouldn't wish to get rid of it, even if we
could. In the words of Mr. John Oakesmith, national patriotism "is not only explicable as a national sentiment, but
justifiable as a reasonable faith." [2] The numerous champions of nationality and national consciousness advance two
major arguments in support of their position, first, that
nationality possesses great spiritual value in that it is a
safeguard against materialistic cosmopolitanism, and, secondly, that nationality possesses high cultural value. The
most eloquent and convincing exponent of the first point
is undoubtedly Mr. Alfred Zimmern, and we may properly
set forth his argument in his own words:

"Nationality, in fact, rightly regarded, is not a political
but an educational conception. It is a safeguard of self-
respect against the insidious onslaughts of materialistic
cosmopolitanism. It is the sling in the hands of weak un-

[1] A. van Gennep, *Traité Comparatif des Nationalités*, vol. i (1922),
pp. 12-13. The translation is not literal. It has been adapted to our
present purposes but without doing injustice, we believe, to Professor
van Gennep's thought.

[2] *Race and Nationality* (1919), p. 116.

developed peoples against the Goliath of material progress.
. . . The vice of nationalism is jingoism, and there are always good Liberals amongst us ready to point a warning finger against its manifestations. The vice of internationalism is decadence and the complete eclipse of personality, ending in a type of character and social life which good Conservatives instinctively detest, but have seldom sufficient patience to describe. Fortunately we possess in Sir Mark Sykes a political writer who has the gift of clothing his aversions in picturesque descriptive writing, and in his books on the Near East English readers can find some of the best examples (which might be paralleled from other continents, not least from America) of the spiritual degradation which befalls men who have pursued 'Progress' and cosmopolitanism and lost contact with their own national spiritual heritage. . . . No task is more urgent among backward and weaker peoples than the wise fostering of nationality and the maintenance of national traditions and corporate life as a school of character and self-respect." [1]

"It is for this problem of the man without roots that nationality provides a solution. Nationality is the one social force capable of maintaining, for these people, their links with the past and keeping alive in them that spark of the higher life and that irreplaceable sentiment of self-respect without which all professions of fine ideals are but as sounding brass or a tinkling cymbal. It is the one force capable of doing so, because it is the one force whose appeal is instinctive and universal. . . . Nationality is more than a creed or a doctrine or a code of conduct, it is an instinctive attachment; it recalls an atmosphere of precious memories, of vanished parents and friends, of old custom, of reverence, of home, and a sense of the brief span of human life as a link between immemorial generations, spreading backwards and forwards. 'Men may change their clothes, their politics, their wives, their religions, their philosophies,' says a Jewish-American writer, 'they cannot change their grandfathers.

[1] A. E. Zimmern, *Nationality and Government* (1919), pp. 53-54.

Jews or Poles or Anglo-Saxons, in order to cease being Jews or Poles or Anglo-Saxons, would have to cease to be.' " [1] It is Mr. Zimmern's conclusion "that the road to internationalism lies through nationalism, not through levelling men down to a grey indistinct cosmopolitanism, but by appealing to the best elements in the corporate inheritance of each nation." [2]

Perhaps another way of putting the argument in behalf of nationality as a safeguard against spiritual degradation would be to say simply that "charity begins at home." We have reason to distrust the person who loves man in general and despises individual men, who prates so much about his duties to humanity that he has no time to serve his next-door neighbour. Nationality may well be a sufficiently definite, limited field in which the individual can school himself in the exercise of those virtues which are directly serviceable to his immediate fellows, but which in the long run inure to the advantage of the race. Likewise it may well be, as Mr. Zimmern has intimated, that nationality is a spiritual protection against material aggression, that more and more as time goes on it will inspire and enable so-called "backward" peoples to put an end to the economic exploitation from which they suffer, and will eventually save the whole world from being turned into a cockpit for capital and labour.

On the cultural value of nationality a vast deal has been written during the last hundred years. Much of it is over-drawn and exaggerated. Litterateurs and even scholars frequently fall into the error of ascribing to nationality the formation of a distinctive culture which could more

---

[1] A. E. Zimmern, "True and False Nationalism," *op. cit.*, pp. 77-78. The quotation he gives is from an essay by Mr. Horace M. Kallen, "Democracy versus the Melting Pot," New York *Nation*, vol. c, p. 220 (Feb. 25, 1915). The same theme has been developed at length and with all the clear beauty of which French prose is capable in the writings of Maurice Barrès. See especially *Les Deracinés* (1897), *Scènes et Doctrines du Nationalisme* (1902), *Les Amitiés Françaises* (1903), *Colette Baudoche* (1909), *Le Génie du Rhin* (1921).

[2] A. E. Zimmern, *op. cit.*, p. 85.

properly be attributed to the influence of an international religion or to a cosmopolitan revolution in the industrial arts. But after making due allowance for error and exaggeration, we must yet acknowledge that nationality has been throughout the ages a great conserver of human differences in architecture, in literature, in the plastic and pictorial arts, in music, in dancing, in all aesthetic manifestations of man's civilisation, and also in modes of thought which enrich his being and in customs and manners which embellish his life. To the common store of the world's civilisation, the several self-conscious nationalities undoubtedly have made, and are still making, significant special contributions; undoubtedly, too, the common store of the world's culture is all the larger by reason of past and present cultural competition among the contributing nationalities.

Besides, some of us like differences and contrasts, and I, for one, sympathise cordially with those who rebel at the prospect of a drab uniformity of manners, customs, and arts from New York to Singapore, and from Helsingfors to Valparaiso. I do not look forward with pleasure to seeing each mark of civilisation to which I am accustomed at home photographically reproduced in every town in France, Holland, Russia, Turkey, India, Abyssinia, and Japan. I have no fancy for absolute uniformity, and if it is a question between uniformity and what some cosmopolitan businessmen of the present age term "inefficiency," my suffrage can be counted on the side of inefficiency. More than ever today, when the Industrial Revolution is devastating localism everywhere, and piling up the same sort of brick and steel girder in Asia and Africa as in Europe and America, when hotels the world over serve in the same way from *hors d'oeuvres* to coffee the same kind of dinner, when men universally array themselves in like ugly habilaments, at this very time it is a comfort that nationality still endures and still performs its delightful and wholesome function of encouraging at least minor differences in civilisation and culture.

In the light of the cultural and spiritual worth of nationality as well as in the light of its instinctive and universal
character, it would seem not only utopian and idle but
downright wrong-headed and mistaken to advocate a super-
session of nationality by cosmopolitanism or imperialism.
Some type of internationalism may be desirable and obtain-
able, but we shall be reasonable and practical if we accept
the dictum of the friends of nationality and construct our
internationalism of the future from the building-blocks
of existing nationalities and even of existing nationalisms.

The qualities and the nature of nationality constitute
one reason why some form of nationalism is likely to continue indefinitely.   Another reason is the contemporary
vigour of the political institution of the national state. This
institution, unlike national consciousness, is neither instinctive nor eternal.   It is mainly an invention of modern times, a fashion preëminently of recent times. So episod-
ical is it in the whole complicated history of the human
race that we cannot affirm with the same degree of conviction of it as of nationality that it will last so long as human
nature remains unchanged.   But what the national state
of the present age lacks in the way of roots reaching far
back into history and deep down into human nature, it
compensates for in the wide spread of its branches and the
rich greenness of its foliage.   So sturdy has grown of late
the national state that none can fell it in a day.   And we
now live so completely under its shadow that perhaps none
will wish to fell it.

The factors which have evolved the national state are
still operative; the conveniences and the benefits of political
unity for a people who speak a common language are still
manifest.   It is certainly both a convenience and a benefit for each government to transact its business in a single
language, and it is difficult to perceive how political democracy, upon which we have set our hearts, can be conducted
most advantageously in a country of many and varied nationalities.   The old Habsburg Empire, as it existed down

to 1918, was an eloquent witness to the incompatibility of political democracy and national disunion. Nor is it easy to imagine how universal formal education, to which equally with political democracy we now pin our faith, can be expeditiously assured in a polyglot empire. To realise the contemporary ideals of universal literacy and popular sovereignty, the national state is far better adapted than any other political institution which the world has ever known.

Another source of strength to the modern national state inheres in economic circumstance. It has been the rising national state which has most fully exploited the commercial and financial revolutions of the sixteenth century and the industrial revolution of more recent times, and to-day the average manufacturer, trader, banker, farmer, and workingman looks to the national state for economic guidance and control. It may be that eventually the international, even the cosmopolitan, aspects of modern industrialism will come to predominate over its national aspects and that world-wide economics will then outgrow and slough a political institution so confining and cramping as the national state, but to me at least such a development seems remote. The contemporary labour movement is not cosmopolitan, and it is international only in a platonic sense; in thought and deed it is fundamentally national. Even Marxian Socialism, despite its international programme and its cosmopolitan slogans, is essentially national: it propagates its doctrine within the framework of the national state; it coöperates with nationalists in the destruction of imperial states; and when it ascends to political power, as in Russia, it exalts, rather than abases, the national state. Bolshevist Russia furnishes but a recent and extreme instance of that *étatisme* which, following the national state, has gloriously magnified it. Not alone to the popular education and political democracy of today is the national state of indispensable service, but likewise to the socialising tendencies and economic egalitarianism of tomorrow.

Moreover, it is on the national state that in recent times

all sorts of patriotism have focussed. Patriotism of some kind or variety has been a mark of human beings from prehistoric times. It has always been an emotional factor of great force and strength. It is, in truth, an aspect of loyalty, an aspect of that prized attribute of man which facilitates his gregariousness and socialises his life and being. Normal man has always been, and doubtless always will be, loyal to something or somebody outside of himself. Patriotism, like sex, is liable to abuse, but it is needful to the life of the race and it is capable of inspiring the finest sentiments and the noblest deeds.

That this great vital and emotional force of patriotism should *in toto* have been appropriated in modern times by the national state, is at once a tribute to the current attraction of the national state and an augury of its future potency. National patriotism may be more artificial than local patriotism; it may require a tremendous stretch of the imagination to love as one's native land a region three thousand miles distant from the place of one's nativity. But apparently the modern imagination can be stretched enormously, and artificiality is no final proof against effectiveness. The fact obtrudes that love of country now means love of all lands subjected to the national state, that love of one's government now denotes love of the government of one's national state, that love of one's countrymen now signifies love of all one's fellow citizens in the national state. In a word patriotism in our day has become synonymous with devotion to nationality and the national state. This consummation of patriotism is the ultimate evidence that nationalism cannot, if it should, be forthwith abolished, and that, on the contrary, some form of nationalism will continue indefinitely in the future.

3

Nationalism is too firmly entrenched in the primitive popular principle of nationality and in the powerful political organisation of the modern national state to be dislodged immediately or routed utterly. Yet, unless we look forward with equanimity to a worsened world, we shall eagerly desire some mitigation of nationalism. For in present-day nationalism there are grave abuses which, unless they are removed or remedied, will almost certainly plunge the several nationalities and the several national states into madness and ruin.

That there are evils in nationalism has been recognised by numerous critics. Lecky and Lord Acton, both brought up in the traditions of Liberalism and both writing in the third quarter of the nineteenth century, were conspicuous apologists for the beneficent civilising influence of an expansive imperial state and fearful of the "little mindedness" and intolerance which would result from a world broken up into fragmentary national states; if the one was moved mainly by dread of a nationalist disintegration of the British Empire, the other was actuated primarily by the threat of nationalism against the Austrian Empire; both viewed nationalism as a dangerous and destructive principle which would make empire impossible, reduce government to an absurdity, and end in general chaos. By most Liberals nowadays, however, other evils are emphasised, including some which are diametrically opposed to those detected by Acton and Lecky. It is now not the weakening of government but the undue strengthening of government which is most apprehended, not the ending but the begetting of imperialism, not chaos in general so much as a series of international wars, highly organised, highly efficient, and progressively more destructive.

Contemporary critics who perceive these evils in the whole complex which we have labelled nationalism, do not agree, nevertheless, as to the exact part of the complex with which the evils are chiefly associated. Mr. Sydney Brooks thinks that war—the greatest curse of nationalism—is the result of the union of nationality and patriotism. "Patriotism or nationality," he says, "was never a more stubborn or more jealous fact than it is today. . . . To those who believe in and dream of and work for a coming time of universal peace, I would say, 'Nationality, there is the enemy.' . . . [There is] a fundamental antinomy between peace and patriotism. . . . Universal peace may come as the result of a world-wide despotism, through the undermining and destruction of the sentiment of nationality, and the substitution therefor of a patriotism coëxistent with humanity, or by means of a transformation in the moral values, judgements, and instincts of mankind; but in no other way." [1] Mr. John Oakesmith, on the other hand, maintains that "it is a flagrant abuse of terms to say that nationality is the cause of war; it is diseased and corrupted nationality. It is pride, ambition, selfishness, inordinate lust of power. The so-called antinomy between peace and patriotism does not exist; what does exist is the eternal antinomy between passion and self-control, between madness and sanity, between wisdom and folly." [2]

Contrary to Mr. Oakesmith and yet somewhat different from Mr. Brooks, Mr. J. M. Robertson and Mr. Norman Angell have argued that the sentiment of nationality lies at the root of all international animosities, the one claiming that the sentiment is a mere hallucination and the other that it is an uncontrolled irrational instinct. Mr. Thorstein Veblen and Mr. J. A. Hobson have connected national patriotism with the economic causes of war, suggesting that it is utilised as a kind of idealistic camouflage for the advancement of economic imperialism and for the promotion of selfish interests of particular classes and persons.

Mr. Zimmern, however, applauds the sentiment of na-

[1] "The Dream of Universal Peace," *Harper's Monthly Magazine*, vol. cxxxiii, pp. 862-869 (November, 1916). *Cf.* also, in this connection, John Oakesmith, *Race and Nationality* (1919), pp. 261-269; J. M. Robertson, *Patriotism and Empire* (1899), and *Evolution of States* (1912); Norman Angell, *The Great Illusion* (1914); Thorstein Veblen, *An Inquiry into the Nature of Peace* (1916); J. A. Hobson, "The Open Door," *Towards a Lasting Settlement,* ed. by C. R. Buxton (1916); A. E. Zimmern, *Nationality and Government* (1919); J. L. Stocks, *Patriotism and the Super-State* (1920), pp. 62-69; G. L. Dickinson, "The Basis of Permanent Peace," *Towards a Lasting Settlement,* ed. by C. R. Buxton (1916).

[2] *Op. cit.,* p. 269.

tionality and extolls a certain type of national patriotism and then proceeds to contend that nationality is a safe and sane principle only if it is wholly divorced from the state and restricted to the social and educational sphere. Mr. J. L. Stocks, after pointing out that Mr. Zimmern writes as a Jew, with the problems of the Jew in mind, adds, "After all, the Irishman and the Indian get more comfort from Mill and Mazzini than from Marx and Professor Zimmern. The sober nationalism of Jaurès did more to hinder the European war than the theoretic anti-nationalism of the German socialists. If our states are too large, let us try to make them smaller; if they are too proud, let us try to prick their pride. But nothing will be gained by any attempt to ignore the truth asserted by the nationalist, that political boundaries must be determined primarily by the wishes and affinities of the populations concerned." Mr. Zimmern's praise of nationality we may endorse, but it is more difficult for us to accept as practical his proposed divorcement of nationality from politics. He may be right in alleging that the evils of nationalism flow from the political institution of the national state—the trenchant writings of Mr. G. Lowes Dickinson and Mr. Bertrand Russell tend to confirm him here—but the national state is a fact as impressive today as is the older fact of nationality. However much we may desire to confine nationality to an educational and social sphere, we simply cannot do so. Nationality is in politics and in economics; in fine, it is now inextricably interwoven with the *raison d'être* of the modern state, the national state.

We need pursue the critics no farther. To multiply quotations from their writings would but serve to deflect us from our major quest of the evils and abuses of nationalism to a bewildering and very minor search for the exact source of those evils and abuses. It has been a prime purpose of the present study to demonstrate that nationalism is a complex of nationality, national state, and national patriotism. To our way of thinking, none of these elements in itself is moral or immoral, good or bad; each may be put to good use and each is liable to abuse. What basically gives one or another—perhaps all three—an evil appearance today is their intimate association in a new trinity and unity of nationalism. Failure to recognise this fact is probably the most plausible explanation of the differences among recent critics and students of the subject. Nationalism—the combination of nationality, the national state, and national patriotism, as effected in our age—is the indivisible source of grave abuses and evils.

What, in summary, are these grave evils and abuses? First is the spirit of exclusiveness and narrowness. The national state, through education in national school, national army, and national journalism, through the social pressure of national patriotism, inculcates in its citizens the fancy that they are a world by themselves, sufficient unto themselves; it teaches them that they are a chosen people, a peculiar people, and that they should prize far more what is theirs as a nationality than what is theirs as human beings. It is this spirit of exclusiveness and narrowness which thrives on, and in turn nurses, a smugness that is laughable, an ignorance that is dangerous, and an uncritical pride that can be reduced, if at all, only by a beating.

Secondly, nationalism places a premium on uniformity. It prescribes national models of art, national standards of thought, and national norms of conduct, and to these it expects all the inhabitants of each national state to conform. Individual differences, class differences, religious differences, are alike deemed unfortunate; and the individual of genius is suspect, especially if his genius displays itself in criticism of national uniformity. If nationality does something to prevent the reduction of the whole world to a drab sameness, then nationalism does much more within a nationality to overlay local colour with its own dull greyness.

Thirdly, nationalism increases the docility of the masses. As a result of their national upbringing and their life-long nationalist education, they are seldom inclined to question the providential character of their nationality, of their state, of their government, or of the economic circumstances in which they live. If only a leader appeals to them in the cause of national patriotism, they are prepared to follow that leader unquestioningly and unhesitatingly into any undertaking upon which he has set his heart. In the name of national rights, national interests, and national honour, they will forego their own individual rights, sacrifice their own individual interests, and even forswear their own individual honour. They are ready in the name of the liberty and freedom of their nationality to abridge the liberty of fellow citizens and to take away the freedom of other nationalities. They have, in supreme degree, the will to believe, and this will to believe renders them easy dupes of nationalist propaganda in support of imperialism and war.

Fourthly, nationalism in its present form focusses popular attention upon war and preparedness for war. War is that historic tradition of a nationality which the national state, under present conditions, does most to keep alive and active in the minds and hearts of its citizens. Military heroes outrank in national pantheons the heroes of science and art and learning. Baseball or cricket or mah-jong may be a national game of a particular people, but of all nationalists the world over the biggest and best sport is national fighting. But the more the people train for the great sport of fighting, the more they deify their soldiers, and the more they cherish the memory of the prowess of their ancestors, the less disposed will they be to give time or thought to social reform and preparedness for enduring peace. It is notorious how quickly a popular interest in some educational or economic problem evaporates when confronted by the fierce heat of nationalist passion for military "defence."

From the foregoing general evils and abuses of nationalism proceeds the impulse toward those specific abuses and evils which have been discussed at length in earlier essays —intolerance, militarism, and war. Or, if one likes, one may reorganise the material in those essays and deduce from it, as the fifth, sixth, and seventh outstanding evils of nationalism, respectively Jingoism—Imperialism—Intolerance.

An intolerant attitude and behaviour towards one's fellows; a belief in the imperial mission of one's own nationality at the expense of other, particularly at the expense of backward, peoples; a habit of carrying a chip on one's national shoulder and defying another nationality to knock it off; a fond dwelling on the memory of past wars and a feverish preparing for future wars, to the neglect of present civil problems; a willingness to be led and guided by self-styled patriots; a diffidence, almost a panic, about thinking or acting differently from one's fellows; a spirit of exclusiveness and narrowness which feeds on gross ignorance of others and on inordinate pride in one's self and one's nationality: these are all too prevalent aspects of contemporary nationalism. If in these respects nationalism is not mitigated it will be an unqualified curse to future generations.

4

Some mitigation of nationalism is desirable—and possible. To this very end, in fact, certain forces in the world today are operating, or can be made to operate, though let us not be too comfortably optimistic about the ease or speed with which such forces are likely to counteract the forces which have constructed nationalism and now sustain it. And, above all, let us not be so incorrigibly optimistic as to imagine that the most desirable mitigation of nationalism can be brought about by an interplay of blind forces of nature without conscious effort or direction on our part.

It has ever been fashionable in some quarters to wash human hands—and heads—of all responsibility for what befalls man and to refer the credit and especially the debit variously to Providence or God or Nature or Fate or Progress or (model of A.D. 1926) Infantile Complexes. In line with this general fashion, learned persons have said a good deal about a natural evolution and an inevitable progress, by means of which automatically a tribe evolves into a city-state and then a city-state evolves into a national state, and also by means of which, with the same inevitability, the national state must evolve into a world-state, the whole evolutionary process being a progress steadily onward and upward. Professor Novicov, for instance, has magisterially proclaimed that "the tribe, the state, and the nationality are the three principal degrees of social evolution; . . . when that particular organ which we call the intellectual élite or the social brain is completely differentiated, when it suitably discharges the functions which have devolved upon it, we find ourselves in the presence of a nationality." [1] Professor Novicov's metaphysics are carried to an optimistic if not an exactly logical conclusion by Professor J. Holland Rose, according to whom, the "national instinct," when it is fully "satisfied," begins to age and atrophy and the social brain, emptied of nationalism, is thereupon recharged with "internationalism." [2] All of which may be true, and all of which may be buncombe. Who knows? Even if there be a "natural law" of progress governing the mutations of human society, how do we know that it produces a sequence such as that indicated by Professors Novicov and Rose? Is there not equally good evidence of the sequence suggested by Franz Grillparzer, "from Humanity through Nationality to Bestiality"? All I would hazard concerning an inevitable progress of peoples is this: perhaps, if we turn fatalist and sit idly by, nationality will lead to bestiality; perhaps, if we try, we can make nationalism a stepping stone to internationalism.

There can be little doubt that the Industrial Revolution has provided us with a large number of forces which we can turn to account, if we are so minded, for the mitigation of nationalism. It is an arresting fact that recently during the very period of history in which our schools and armies

[1] *La Politique Internationale* (1886), p. 25.
[2] *Nationality in Modern History* (1916), lecture x, especially pp. 200-202.

and newspapers have been inculcating the notion that humanity is dissoluble into little fighting groups of self-content and self-sufficing nations, a profound economic transformation has been conferring upon all of us the steamship, the steam locomotive, the electric motor, the gasoline engine, the automobile, the telegraph, the telephone, the radio. These things, accompanied by large-scale machine-production, vast world-commerce and international finance, have come so universally and so recently that few of us yet realise their full import. The truth of the matter is that the Industrial Revolution has been laying the economic foundations of *world* citizenship. It now invites us, unless we perish or unless we destroy all industry and trade, to square our political superstructure with its economic foundations and our idea of the national state with the requirements of world citizenship.

The Industrial Revolution, it is true, has been put to nationalist use; it has been an important factor, as we have observed elsewhere, in the development of nationalism. But it has reached the stage now where it may be put increasingly to international use, where it should prove to be a most significant factor in the mitigation of nationalism. Under existing economic conditions, no nationality can be entirely self-sufficing, no national state can be really sovereign and independent of the rest of the world. Bound and contracted by steel rails and copper wire and electric current, the globe has shrunken rapidly during the last hundred years, until now it is easier and more necessary for a Californian to trade with Europe, Asia, and Africa than it was in the eighteenth century for a New Englander to communicate with a Virginian. The globe has shrunken so small, in truth, that it may be handled by children, and, if we are going to instruct the children of our generation in what is likely to be most useful to them in their bread-winning throughout life, then we shall teach them the economic interdependence of all countries and all nations and all races. To teach this to children of the twentieth century will be less of a feat than it was to teach children of the eighteenth century to perceive among their several localities a national unity and solidarity.

The Industrial Revolution has created world markets not only for economic goods and capital, but also for ideas. No idea has ever been the exclusive property of a single nationality, and ideas have always had a tendency to accompany man wherever he has travelled and to infect whomsoever he has come in contact with. Particularly now, when the earth is girdled with telegraphic and telephonic wires and strewn with books and papers, there is an unprecedented transit of ideas.

This fact means that most ideas, which under our nationalist scheme of education appear to be distinctive of a given nationality, are actually the common property of mankind. For example, Americans still talk as though they were the only people in the world who understood and practised political democracy, although Frenchmen, Englishmen, Finns, Dutch, and most other nationalities make the same claim, as absurd in its exclusive aspect as it is true in its general application. For, generally speaking, political democracy is now understood and lauded throughout the world. It is almost the same with the idea of republicanism and with the idea of liberty and with the idea of equality.

It is similar with ideas of religion. The Industrial Revolution, in expediting the spread of ideas in general, has promoted the spread of religious ideas in particular and has stimulated missionary enterprise on a scale hitherto unknown. It may well be that great religious systems of the world will be enabled in the next generation to resume their historic rôle of cementing nationalities and strengthening the spiritual brotherhood of mankind.

Science, too, may be put to constructive and unifying uses. It is impossible in our industrial age to restrict either experimental science or applied science to any particular nationality. The first successful steamboat was invented by an American of Irish stock, the first telephone by an American of Scottish stock, and the first successful airplane by Americans of English stock, but airplanes, telephones, and steamboats are now operated in all civilised countries. The gasoline engine was invented in Germany and first applied to carriages in France, but more automobiles are now made in America than in any other country. Americans know, or think they know, what a germ is, and most Americans seem to enjoy the radio; for their knowledge of the one they are indebted to a French scientist and for their enjoyment of the other they are under obligations to an Italian. It was a fine and fruitful interruption of political nationalism not long ago when American women purchased almost priceless radium and presented it for scientific purposes to a distinguished Polish woman living in France and labouring for humanity. The teaching of science can be made an antidote to narrow nationalism, and when it is so dealt with it may prove less serviceable in forging engines for death and destruction among the several national states, but it will almost certainly prove more blessed to humanity at large.

The Industrial Revolution, then, has greatly expedited not only an international traffic in commodities but also a world-wide transit of ideas—ideas of science, religion, philosophy, economics, and politics. It has created a new interdependence of nationalities and individuals. It has provided at once the need and the means of mitigating nationalism. Nor has the need been entirely ignored or the means completely neglected. There has been a good deal of quickened and quickening international coöperation during the last hundred years—too much, in fact, to recount here. Suffice it to mention a few kinds.

Joint action by national states has been growing more and more prevalent. Thirty nations formed the Universal Telegraph Union (1875); twenty-three adopted a convention regarding the common use of the metric system of weights and measures (1875); sixty adhered to the Universal

Postal Union, which was created in 1878, with headquarters at Berne; five joined the Latin Monetary Union (1865) for the regulation of an interchangeable coinage; nineteen ratified the Berne Convention of 1883 for the standardisation of patent laws; and fifteen signed the Berne Convention of 1887, providing for practically uniform copyright laws. These were a few instances of joint action for economic purposes in the second half of the nineteenth century. And before and since has been the constant activity of a staff of diplomatic agents, not least among whose achievements has been the negotiation of a host of international treaties regulating commerce, naturalisation, and extradition, and providing occasionally for arbitration of disputes.

There grew up, too, among the Great Powers of Europe a "Concert," which, though always quite informal and sometimes reduced to impotence by war and other effects of domestic nationalism, performed valuable service by emphasising inter-state interests and by seeking to prevent war or to alleviate its miseries. Thus the representatives of the Great Powers and of Turkey, meeting to conclude the Crimean War, signed the so-called Declaration of Paris (1856), for the protection of neutral trade in times of war, and authorised the establishment of an international commission for the regulation of navigation on the lower Danube. In 1864 the Powers signed a convention at Geneva, in accordance with which the International Red Cross Society was organised, with branches in all European countries and with an international flag. In 1882, largely through the enthusiasm and energy of Clara Barton, the United States ratified the Geneva Convention; and later, both Turkey and Japan established local branches of the Red Cross Society, though under flags slightly modified so as to satisfy the religious scruples of their non-Christian populations.

The principle of the Concert of Europe was invoked repeatedly to halt war: in 1878, to prevent the Russo-Turkish War from precipitating a much vaster struggle; in 1885-

1886, to restore peace between Serbia and Bulgaria; in 1897, to arrest Turkish aggression against Greece. It was under the auspices of the Concert that the Balkan states drew up their treaty with Turkey at London in 1913 and that the autonomous principality of Albania was erected. Nor was southeastern Europe the only field of concerted action by the Great Powers. In central Africa and in China the freedom of commerce of all nations was protected by international agreement. Central Africa was amicably partitioned, the middle part of it being established as the mutually guaranteed Congo Free State. In China, the Great Powers, including the United States and Japan, united in an expedition which suppressed the Boxer insurrection.

In the meantime, in 1881, James G. Blaine, United States Secretary of State, invited the several independent states of the New World to participate in a conference at Washington "for the purpose of considering and discussing the methods of preventing war between the nations of America." The conference, which for a variety of reasons was delayed until the autumn of 1889, drew up a plan for the obligatory arbitration of all controversies, whatever their origin, with the single exception that it should not apply where, in the judgement of any nation involved, its national independence was imperilled; and even in such a case, arbitration, though optional for the nation so judging, was to be obligatory for its adversary. This plan was not generally ratified, but the conference in which it was drafted proved to be the precursor of a series of conferences—at Mexico City in 1901, at Rio de Janeiro in 1906, at Buenos Aires in 1910, *etc.*—which served to accentuate the desire of the American republics for common peaceful development and to strengthen the sentiment of Pan-American solidarity. Argentina and Chile concluded in 1902 a treaty of arbitration for the settlement of all controversies between them and jointly erected an heroic statue of Christ on a lofty peak of their Andean boundary.

More general international conferences were held at The Hague in 1899 and 1907. At the earlier one, twenty-six Powers were represented; at the later one, there were forty-four—this time practically the whole world. The Hague conferences failed to reduce armaments or "to make the great idea of universal peace triumph over the elements of trouble and discord," [1] but they established international courts to which disputes between states might be submitted and drafted rules of international behaviour in the event of future war.

Far in advance of the Concert of Europe, the Pan-American Conferences, and The Hague Conferences, is the League of Nations, set up in 1920, after the conclusion of the Great War, mainly through the instrumentality of Woodrow Wilson. The League of Nations now embraces almost all the national states of the world, and it acts directly and constantly as an elaborate organism, with a permanent capital and secretariat at Geneva, with a small frequently assembling Council, with a general annual Assembly, with a permanent court of international justice, with an international labour office, and with a host of international commissions. The League has not fulfilled all the hopes of its most sanguine supporters; it has not reduced national armaments, established mutual security, or put an end to war and threats of war. But it has already done a tremendous amount to coördinate numerous international agencies, to train a staff of officials to view matters from an international, rather than from a nationalist, standpoint, and to accustom representatives of the several national states to meet together regularly, to express themselves freely, to learn from one another, and to collaborate frequently; in a word, the League is fostering a spirit of international co-

[1] Words from the Rescript of the Tsar Nicholas II, convoking the First Hague Conference.

operation. To stop the deluge of war, once the thunder-
clouds are black upon the horizon, may be an impossible
task for the League of Nations, but a greater and more
practical, if less ostentatious, work it accomplishes by sharpening both an international consciousness and an international conscience and by providing definite means and opportunities for popular education in internationalism.

Means and opportunities for the mitigation of extreme
nationalism have latterly been provided by a vast array
of popular international movements outside the immediate
sphere of governmental action. The international character of the problems and interests of workingmen throughout the world has been stressed, not only by international
congresses of Socialists, but also by international organisations of the several coöperative societies, trade-unions, and
mutual benefit associations. Similarly, earnest advocates
of democracy have established and arranged periodic meetings of an International Parliamentary Union; and agitators of woman suffrage and feminism have held international women's congresses. Religion has felt the general
impulse: Protestant Christians of a hundred divergent
sects and of a thousand shades of individual opinion have
met in world congresses and made friendly agreements for
the parcelling out of heathen lands among their several
local and national bodies for missionary purposes; Catholic
Christians, never quite forgetful of the universal traditions
of their faith, have met in numerous international conferences at Rome and elsewhere for a great variety of purposes and, since 1881, have held a series of Eucharistic
Congresses which have drawn large numbers of clergy and
laity from many climes now to Paris, now to London, now
to Jerusalem, now to Montreal, now to Amsterdam, now to
Chicago; even a World's Parliament of Religions has been
projected and actually convened.

For the advancement of learning, regardless of national
frontiers of language, tradition, and political sovereignty,

much has been planned and discussed and done. There have been periodical international conventions of distinguished physicists, chemists, biologists, historians, economists, physicians, and jurists. There has been exchange of professors and students between universities and schools of different countries. There has been steadily developing around the globe a conscious community of intellectual interests, the product of what has happily been described as "the international mind." [1]

It is possible, with a certain amount of popular international mindedness, to join nationalities politically, even if the nationalities so joined are quite self-conscious and possess a considerable degree of nationalism. Something of the sort has been exemplified in the international alliances of the last hundred years—the alliance of France and Italy, of Italy and Germany, of Great Britain and Japan—and perhaps most strikingly in the recent alliance of France with Belgium and Poland and in the contemporary "little entente" of Czechoslovakia, Rumania, and Yugoslavia. But after all, these alliances and ententes have been limited in duration and restricted to very specific objects. They are based upon a temporary community of particular interests, and they are contracted by sovereign states by whom they may be cancelled. Examples of a closer and more effective political internationalism are afforded by modern federalism.

The United States under the Constitution of 1787 formed a close league of nations, and likewise the German Empire under its Constitutions of 1871 and 1919. In both instances, each component state, whilst retaining many powers and considerable prestige, whilst continuing to command a special patriotism of its inhabitants, surrendered large powers, capital prestige, and the paramount patriotism of its population to the federal government. It may be objected that these instances are beside the point, in-

[1] N. M. Butler, *The International Mind* (1912).

asmuch as they are instances of states of common nationality whose people, by forming a federal state, merely created a nationalist state. But no such objection can be raised against certain other instances of political federalism.

Switzerland is an outstanding example of a successful political federation of three nationalities; each canton is nationally homogeneous, German or French or Italian; each canton has its own national language, national traditions, and national patriotism; and each canton has a liberal measure of local autonomy; but the tie which binds all these cantons together in the Swiss Confederation serves not only to promote their joint interests but also to mitigate the nationalism of each through the internationalism of all; there is a Swiss patriotism which in Switzerland is a sedative to German nationalism, French nationalism, and Italian nationalism. Canada is another conspicuous example of the same kind of close international federation; most of the Canadian provinces are predominantly British in nationality, but one large province is French; yet side by side with the French nationalism of Quebec and the British nationalism of, say, Ontario, exists a common Canadian patriotism. The Union of South Africa is also a corporate union of two nationalities—British and Dutch—with a measure of national autonomy and even a degree of nationalism for each, but with a common South African patriotism for both. In fact, the whole British Empire, in so far as its self-governing Dominions are concerned, is a federation of nationalities and national states, in which divergent local and national differences are not altogether incompatible with the claims of a unifying patriotism.

May we not have here an index to the future development of the League of Nations? May we not have here the most practical means of squaring existent political institutions with the economic and spiritual needs of the world? May we not have here the most promising means of supplementing nationalism by internationalism, and thus of mitigating nationalism?

5

The popular and governmental "internationalism" of the last generation must not be confused with "cosmopolitanism." Cosmopolitanism, as understood by ancient philosophers and eighteenth-century rationalists, carried with it a decrying of local and national distinctions and of patriotism; the unit of its ideal world-state was the individual or the social class and not the nationality or the national state. Internationalism, on the other hand, presupposes a prime loyalty of the individual to his national state, a cherishing by him of his national language and his national traditions, a lively patriotism within him; the internationalist aims to build his world-state with national blocks. And, whatever academic reflections may be indulged on the relative ideal merits of cosmopolitanism and internationalism, it is the latter, and not the former, which will appeal to the practical realist of the present generation as the possible and desirable antidote to the poison of nationalism. To go from nationalism to cosmopolitanism is to hurdle from a familiar path and start off in an opposite direction along a path that is strange and choked with underbrush. To go from nationalism to internationalism is merely to take a well-marked turn on the very highway on which the modern world is travelling.

So, let us continue to be patriotic citizens of our respective national states. Let us cherish our national language, our national traditions, and our national ideals. Only, let us clearly recognise and frankly acknowledge that there are faults in contemporary nationalism and let us sincerely endeavour to remedy such faults by combining our nationalism with internationalism, by tempering our national loyalty with an honest and reasoned respect for all other nationalities. As the venerable Professor John Watson has strikingly phrased it:[1] "The feeling of loyalty must be sublimated into a form of patriotism which combines the

---

[1] *The State in Peace and War* (1919), p. 261.

most intense love of country with the desire to do justice to other nations. There are tasks enough for men to do without wasting their emotions on evil feelings against the citizens of a foreign nation, and really vigourous life is not to be expected from those whose devotion to humanity makes them indifferent to the immediate problems of their own country. The union of love of country with devotion to the cause of humanity is the true ideal, and neither a selfish patriotism nor a vague humanitarianism that leads to nothing but neglect of the duty that lies nearest."

The mitigation of ignorant, boastful, and intolerant nationalism by wholesome internationalism will not be effected by forces outside of our own consciousness. International mindedness is not a dew which falls from heaven gently and equally upon the just and the unjust. It can be acquired only by gradual education within the several nationalities and national states. As popular education in the nineteenth century has been bent to the service of nationalism, so popular education in the twentieth century, if we will, can be made to serve the ends of internationalism. Education we must have in school, in press, and in pulpit, more rather than less education, but it must be an education which aims to surmount exclusiveness and to inculcate mutual understanding and coöperation, an education which seeks to overcome docility, to foster the critical spirit, and to encourage independence of judgement. Of this newer ideal education every person of intelligence is summoned to be a standard-bearer.

We must start by recognising what nationalism is and what internationalism is. We must then acquire a vast deal of sound information not only about our own country but about other countries and other peoples as well. With knowledge we must acquire understanding and sympathy and respect and tolerance. Especially must we be on our guard against contributing unwittingly to the weakening of any force or factor or instrument which makes for internationalism, whether it be a world religion, an international labour movement, or the universal interchange of persons and commodities and ideas. When we shall have gained this equipment and this habit of mind ourselves, we shall then be ready and, I hope, zealous to preach them to our fellow citizens and to do our bit individually and collectively to make them part and parcel of our system of national education.

Almost everything depends, in last analysis, upon our national schools, and particularly upon the teaching of the social sciences within our national schools. For above our nationality, above all nationalities, though many persons of our age forget it, there still is humanity; and humanity is the very stuff of the social sciences. Geography describes man's habitat. Psychology deals with man's mental processes and man's behaviour. Economics concerns itself with man's ways of gaining a livelihood. Civics treats of man's political institutions, and sociology of man's social institutions. History tells what man has thought, said, and done. With all the social sciences it is basically not Frenchmen, Englishmen, or American men, but *men,* the individual members of humanity. Science, religion, art and learning, all ideas, are the common heritage of humanity, and teachers of the social sciences are cheating pupils of the best part of their heritage as human beings if their information and their interest are limited to such matters and such interpretations as are compatible only with narrow nationalism. In any struggle between nationalism and humanity, those teachers who are truly progressive, those teachers who have some insight into the terrible fate awaiting an utterly triumphant nationalism must surely be on the side of humanity, must surely merit and receive the encouragement and active aid of fellow citizens of intelligence, sound information, and good will.

We should feel so keenly the ravages in humanity that nationalism has already made and foresee so clearly the awful final outcome of unmitigated nationalism that if we thought the school curricula, and especially the social sciences, would be employed further to strengthen and exalt it, we should urge the exclusion of all social studies from the schools. As a counsel of despair, we should wish to go farther and to close the schools altogether. Better an illiterate nation than a nation taught to hate and exterminate others.

But to such a sorry choice we have not as yet come. There is still hope, and the great hope, let me repeat, resides in education. In fact, a great race even now is beginning, a race that will be run throughout the next generation or two, between the forces of nationalism and the forces of humanity, toward the respective goals of destruction and salvation. In such a race the schools will play a transcendent rôle, for in them the runners will be trained. And with the assistance of economic internationalism and intellectual interdependency, with due attention to the influence of the Industrial Revolution in world-geography, in world-economics, in world-civics, and in world-history, with a reasoned tolerance of all religious, social, and political agencies working in the same direction, and, most of all, with the earnest consistent backing of right-minded citizens, the teachers of the social sciences should and, I believe, can perform heroic service in the training of runners for the race in behalf of humanity, the race that leads to salvation. It will be a hard race; its event is not certain. But the very doubt concerning its outcome may fire our imagination as the stakes of the race must appeal to our reason.

6

To urge the mitigation of nationalism and the propagation of internationalism is not to decry patriotism. Rather, it is to purify and exalt true patriotism. For it should ever be remembered that critics of public policy, even more than blind devotees, may be inspired by the truest love of native land, by real patriotism. Patriotism is love of one's country, and, as has been suggested earlier, love of one's country is a peculiarly natural and ennobling expression of man's primitive sentiment of loyalty.

Nationalism is partly love of country, but chiefly something else. Nationalism is a proud and boastful habit of mind about one's own nation, accompanied by a supercilious or hostile attitude toward other nations; it admits that individual citizens of one's country may do wrong, but it insists that one's nationality or national state is always right. Nationalism is either ignorant and prejudiced or inhuman and jaundiced; in both cases it is a form of mania, a kind of extended and exaggerated egotism, and it has easily recognisable symptoms of selfishness, intolerance, and jingoism, indicative of the delusions of grandeur from which it suffers. Nationalism is artificial and it is far from ennobling; in a word, it is *patriotic snobbery*.

True patriotism, on the other hand, involves *humility*. If we really love our country, we shall be bowed in humility in its presence and in its service, and in humble fashion we shall labour to bring to it all the blessings and hopes of humanity and to promote the happiness and well-being of all its citizens. We shall be so intent upon improving our country, spiritually, intellectually, and physically, and upon making it a fit habitation for fellow human beings that we shall not have the time or the inclination to attack other countries or other peoples in thought, word, or deed. If we have the virtue of humility in sufficient degree, we shall eventually learn the great and divine secret that we are not worthy of our country, that no man is worthy of what he loves. When that time comes, we shall have a real understanding of the basis of perpetual peace; we shall then have a true sympathy not only for our fellow nationals but likewise for the foreigner afar and for the stranger within our gates. Nationalism, when it becomes synonymous with the purest patriotism, will prove an unique blessing to humanity and to the world.

BIBLIOGRAPHICAL NOTE

There is no profound systematic treatment of the subject of nationalism in any language. A beginning of scholarly study of nationality has been made by Arnold van Gennep in his *Traité Comparatif des Nationalités*, a projected anthropological treatment, of which volume i, *Les Élements Extérieurs de la Nationalité*, has already appeared (1922); by Waldemar Mitscherlich in several writings, *Der Nationalismus und seine Wurzeln* (1912), *Fehlerquell und Statistik des Nationalismus* (1914), *Nationaler Staat und Nationale Wirtschaft* (1915), and, especially, *Der Nationalismus West-Europas* (1920), an historical and descriptive survey; and by J. Holland Rose, *Nationality in Modern History* (1916), a collection of lectures, of which i-v have some permanent value.

Several volumes of real worth deal with particular nationalities and nationalisms. With special reference to the French, the best is René Johannet, *Le Principe des Nationalités*, 2nd ed. (1923), and a good brief resumé is Henri Hauser, *Le Principe des Nationalités, ses origines historiques* (1916), while on specific periods of French history we have an important volume by A. Aulard, *Le Patriotisme Français de la Renaissance à la Révolution* (1921); a collection of source-material covering the years 1789-1830, edited with an interesting prefatory essay by H. F. Stewart and Paul Desjardins, *French Patriotism in the Nineteenth Century* (1923); and illuminating studies of more recent phases by E. R. C. Curtius, *Maurice Barrès und die geistigen Grundlagen des französischen Nationalismus* (1921), and by Joachim Kühn (ed.), *Der Nationalismus im Leben der dritten Republik* (1920). There is a good account of Pan-Slavism, with some attention to the development of nationalism among the several Slavic peoples, by Alfred Fischel, *Der Panslawismus bis zum Weltkrieg* (1919). Serbian and Yugoslav nationalism is specially dealt with by Vidan Blagoyévitch, *Le Principe des Nationalités et son application dans les Traités de Paix de Versailles et de Saint-Germain* (1922); Rumanian, by Alexandre Suciu, *De la Nationalité en Roumanie* (1906), and by M. A. Laurian, *Le Principe des Nationalités et l'Unité nationale rou-*

maine (1923); Armenian, by Jacques de Morgan, *Essai sur les Nationalités* (1917); nationalism in the former Habsburg Empire, by Bertrand Auerbach, *Les Races et les Nationalités en Autriche-Hongrie,* 2nd. ed. (1917), and by R. W. Seton Watson, *Racial Problems in Hungary* (1908) and *The Southern Slavs* (1911); in Switzerland, by Louis Dumur, *Les deux Suisses* (1917); in Belgium, by Jules Destrée, *Wallons et Flamands, la Querelle linguistique* (1923); in the Near East, by Arnold Toynbee, *The Western Question in Greece and Turkey* (1922).

Psychological factors in nationality and nationalism are discussed in several well known works: G. E. Partridge, *The Psychology of Nations* (1919); W. B. Pillsbury, *The Psychology of Nationality and Internationalism* (1919); Gustave Le Bon, *The Psychology of Peoples,* Eng. trans. (1899); William McDougall, *Group Mind* (1920), *National Welfare and National Decay* (1922), and *Ethics and Some Modern World Problems* (1924). Racial factors are criticised by John Oakesmith, *Race and Nationality, an Inquiry into the Origin and Growth of Patriotism* (1919), with special reference to English patriotism; by Jean Finot, *Race Prejudice,* Eng. translation by Florence Wade-Evans, new ed. (1924); by Arthur Keith, *Nationality and Race* (1919); and by L. Le Fur, *Races, Nationalités, États* (1923). Economic factors are suggested by Thorstein Veblen, *An Inquiry into the Nature of Peace and the Terms of its Perpetuation* (1916); by Waldemar Mitscherlich, *Nationaler Staat und Nationale Wirtschaft* (1915), and by Otto Bauer, *Die Nationalitätenfrage und die Sozialdemocratie* (1909). Geographical factors are discussed by Leon Dominian, *Frontiers of Language and Nationality* (1917) and *The Nationality Map of Europe* (1917), and by Sir Thomas Holdich, *Boundaries in Europe and the Near East* (1918). For an introductory account of the influence of public schools in western Europe and the United States, see E. H. Reisner, *Nationalism and Education since 1789* (1922). The relations of nationalism to Christianity are treated by F. N. Figgis, *Churches in the Modern State,* 2nd ed. (1914); Lord Hugh Cecil, *Nationalism and Catholicism* (1919); William Cunningham, *Christianity and Politics* (1915); S. Mathews, *Patriotism and Religion* (1918); A. Lugan, *La grande Loi Sociale de la Justice,* vol. v (1925); and M. Vaussard (ed.), *Enquête sur le Nationalisme* (1924).

There are many fragments on the political philosophy of nationalism—among the writings, for example, of Herder, Fichte, Bluntschli, Lieber, Mazzini, Mancini, J. S. Mill, Renan, Laveleye,

Acton, and Masaryk. A brief survey of some phases of the political speculation on the subject is presented by W. A. Dunning, *A History of Political Theories from Rousseau to Spencer* (1920), ch. viii. Other summaries are given in some of the works cited above, for example, in those of René Johannet and Vidan Blagoyévitch. Reference may also be made to H. J. Laski, *Grammar of Politics* (1925), ch. vi; to F. Rosenbluth, *Zur Begriffsbestimmung von Volk und Nation* (1910); and to writings of such extreme nationalists as Maurice Barrès (see especially his *Scènes et Doctrines du Nationalisme* 1902), Charles Maurras, Gabriele D'Annunzio, Benito Mussolini, *etc.*

Among a host of brief and semi-popular books and essays in English, the following are fairly typical: G. P. Gooch, *Nationalism* (1920); J. L. Stocks, *Patriotism and the Super-State* (1920); Israel Zangwill, *The Principle of Nationalities* (1917); A. E. Zimmern, *Nationality and Government*, 2nd ed. (1919); Ramsay Muir, *Nationality and Internationalism* (1917); S. Herbert, *Nationality and its Problems* (1920); C. D. Burns, *The Morality of Nations* (1915) and *International Politics* (1920); Norman Angell, *The Fruits of Victory* (1921); T. Ruyssen, "The Principle of Nationality," *Publications of the American Association for International Conciliation* (1916-1917); Leo Perla, *What Is National Honor?* (1918).

Additional bibliographical aids are furnished by E. B. Krehbiel, *Nationalism, War, and Society* (1916); by H. E. Barnes, article "Nationalism" in *Encyclopedia Americana* (1919 ed.), vol. xix, pp. 743-765; and by P. T. Moon, *Syllabus on International Relations* (1925), pp. 8-36.